ITALIAN COOKING
Classic Recipes and Techniques

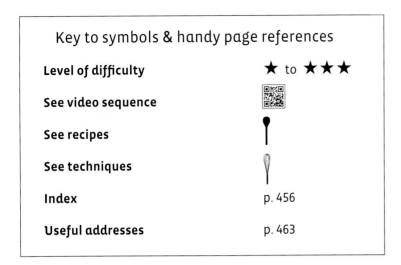

Key to symbols & handy page references

Level of difficulty	★ to ★ ★ ★
See video sequence	
See recipes	
See techniques	
Index	p. 456
Useful addresses	p. 463

Translated from the French by Julia Chalkley
Design: Alice Leroy
Copyediting: Penelope Isaac
Typesetting: Gravemaker+Scott
Proofreading: Nicole Foster
QR codes: BookBeo
Indexing: JMS Books
Chef's interviews: Stefano Palombari
Color Separation: LCT Angoulême, France
Printed in China by Toppan Leefung

Originally published in French as
Encyclopédie de la gastronomie italienne
© Flammarion, S.A., Paris, 2013

English-language edition
© Flammarion, S.A., Paris, 2014

editions.flammarion.com

14 15 16   3 2 1

ISBN: 978-2-08-020189-8

Dépôt légal: 10/2014

Mia Mangolini

Photographs by Francesca Mantovani

ITALIAN COOKING
Classic Recipes and Techniques

Flammarion

How to use this book

Techniques (pp. 11–153)

All the basic techniques, with specialist step-by-step explanations

Step-by-step photos
referring to the text

Level of difficulty

Easily visible page numbering

Chef's notes

Useful tips

Access to video sequences

Scan the QR codes with the BookBeo app, free for iPhone and Android. When you have read the explanation, watch the sequence and/or download it to view as convenient. Use Wi-Fi for faster viewing and downloads.

You can also:

• use another QR code reader compatible with your smartphone;

• copy the URL below the codes to browse on your PC/Mac or smartphone.

Techniques

140

Scaloppine

Saltimbocca ⊛

Saltimbocca is one of the signature dishes of Roman cooking. It is prepared with very thin scaloppine cut from a leg of veal that are covered with ham and sage and held together with a toothpick. It is a dish that's easy and quick to cook.

Serves 4
Preparation time: 10 minutes
Cooking time: 20 minutes

Ingredients
12 oz. (300 g) veal scaloppine
4 oz. (120 g) dry-cure ham
⅔ stick (3 oz./80 g) butter
8 fresh sage leaves
½ cup (100 ml) white wine (ideally Vino dei Castelli Romani)
Salt, pepper

Flatten the scaloppine finely in such a way as to give you approximately 5 in. (10 cm) squares (1).
Season lightly with salt and pepper.
Place a slice of ham and a sage leaf on each one (2), fixing them in place with a toothpick (3).
Heat half the butter in a skillet and brown them for 2 minutes on each side, beginning with the ham side down (be careful that the ham does not cook too fast, it can become very dry) (4).
Deglaze with the white wine and finish cooking. Remove the saltimbocca and keep warm. Dilute the juices on the base of the pan with 2 tablespoons of water and add the rest of the butter to bind the sauce.
Serve the saltimbocca coated with the sauce.

● **Chef's notes**
You can accompany the saltimbocca with green beans, peas, spinach, potatoes, etc.
Saltimbocca is often confused with involtini: these are scaloppine rolled around a stuffing, usually made with cheese.

● **Did you know?**
Saltimbocca literally means "jumps in the mouth" in Italian, because the dish is regarded as so tasty.

http://flamm.fr/ic01

Recipes (pp. 185–455)

More than one hundred basic recipes, with twelve additional recipes created and tested by renowned Italian chefs

Easily visible page numbering

Level of difficulty

Ingredients
12 oz. (350 g) loin of veal
2 cloves garlic
1 lemon
1 white truffle, preferably from Alba
2 tablespoons olive oil
Salt and freshly ground pepper

Equipment
1 truffle mandolin

Veal *Tartare* with White Truffle ⭐

Carne all'Albese

*All'Albese means typical of Alba, a town in Piedmont.
This is a recipe that shows off the famous white truffle to great advantage.
Veal is the ideal meat for this dish.*

Serves 4
Preparation time: 20 minutes
Marinating time: 1 hour

Peel the garlic and chop. Squeeze the lemon juice.
Clean the truffle with a dry brush to remove the soil, using the tip of a knife to help if necessary. Wipe it with a damp cloth and pat it dry.
You can ask your butcher to chop the veal for the *tartare* by hand. Otherwise cut it up yourself into small pieces, then, with a very sharp large-bladed knife, chop it more and more finely.
Prepare a sauce with the garlic, olive oil, salt, and pepper. Mix well with the meat to season it. Marinate for about 1 hour. Only add the lemon juice just before serving, to prevent it from "cooking" the meat, which should remain pink.
Divide the *tartare* between the plates. Sprinkle with petals of white truffle finely shaved with a truffle mandolin.

● **Suggested food/wine match**
Barbaresco, DOCG red

🍴 **Techniques**
Anchovies in Salt ›› p. 26
Crudités ›› p. 15
Polenta ›› pp. 100–107

Piedmont • Val d'Aosta   Recipes

193

Ingredients

Cross-references to the techniques used in this recipe

Contents

Recipes

Appendixes

Foreword

By Carlo Petrini

Journalist and gourmet critic
Founder of the Slow Food movement

Mia Mangolini's work is a valuable tool for preparing an exceptional selection
of Italian dishes. Techniques and difficulty ratings, utensils and methods,
suggestions and preparation times are all fully explained and illustrated
using detailed photography.

To testify to this great Italian culinary heritage, a dozen prestigious chefs
have been selected to represent the current expertise of a country in which
the diversity of regional cooking is expressed in very different ways.
Unity in diversity is a distinctive Italian feature, a feature destined to
become the future for the whole of European gastronomy.

Techniques

Antipasti
and preserves

Antipasti

Antipasti dishes are very varied, served in small portions and decorated with care. Their quantity varies depending on the context.

Only one is served at a simple meal, two or three for a more ambitious meal, and many more (usually seven) for a formal or ceremonial meal.

At cocktail receptions or buffets, antipasti are now becoming the norm. The best-known selection is undoubtedly a plate of charcuterie accompanied by marinated vegetables. Depending on the quality of the ingredients, this can be a sophisticated and refined dish.

A little bit of history

The word antipasto (antipasti, in the plural) comes from the Latin *ante pastus* and means "before the food." In Italy, the terms *principii* (a rather outdated term from Pellegrino Artusi's book *Scienza in Cucina e l'Arte del Mangiar Bene* [*The Science of Cooking and the Art of Fine Dining*]), *stuzzichini*, or finger food are also used.

Their existence dates back to the time of the Romans. In the fourth century BCE, Filosseno, in his poem "Convito," evoked delicious food that stimulated the appetite before a meal. This usage became obscure in the Middle Ages and resurfaced later during the sixteenth century when, for wealthy people, it became used to describe the sampling of all kinds of previously unknown foods.

Preparing antipasti

Presentation

The aesthetic aspect of antipasti should not be underestimated, as a few beautifully presented dishes attract the eye before stimulating the appetite. Therefore it is important to choose an appropriate serving dish. For example, a compartmented dish can be very useful for presenting different vegetables.

Sequence of ingredients

As the introduction to the meal, antipasti should be in harmony with it, and initiate a balanced progression. The most delicate flavors should precede more intense tastes. Vegetables naturally precede meat or fish. A fish dish may introduce a meat dish; a white meat dish can, more rarely, introduce a highly flavored fish dish.

Cold or hot

In general, antipasti are served cold in summer and hot in winter. But, in a selection, it is common to serve the two—the cold first and then the hot.

Ingredients

All types of foods can be prepared as antipasti: bread and pizza, cereals, vegetables, eggs, fruit, charcuterie, cheeses, fish, and meat.

A few examples of classic antipasti

Parma ham and melon; dry sausage and figs; pears and Parmesan; *pinzimonio* (p. 15); anchovy fondue (p. 191); langoustine carpaccio (p. 132), sea bream, or other fish; seafood salad (p. 128); cuttlefish (p. 239); *crostini* (p. 300); *bruschette* (p. 300); meat and fish pâtés; Cipriani's carpaccio (p. 242) or vegetable carpaccio; pecorino cheese accompanied by jellies (p. 22), chutney, and chocolate sauce, etc. For cold buffets, brunch, or cocktail receptions, main dishes (pasta, gratins, roasts, and so on) can be divided into very small portions and beautifully presented as antipasti.

Crudités ★

Pinzimonio

Pinzimonio, known as *cazzimperio* in Roman dialect, is a preparation of raw vegetables served with an olive oil dressing.

Serves 4
Preparation time: 10 minutes

Ingredients
1 baby artichoke
1 fennel bulb
1 endive
1 carrot
1 cucumber
1 bell pepper, red, yellow, or green
8 radishes
4 scallions
Juice of ½ lemon
7 tablespoons (100 ml) olive oil
Salt, pepper

Clean the vegetables and cut the largest into quarters (artichoke, fennel, endive), or sticks (carrot, cucumber, bell pepper).
Season the lemon juice with salt and pepper then gradually incorporate the olive oil, using a fork.
Arrange the vegetables in a serving dish, in small bowls or a basket, or on a tiered serving stand.
Divide the olive oil and lemon dressing between individual bowls in which guests can dip their vegetables.

● Chef's note
The lemon juice can be replaced by 4 tablespoons of balsamic vinegar. You could also leave out the acidifier altogether, so as to highlight the quality of the olive oil and fresh vegetables.

Grilled Vegetables ★

Verdure grigliate

This is a very simple recipe, which can introduce a meal, embellish a salad, or accompany a main dish. The quality and choice of seasonal vegetables determine the success of the recipe.

Serves 4
Preparation time: 20 minutes
Cooking time: 10 minutes

Ingredients
Depending on the season
1 eggplant
2 zucchini
1 bell pepper, red, yellow, or green
or
4 endives
8 mushrooms
1 radicchio

Scant ½ cup (100 ml) olive oil
Salt
2 tablespoons chopped herbs (thyme, oregano, marjoram, parsley, etc.)

Clean the vegetables. Cut into approximately ¼ in. (5 mm) slices (eggplants, zucchini), in quarters (endives, radicchio), or in strips (bell peppers) (1).
Oil a ribbed grill pan and place over a high heat until hot. Grill the vegetables for 3 minutes on each side (2), turning only once with tongs or a fork.
Microwave the bell peppers for 4 minutes to complete their cooking process.
Once cooked, place in a dish and season immediately with the olive oil, salt, and chopped herbs.
Serve hot or cold.

1

2

Stuffed Vegetables ★

Verdure ripiene

Small stuffed vegetables (or flowers) are often included in antipasti throughout Italy. Stuffing and vegetables vary from one region to another and according to the season. Here is a recipe from Liguria.

Serves 4
Preparation time: 20 minutes
Cooking time: 35 minutes

Ingredients
2 floury potatoes (e.g. Russet, King Edward, or Maris Piper)
2 zucchini
2 large onions
½ cup (3 oz./80 g) green beans
1 egg yolk
1 clove garlic
⅓ cup (2 oz./60 g) grated Parmesan cheese
¼ cup (60 ml) olive oil
⅛ cup (½ oz./10 g) dried porcini (soaked for 15 minutes in lukewarm water)
A few basil leaves
1 teaspoon marjoram
4 zucchini flowers
Salt, pepper

Clean the vegetables.
Peel the potatoes and cut them into pieces.
Cut one of the zucchini in two lengthwise.
Cut the onions in half, then scoop out the insides to make four shells.
Remove stalks from the green beans and cut them into pieces.
Steam all the cleaned vegetables for approximately 20 minutes.

Prepare the stuffing.
Press the green beans, potatoes, and zucchini through a coarse sieve or vegetable mill (1).
Add the egg yolk, crushed garlic, grated cheese, 2 tablespoons (30 ml) of the olive oil, the drained porcini, and chopped herbs (2). Season with salt and pepper.

Prepare the vegetable shells.
Remove the pistils from the flowers. Cut the second zucchini in two, lengthwise. Scoop out the seeds and cut each half into two. Fill the flowers, the zucchini, and the onion shells with the stuffing (3). Place them on an oiled baking sheet. Bake for 15 minutes at 400°F (200°C).
Serve the stuffed vegetables hot or cold.

Flavored Olives ★

Olive aromatiche

Olives can be drained and served just as they are, or flavored
very simply with the addition of a few ingredients (vegetables
in oil, chilies, garlic, citrus zest, herbs, spices, etc.). Here is
a recipe from Umbria.

Serves 4
Preparation time: 20 minutes
Cooking time: 40 minutes
Marinating time: at least 6 hours

Ingredients
²/₃ cup (4 oz./120 g) black olives
Zest of 1 orange
1 clove garlic
1 bay leaf
Salt
1 tablespoon olive oil

Mix the olives with the orange zest (1), the peeled
and crushed garlic, and the chopped bay leaf.
Season with salt, add the olive oil (2), and mix.
Marinate for at least 6 hours before serving (3).

Charcuterie

The way charcuterie is cut is fundamental for optimizing taste. Italian charcuterie, for the most part, must be cut very thinly with a meat-slicing machine. Whether it is a portion of charcuterie or a whole piece, the preparation and slicing require care.

For example, the Consortium of Parma Ham (Prosciutto di Parma), guarantor of the quality of this Protected Designation of Origin (PDO), the most consumed in Italy, gives the following instructions:
• **Partial removal** of the outer layer of rind from the piece to be sliced ½–¾ in. (10–20 mm).
• **Partial removal of the fat**: leave half the thickness of fat. The fat from Parma ham, rich in unsaturated fatty acids, contributes to the softness of its texture and to its sweet flavor. It is therefore better to leave some fat surrounding the lean.
• **The thickness of each slice**, to be cut by machine only, should be the same as a sheet of paper; this reveals the ham's subtlety and its fine aromas and flavors.
• **Slicing** should only be done as required; this guarantees the freshness of each slice and the intensity of its flavor.

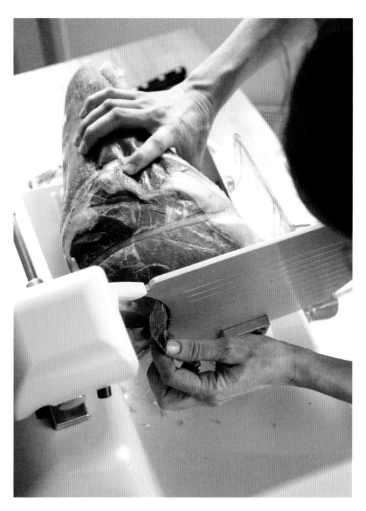

Which method is required to guarantee the ideal preservation of Parma ham?

Parma ham	Temperature	Residual moisture	Shelf life
Whole, bone in	60°F–140°F (14°C–18°C)	55–65%	• From a hygiene point of view: unlimited • From a taste point of view: 24 months or more, depending on weight
Boneless (packaging intact)	30°F–50°F (1°C–10°C)		6 months maximum
Boneless (packaging removed)	30°F–40°F (1°C–6°C) with meat area covered to prevent oxidation and incrustations		1 month maximum
Pre-sliced (prepacked)	30°F–50°F (1°C–10°C)		3 months maximum

Bread Sticks ★★★

Grissini

Grissini are crisp bread sticks for serving with charcuterie and other antipasti.

Serves 4
Preparation time: 20 minutes
Rising time: 1 hour
Cooking time: 20 minutes

Ingredients
1 ⅓ teaspoons (⅕ oz./6 g) fresh yeast
½ cup (100-120 ml) water
2 cups (7 oz./200 g) all-purpose flour
1 teaspoon (4 g) brown sugar
1 teaspoon (5 g) salt
3 ½ tablespoons (50 ml) olive oil (+ oil for the dough)
1 tablespoon (10 g) semolina

Dissolve the yeast in the water. Place the flour in a large bowl and make a well in it. Add the dissolved yeast (**1**), sugar, salt, and olive oil to the well (**2**). Mix everything together to form a compact mixture, then knead vigorously until a smooth dough is formed (**3**).
Place the dough on the counter and shape it so that it is longer than it is wide (**4**). Lightly oil its surface (**5**) and sprinkle with the semolina. Let rise for approximately 1 hour.
Cut the dough into stick shapes across its width (**6**) and stretch them gently by hand lengthwise, starting from the middle and working toward the ends. Place them on a baking sheet lined with parchment paper (**7**). Bake for 15 to 20 minutes at 400°F (200°C) until the bread sticks are well browned.

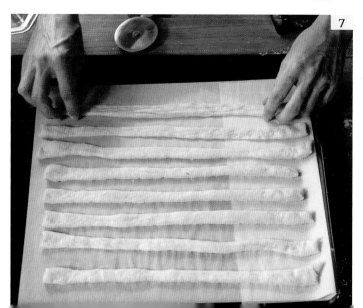

Cheeses and jellies

It is very common today to serve cheeses (especially hard cheeses) as antipasti, accompanied by jelly, chutney, chocolate sauce, or traditional balsamic vinegar. Here is a recipe for chili jelly, which would accompany a maturing pecorino very well, but could also be used as an accompaniment to roast meat.

Chili Jelly ★

Marmellata di peperoncini

Makes one 14 oz. (385 ml) jar
Preparation time: 20 minutes
Cooking time: 1 hour

Ingredients
9 ½ oz. (270 g) fresh red chilies
9 oz. (250 g) apples
1 cup (7 oz./200 g) granulated sugar
⅔ cup (2 ½ oz./70 g) brown sugar
Salt
10 coriander seeds
3 cloves
3 juniper berries
1 stick cinnamon
1 blade mace

Wash the chilies and remove the stems and seeds (all or only some, depending on how spicy you want the jelly to be) (1). Wash the apples, peel, quarter, and remove the seeds. Cut the quarters into pieces.
Place the apples and chilies in a saucepan with the granulated and brown sugars, a pinch of salt, and the spices (2).
Leave to cook for 1 hour over low heat (3). Remove the froth on the surface and pour into presterilized jelly jars while still hot. Close the jars hermetically, turn them upside down, and leave to cool. You can turn them upright once completely cooled.

Preserves

This is an ideal method for preparing antipasti in advance using different seasonal vegetables; preserving them also enriches their flavor. When it's time to taste, you can open your own homemade preserves for your guests to enjoy!

Artichokes in Oil ★

Carciofini sott'olio

Artichokes in oil are traditionally prepared at the end of their season, from April to May.
At the end of its growing cycle, the plant produces many small artichokes, which can be left whole. It is possible to prepare this preserve with slightly larger artichokes, but they should be quartered.

Makes one 1 lb. (500 g) jar
Preparation time: 40 minutes
Cooking time: 4 minutes
Drying time: 2-3 hours
Sterilization time for jar: 10-15 minutes

Ingredients
12 oz. (800 g) baby artichokes
Juice of 1 lemon
6 ⅓ cups (1.5 liters) white wine vinegar
4 cups (1 liter) water
2 bay leaves
20 peppercorns
Salt
1 ½ cups (350 ml) olive oil

Clean the artichokes, remove the toughest leaves, cut off the tips and the stalks, and cut into quarters if large (1). Put them in water to cover, and acidify with the lemon juice. Bring the vinegar to a boil with the water, one of the bay leaves, 10 peppercorns, and a big pinch of salt. Drain the artichokes, add to the vinegar solution, and blanch for 4 minutes (2). Drain and dry them upside down on absorbent paper (2 to 3 hours) (3).
Once dry, place the artichokes in a sterilized jar with the second bay leaf and remaining 10 peppercorns (4). Cover with plenty of olive oil, removing any air trapped in the middle of the artichokes with the blade of a knife (5). Close hermetically and sterilize the jar for 10 to 15 minutes to preserve for several months.

● **Chef's note**
The same process can be applied to other vegetables, with the spices varied accordingly (for example, garlic, cloves, thyme for porcini, and so on).

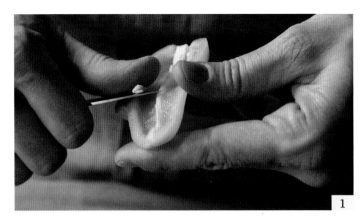

Bell Peppers in Vinegar ★

Peperoni sott'aceto

Vegetables preserved in vinegar go very well with charcuterie, but can also enhance a green salad or rice salad, or be included in the ingredients for a meat stew, such as pork *alla Lucana* (p. 405).

Makes one 2 lb. (1 liter) jar
Preparation time: 20 minutes
Cooking time: 2 minutes
Drying time: 2-3 hours

Ingredients
1 ½ lb. (700 g) bell peppers
Salt
1 tablespoon (10 g) sugar
3 bay leaves
A few basil leaves
10 peppercorns
5 cups (1.2 liters) white vinegar

Clean the bell peppers, cut them into strips, and remove the white pith as well as the seeds **(1)**.
Place in salted boiling water for 2 minutes (4 teaspoons/20 g salt to 4 cups/1 liter water) **(2)**, then add the sugar.
Drain and dry well on kitchen towel (2 to 3 hours) **(3)**.
Once dry, layer them with the bay leaves, basil leaves, and peppercorns in a previously sterilized jar **(4)**.
Add enough vinegar to cover generously, pressing down well to remove any air trapped in the middle of the bell peppers. Seal hermetically; they will keep for several months in a cool, dry place away from the light.

Recipe idea
Pork *alla Lucana* >> p. 405

Anchovies in Salt ★

Acciughe sotto sale

Anchovies in salt are used in a number of recipes (e.g. anchovy fondue, p. 191). They can also be served simply on crostini spread with butter.

You can transform them into fillets of anchovies in oil, even more useful in the kitchen.

Anchovies in salt are traditionally prepared in *arbanelle*—wide, straight jars made of thick glass.

Makes one 2 lb. (1 kg) jar
Preparation time: 20 minutes
Cooking time: 2 minutes
Salting time: 2 months

Ingredients
2 ¼ lb. (1 kg) very fresh anchovies
4 cups (2 ¼ lb./1 kg) sea salt

Remove the head and intestines of the anchovies. To do this, detach the head with your fingers and pull away what comes with it (1). Do *not* rinse the anchovies in water.

Place the anchovies in a dish. Spread a layer of salt in the bottom of the jar; arrange a layer of anchovies on top without leaving any space between them (2, 3).

Sprinkle with another layer of salt (4), then alternate layers of anchovies and salt, finishing with a layer of salt, taking care to press down well (5).

Place a weight (flat stone, glass disk, piece of slate, etc.) on top of the contents. Do not close the jar hermetically but cover it with a circle of parchment paper held in place by a rubber band.

Stand in a dish and put in a cool, dry place away from the light. You can use these anchovies after 2 months but do not keep longer than 2 years.

Check the jar from time to time: if any water has formed and is tending to leak, empty the jar slightly; if the anchovies become too dry, add a little brine prepared with boiled and cooled salt water (4 teaspoons/20 g of salt to 4 cups/1 liter water).

To make anchovy fillets in oil.
Remove the central bones of the salted anchovies and rinse with a mixture of half water, half vinegar.

Spread out on absorbent paper to dry (2 to 3 hours).

Layer them with a few bay leaves in a previously sterilized glass jar.

Cover with olive oil and close hermetically.

Anchovy fillets prepared in this way will keep several months in a cool, dry place away from the light.

Preserves: method of preparation

• Only use ingredients that are very fresh, in perfect condition, and not too ripe. Wash, wipe dry, and trim carefully.

• Wash the jars with boiling water before adding the ingredients. The jars must be perfectly clean and dry. Always use new seals or lids for each new batch.

• Do not fill the jars to the brim—leave $1/3$ to $2/3$ in. (1 to 2 cm). Remove any air bubbles by firmly pressing the contents down to the bottom of the jar. If the contents leak in the upside-down position, wipe with a clean, damp cloth.

• Label the jars with the date of preparation and the contents and keep in a cool, dry place away from the light.

• Wait at least 2 months before sampling your preserves; do not keep longer than 1 year (except salted anchovies).

• Once opened, the jars must be kept cool and the contents consumed as soon as possible.

• To sterilize the jars and vacuum-seal the contents, place in a pan and stabilize them with a cloth or piece of card. Cover the jars with water to come about 1 to 2 in. (2 to 5 cm) above the lid and bring to a boil. Allow 20 to 60 minutes cooking time, depending on the size of the jars (20 minutes for jars up to ½ lb. [250 g], 30 minutes for jars up to 1 lb. [500 g], 45 minutes for jars up to 2 lb. [1 kg], and 60 minutes for jars up to 3 lb. [1.5 kg]). Let the jars cool in this water. If the sterilization process has happened correctly, the lid will be slightly depressed. Remove the jars from the water and wipe them dry carefully before storing them.

• Jellies and preserves in vinegar do not require sterilization.

• For preserved vegetables it is always necessary to boil the vegetables in an acidulated solution. This is to avoid contamination from botulism. The solution must contain a ratio of at least $2/3$ vinegar to water (or the juice of 3 lemons for 4 cups/1 liter water). Salt is also important for the preserving process. The cooking time will vary, depending on the size of the pieces of vegetables, but it is preferable to leave them al dente, because they will continue to "cook" during the preserving process. Vegetables prepared in this way can be kept in this same solution, or removed and dried well, before being covered with olive oil to preserve them.

• When opening jars of preserves, discard any contents that do not seem to have vacuum-sealed successfully, appear to have deteriorated, or give off an unpleasant smell.

• Add a few spoonfuls of soybean oil to your preserves in olive oil to prevent them from solidifying in the refrigerator.

Pizza

Traditional pizza

Pizza certainly originated in Naples, making Neapolitan pizza worthy of the title TSG (Traditional Specialty Guaranteed) since 2010. The recipe is protected and promoted throughout the world by the True Neapolitan Pizza Association (Associazione Verace Pizza Napolitana), founded in 1984. The pizzerias that comply with the specifications laid down for this recipe receive a numbered logo from the association to display on their storefront. There are more than 400 affiliations in the world. Approval is given to the pizzerias by the *pizzaioli* of Naples. It is mandated that the pizza should be baked in wood-fired ovens. The method outlined here, slightly revised for domestic use, is for the preparation of authentic Neapolitan pizza. Olive oil needs to be added to the dough to compensate for the longer cooking needed in an electric oven; this helps to prevent it from becoming dry. It is also necessary to adapt the method of stretching to the so-called "DJ" method (turning and stretching the dough on the counter—see the step-by-step photographs p. 33) whereas the traditional method is called the "slap" technique (*schiaffo*), where the dough is alternatively slapped between the hands and the counter.

Original recipe for traditional Neapolitan pizza dough, cooked in a wood-fired oven

Pasta per pizza per cottura a legna

Ingredients
4 ¼ cups (1 liter) water
3 ¼ tablespoons (2 oz./50-55 g) sea salt
²/₃ teaspoon (3 g) fresh yeast
17-18 cups (3 ¾-4 lb./1.7-1.8 kg) bread flour or 00 flour

Preparation time for dough: 10 minutes
Mixing time: 20 minutes
First rising time: 2 hours
Second rising time in pizza pans: 4-6 hours
Rising temperature: room temperature (77°F/25°C)
Keep at room temperature: maximum 6 hours

Mix the ingredients together (see facing page). Shape balls of ¹/₃-½ lb. (180-250 g) each by hand.

Advice on making a successful pizza

Cooking

One of the most important factors when preparing pizza is the cooking temperature. The quicker the pizza is cooked, at the highest possible temperature, the softer and crisper it will be. Therefore the optimal cooking method is in a wood-fired oven. Wood-fired ovens heat to an average temperature of 905°F (485°C), cooking the pizza in 60 to 90 seconds. Most pizzerias that do not possess a wood-fired oven are equipped with electric ovens with a floor covered with refractory stones. These ovens can reach temperatures close to 750°F (400°C) and the pizza will cook in about 3 minutes, but they will lack the aroma and color (small, charcoal-colored spots) typical of pizza cooked in a wood-fired oven. Even in the hottest of domestic ovens, the temperature does not exceed 540°F (280°C). To cook the pizza as rapidly as possible, it is best to buy a refractory baking stone (from hardware stores or available on the Internet) to install on the floor of the oven, which will act as an accumulator of heat. You can bake the pizza directly on the stone, placing it there with a pizza peel (or with the removable flat base from a metal tart mold). The pizza will then cook in 5 to 6 minutes. It is also possible to cook the pizza on a metal baking sheet, or in a pizza pan, but the cooking time will lengthen to 12 to 15 minutes. The result will be most noticeable in the way the dough cooks: it will become drier and more brittle.

Mozzarella

It is always better to use mozzarella that is at room temperature, both to appreciate its flavor, and to avoid a dramatic change in temperature that risks spoiling it. When making pizza at home, use a mozzarella that does not contain too much water; this will prevent the pizza becoming soggy during cooking. With a wood-fired oven, the water in the fresh mozzarella cheese evaporates very quickly, but less so at 540°F (280°C). Therefore use a processed mozzarella or well-drained braid (*treccia*, see p. 159) of fresh mozzarella. It is also better to cut the mozzarella into small pieces so that it melts in 5 minutes without burning (sliced mozzarella scorches as it melts which is very unpleasant). If you want to use fresh buffalo (*bufala*) mozzarella or fresh cow's milk (*fior di latte*) mozzarella, it is advisable to drain it as thoroughly as possible using paper towel before laying it on the pizza. The same thing can be done with slices of fresh tomato, which also tend to give out water during the cooking process.

Tomato sauce

The True Neapolitan Pizza Association specifies the use of good-quality peeled tomatoes for the preparation of pizza. Sieved tomato (*passata*) is too liquid and chopped tomato is not suitable; it is only by crushing peeled tomatoes with a fork or blender that the consistency of a sauce perfectly suited to Neapolitan pizza can be achieved. There is no need to precook the tomato sauce; it cooks with the other ingredients directly on the pizza. To correct the acidity of a tomato sauce of poor quality, one spoonful of sugar or a pinch of baking soda can be added. Oregano should not be used—with certain exceptions, e.g. on a marinara pizza; according to Neapolitans, oregano absolutely does not go with cheese.

Yeast and rising times

For making pizza dough, fresh baker's yeast should be used, as it gives the best results for raising the dough. The amount of yeast used is in inverse proportion to the time planned for the rise. The proportions of the recipe are planned for a rising time of 8 hours. If you want dough to rise for 16 hours, divide the amount of yeast approximately in half; if it is going to rise for 4 hours, increase it by a little more than double. The longer it is left to rise, the better the dough will be. Salt is also very important: for the taste, to prevent the fermentation of the dough, and to give it elasticity. The high-gluten bread flours that are available commercially work perfectly but, should you find flour described as "special pizza strength," the result will be slightly superior. Olive oil is only added to the dough when it is to be cooked in an electric oven to make the final result crisp. This use is outlawed in the TSG charter for cooking in a wood-fired oven.

Neapolitan pizza

Pizza Dough ★ ★ ★

Pasta per pizza napoletana

For 1 pizza
Preparation time: 25 minutes
Rising time: 30 minutes

Ingredients
1 ¾ cups (6 oz./170-180 g) all-purpose flour
⅓ cup (100 ml) water at 77°F-83°F (25°C-30°C)
1 teaspoon (5 g) salt
⅕ teaspoon (0.5 g) fresh yeast
1 teaspoon (5 ml) olive oil

Put the water in a mixing bowl and add the salt.
Dissolve the yeast in the salted water.
Taking small amounts at a time, add half the flour in a thin stream, mixing continuously with your fingers. Stir in the olive oil.
Add the rest of the flour and knead the dough until well mixed and coming away from the sides of the bowl. Continue kneading for 10 minutes, until smooth and elastic; it should not stick to your fingers.
Shape the dough into a ball and leave it, lightly floured, in the bowl covered with a damp cloth and leave it to rise for 30 minutes at room temperature, free from drafts, approximately 65°F-70°F (18°C-22°C).
If you have prepared a large quantity of dough for several pizzas, divide it with a knife into the number of pizzas to be made. Shape into tightly formed balls, cover with a damp dish towel and leave to rest for 8 hours at room temperature, free from drafts, at approximately 65°F-70°F (18°C-22°C).

● **Chef's note**
It is always possible to stop the dough rising by putting it in the refrigerator (2 days maximum, if brushed with oil and placed in a hermetically sealed box), or even in the freezer (well covered in plastic wrap). You will then need to restore the dough to room temperature before completing the rising time. However, this will have an effect on the final quality of your pizza.

Tomato Sauce for pizza ★

Pomodoro per pizza

For 1 pizza
Preparation time: 5 minutes

Ingredients
½ cup (3 oz./80 g) good-quality peeled tomatoes
   (canned or fresh)
½ clove garlic
1 teaspoon (5 ml) olive oil
A few basil leaves
Salt

Crush the garlic and very quickly mix all the ingredients together with a stick blender. Season with a pinch of salt.

Mozzarella for pizza ★

Mozzarella per pizza

For 1 pizza
Preparation time: 5 minutes

Ingredients
5 oz. (150 g) ball or braid of mozzarella

Squeeze the water from the mozzarella and chop either in a food processor, or with a knife.

● **Chef's note**
The recipes that follow are all prepared with the pizza dough described on p. 31.

http://flamm.fr/ic01

Margherita Pizza ★★

This pizza was prepared for the first time in 1889 by the chef Raffaele Esposito, for Queen Margherita of Austria, while on holiday in Naples with her husband, King Umberto of Savoy. The *pizzaiolo* wanted to represent the tricolor Italian flag with the colors of his pizza ingredients: the red of the tomato, the white of the mozzarella, and the green of the basil. In the light of the Queen's enthusiasm, he baptized his creation "Margherita." The next day, *Pizza Margherita* was on the menu, and the best seller in the Esposito family's pizzeria.

Makes one pizza approximately 12 in. (30 cm)
in diameter
Preparation time: 5 minutes
Cooking time: 5-6 minutes

Ingredients
1 ball of pizza dough (see p. 31)
1 portion of tomato sauce (see left)
1 portion of mozzarella (see left)
1 teaspoon olive oil
A few basil leaves

Preheat the oven to 535°F (270°C-280°C), choosing the setting for combined top and bottom heating. Place a baking stone on the floor of the oven.
Flour the counter and your hands.
With the help of a spatula, take a ball of pizza and place it on the work surface. With your fingertips, begin to lightly flatten out the ball of dough to create a disk.
Once you can place both hands flat on it, begin to stretch the dough by pulling from the middle toward the outside edge, turning it by 90 degrees with each movement of the hands until you have a disk of approximately 12 in. (30 cm) in diameter.
Using a ladle or spoon, spread the tomato sauce from the center outward with a circular motion.
Add the crumbled mozzarella, and drizzle over the olive oil.
Using a pizza peel, slide the pizza directly onto the preheated baking stone and cook for 5 to 6 minutes.
On removal from the oven, decorate with the basil leaves and serve immediately.

● **Did you know?**
A letter from the royal household, praising the "excellent" pizzas prepared by Esposito, is still on show in the Ancient Pizzeria Brandi in Naples, birthplace of the Margherita.

Neapolitan Pizza ★★

Neapolitan pizza is very rich-tasting, thanks to its seasoning based on capers and anchovies.
It is often prepared without mozzarella, when it is known as *pizza rossa*.

Makes one pizza approximately 12 in. (30 cm) in diameter
Preparation time: 5 minutes
Cooking time: 5-6 minutes

Ingredients
1 ball of pizza dough (see p. 31)
1 portion of tomato sauce (see facing page)
1 portion of mozzarella (see facing page)
5 anchovy fillets in oil
1 tablespoon salted capers (presoaked to remove salt)
1 teaspoon olive oil
A few basil leaves

Preheat the oven to 535°F (270°C-280°C), choosing the setting for combined top and bottom heating. Place a baking stone on the floor of the oven.
Flour the counter and your hands.
With the help of a spatula, take a ball of pizza and place it on the work surface. With your fingertips, begin to lightly flatten out the ball of dough to create a disk (1).
Once you can place both hands flat on it, begin to stretch the dough by pulling from the middle toward the outside edge, turning it by 90 degrees with each movement of the hands until you have a disk of approximately 12 in. (30 cm) in diameter (2).
Using a ladle or spoon, spread the tomato sauce from the center outward with a circular motion (3).
Add the topping ingredients in the following order: chopped mozzarella, anchovies, and capers, then drizzle over the olive oil (4).
Using a pizza peel, slide the pizza directly onto the preheated baking stone and cook for 5 to 6 minutes.
On removal from the oven, decorate with the basil leaves and serve immediately.

● **Did you know?**
Curiously, in Naples, Neapolitan pizza is called pizza Romana— *Roman pizza!*

Calzone ★★

Makes one pizza
Preparation time: 5 minutes
Cooking time: 5-6 minutes

Ingredients
1 ball of pizza dough (see p. 31)
1 portion of mozzarella (see p. 32)
3 fresh mushrooms, sliced
2 oz. (60 g) cooked ham (*prosciutto cotto*), sliced thinly
1 artichoke in oil, cut into quarters
2 teaspoons olive oil
½ portion of tomato sauce (see p. 32)

Preheat the oven to 535°F (270°C-280°C), choosing the setting for combined top and bottom heating. Place a baking stone on the floor of the oven.
Flour the counter and your hands.
With the help of a spatula, take a ball of pizza and place it on the work surface. With your fingertips, begin to lightly flatten out the ball of dough to create a disk **(1)**.
Once you can place both hands flat on it, begin to stretch the dough by pulling from the middle toward the outside edge, turning it by 90 degrees with each movement of the hands until you have a disk of approximately 12 in. (30 cm) in diameter **(2)**.
On one half of the disk of dough, add the pizza toppings in the following order: mozzarella, mushrooms, ham, and artichokes, then drizzle 1 teaspoon of the olive oil over them.
Fold in two **(3)**, press down firmly with your fingertips all around the perimeter to seal the edges well **(4)**.
Spread a spoonful of tomato sauce on the surface of the calzone and drizzle the remaining olive oil over it.
Using a pizza peel, slide the pizza directly onto the preheated baking stone and cook for 5 to 6 minutes.
Remove from the oven and serve immediately.

● Chef's note
Use your imagination when creating pizza—it is open to many interpretations.

Variations

There are countless combinations of ingredients for making a pizza. Here are a few suggestions for the most classic and widely known toppings:

· **Marinara:** tomato sauce, 1 finely sliced clove of garlic, oregano.
· **Regina** (*prosciutto e funghi* in Italy): tomato sauce, mozzarella, very finely sliced fresh mushrooms, cooked ham (*prosciutto cotto*).
· **Capricciosa:** tomato sauce, mozzarella, finely sliced fresh mushrooms, cooked ham (*prosciutto cotto*), artichokes in oil, black olives.
· **Diavola:** tomato sauce, mozzarella, spicy sausage, finely sliced fresh onion.
· **Parma:** tomato sauce, mozzarella; Parma ham and arugula are added after cooking.
· **Caprese:** very little mozzarella, finely sliced fresh tomato, fresh buffalo mozzarella (*di bufala*) cut up small; a few basil leaves added after cooking.
· **Vegetariana:** tomato sauce, mozzarella, zucchini, eggplant, very finely sliced bell peppers.

· **Quattro formaggi:** mozzarella, Gorgonzola, Gruyère, Parmesan cheese. This pizza is generally made without tomato.
· **Scoglio** (with seafood): tomato, garlic, parsley, mussels, clams, rings of squid, shrimp. This pizza is generally made without mozzarella.
· **Salmon:** mozzarella; finely sliced smoked salmon and arugula are added after cooking. This pizza is generally made without tomato.
· **Antica:** mozzarella, *caciocavallo* (or *scamorza*) cheese; *lardo di Colonnata* added after cooking.

Roman-style pizza

We have Roman bakers of the 1950s to thank for inventing this method of making pizza on large baking sheets. It was a gimmick to expand their range of pizza on offer. Today *pizza al taglio* is sold in every bakery in Italy.

Pizza al Taglio with Porcini, Sausage, and Arugula ★★

Pizza al taglio porcini, salsiccia e rucola

Makes one pizza to fit a 12 × 16 in. (30 × 40 cm) baking sheet
Preparation time: 8 minutes
Cooking time: 20 minutes

Ingredients
1 lb. 5 oz. (600 g) pizza dough (i.e. 3 balls Neapolitan pizza dough, see p. 31)
1 ¼ cups (300 ml) pizza sauce (i.e. 2 portions tomato sauce for pizza, see p. 32)
10 oz. (300 g) mozzarella, chopped (i.e. 2 portions mozzarella for pizza, see p. 32)
1 chipolata or plain Toulouse sausage, cut into small pieces
1 porcini, finely chopped
1 tablespoon olive oil
¼ cup (50 g) arugula

Preheat the oven to 400°F (200°C), choosing the setting for combined top and bottom heating.
Flatten out the pizza dough by hand. Lightly oil the baking sheet. Place the flattened ball of dough on a floured counter and begin to make it larger (1). Place on the baking sheet and spread it out to cover the entire surface, creating a shallow rim (2).
Spread over the tomato sauce using a ladle or spoon (3). Add the toppings in the following order: mozzarella, sausage (4), and porcini. Drizzle over the olive oil.
Bake the pizza on the lowest shelf of the oven.
On removal from the oven, decorate with arugula (5).
Cut into slices and serve immediately.

Focaccia

Focaccia is a bread dough enriched with olive oil, found under different names in every region of Italy. However, Genoese focaccia is by far the best known.

Genoese Focaccia ★★★

To fit a 12 × 16 in. (30 × 40 cm) baking sheet
Preparation time: 45 minutes
Rising time: 3 hours
Cooking time: 20 minutes

Ingredients
6 cups (1 lb. 5oz./600 g) all-purpose flour
2 tablespoons (1 oz./30 g) fresh yeast
1 ½ cups (350 ml) water
2 teaspoons brown sugar or honey
1 tablespoon (½ oz./15 g) fine salt + a little extra for baking sheet
2/3 cup (140 ml) olive oil
1 tablespoon (½ oz./15 g) kosher salt

Dilute the yeast in ½ cup (100 ml) of the water at room temperature. Add the brown sugar and 1 cup (3 ½ oz./100 g) of the flour (1). Leave to rest for 1 hour.
Dissolve the fine salt in the remaining water.
Transfer the mixture to a food mixer fitted with a dough hook (or to a large bowl) (2), add the rest of the flour, the salted water, and 3 tablespoons (40 ml) of the olive oil. Turn on the mixer and knead for 10 to 15 minutes. Take the dough out of the mixer (3), form into a ball, place in a bowl and cover with a damp cloth. Let rise for 1 hour.
Pour 2 tablespoons (30 ml) of the olive oil onto a baking sheet and sprinkle with a little fine salt. Place the risen dough on the baking sheet coated with olive oil; spread it out evenly with your fingertips until the baking sheet is covered (4).
Mix the remaining olive oil (5 tablespoons/70 ml) with the same amount of water. Using a brush, glaze with one third of the olive oil and water mixture.
Leave to rise for 2 hours, covered with a damp cloth (5).
Preheat the oven to 400°F (200°C).
Make indentations all over the surface of the focaccia with your fingers (6). Sprinkle with the kosher salt and brush again with another third of the olive oil mixed with water. Check that the surface is well moistened, then bake the focaccia for 20 minutes.
On removal from the oven, lift the focaccia off the baking sheet (7) and place it on a cooling rack. Brush the surface with the remaining olive oil and water mixture one last time.

1

2

3

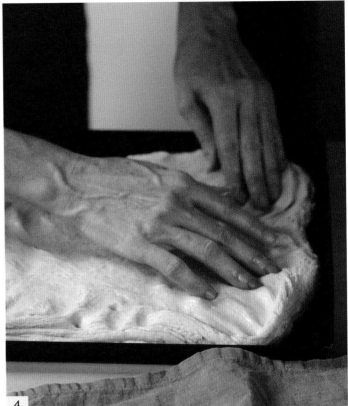

4

5

6

7

Tomatoes

Tomatoes

In Italy, the tomato is known by the name *pomodoro*, meaning golden apple (*mala aurea*, according to the literal wording of botanist Pietro Andrea Mattioli in 1544), from the yellow color of the earliest varieties to arrive in Italy. The red variety became widespread a little later. From the seventeenth century, the tomato was consumed mainly in the South by the poorest of the population, becoming the symbol of popular cuisine. It subsequently spread throughout the rest of Italy to enhance many regional dishes.

We owe the origin of pasta accompanied by tomato sauce to the Neapolitans. The recipe appears for the first time in 1837, in the book *Cucina Teorico Pratica* (The Theory and Practice of Cooking) by the Neapolitan Ippolito Cavalcanti, who was no doubt confirming the existence of a dish that was already widely known.

By the eighteenth century, the scientist Lazzaro Spallanzani had discovered the means of preserving the tomato without altering its taste or appearance. This was the starting point of a flourishing industry. The first Italian tomato sauce factory belonged to Francesco Cirio in Turin. His ideas on the preservation of food were so innovative that they received awards at the Paris Universal Exhibition in 1867. From then on, the tomato became the subject of a substantial processing industry: dried tomatoes, peeled tomatoes in cans, tomato passata, tomato paste, tomato sauces (natural or flavored, ketchup, and so on), and tomato juice.

Today more than 300 species of tomatoes are cultivated. There are all sorts of varieties: round, flattened, oval, elongated (San Marzano, Roma, etc.), smooth or ribbed (beefsteak, etc.). A distinction is also made between tomatoes to be eaten fresh and tomatoes to be preserved. In Italy, some tomatoes receive protected name status; these are ancient species of very high quality less well adapted to the industrial market. Among these are the San Marzano tomato and the del Piennolo del Vesuvio, Fiaschetto, and Pachino varieties.

The tomato is a summer fruit. If grown throughout the year, it matures fully between August and September, when it is at its sweetest and most flavorsome. Its color should be intense and it should be fragrant and firm, but not hard to the touch.

Keep at room temperature in a place that is not too dry, and never in the refrigerator.

Preserves

Peeled Tomatoes ★

Pomodori pelati

San Marzano plum tomatoes are traditionally the most commonly chosen for peeling and bottling. If these are not available, other varieties of plum tomato can be used.

Makes one 8 oz. (250 g) jar
Preparation time: 10 minutes
Cooking time: 1 minute + sterilization of the jar

Ingredients
8-12 plum tomatoes (2 lb./1 kg approx.), preferably San Marzano
A few basil leaves
Salt

Wash the tomatoes and immerse them in boiling water for 1 minute (1), then immerse them in cold water before peeling them (2, 3).

Place them in spotlessly clean preserving jars in alternate layers with the basil leaves and salt (4). Pack them down well, displacing any air bubbles between them. Close the jars and sterilize them in boiling water (5) (30 minutes for 8 oz. [250 g] jars; 45 minutes for 1 lb. [500 g] jars; 1 hour for 2 lb. [1 kg] jars).

If the tomatoes are not juicy enough, you can prepare a brine to add to the jars. To make the brine, boil water with 2 tablespoons (30 g) of salt per 4 cups (1 liter) water.

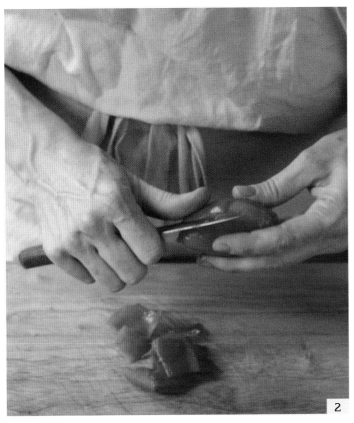

2

3

4

5

Tomato Coulis ★

Salsa (o passata) di pomodoro

For making tomato coulis, it is best to use ripe tomatoes cultivated in open ground in the sunshine, purchased at the end of the summer.

Makes one 8 oz. (250 g) jar
Preparation time: 10 minutes
Cooking time: 1 minute + sterilization of the jar

Ingredients
8–12 plum tomatoes (2 lb./1 kg approximately),
 preferably San Marzano
A few basil leaves
Salt

Wash the tomatoes and immerse them for 1 minute in boiling water, then immerse them in cold water before peeling them. Cook them in a saucepan until they begin to soften, then season with salt.
Press the tomatoes through a coarse sieve and replace over the heat, adding the basil leaves. Bring to a boil and remove from the heat. Pour into spotlessly clean preserving jars. Close the jars and sterilize in boiling water (30 minutes for 8 oz. [250 g] jars; 45 minutes for 1 lb. [500 g] jars; 1 hour for 2 lb. [1 kg] jars).

● **Chef's note**
You can enhance the tomato coulis with other ingredients according to taste: garlic, onion, oregano, thyme, etc. Add all these ingredients at the same time as the basil in the basic recipe.

Oven-Dried Tomatoes in Olive Oil ★

Pomodori secchi sott'olio

Dried tomatoes are produced mainly in the south of Italy, particularly in Calabria, Sicily, Puglia, and Liguria. The tomatoes used are generally San Marzano plum tomatoes, the best being those dried in the sun. The tomatoes are split in two, salted, and placed on wooden lattices in the sun (and brought indoors at night to avoid moisture) for one week, until they have totally lost their juice. At home, this procedure can be done in the oven. You can rehydrate dried tomatoes a little to serve on crostini, or to enhance the flavor of a sauce. You can also preserve them in oil (see below) to enjoy as antipasto or as an accompaniment for other foods.

Makes one 8 oz. (250 g) jar
Drying time: 8 hours
Preparation time: 20 minutes

Ingredients
6–8 meaty plum tomatoes, cored and cut in half lengthwise
1 tablespoon olive oil, plus more for the jar (about 2/3 cup/150 ml)
A few basil leaves
2 cloves garlic, thinly sliced
Salt

Place the tomatoes on a baking sheet covered with parchment paper, drizzle them with a tablespoon of olive oil, sprinkle with a little salt and dry them out at 200°F (100°C) for approximately 8 hours.
Place the oven-dried tomatoes in a preserving jar (1) in alternate layers with the basil leaves and garlic (2). Press everything down well and cover with the olive oil (3). Slide the blade of a knife around the inside of the jar to help remove any air bubbles (4). Wait for 2 weeks before use.
If the tomatoes appear too dry before adding the oil, you can rehydrate them a little by soaking them for 10 to 20 minutes in a mixture of two parts vinegar to one part cold water. Drain and dry them well before placing in the preserving jar.

● **Chef's note**
According to your taste, you can add peppercorns, dried chilies, salted capers, anchovies, wild fennel seeds, oregano, etc.

1

2

3

4

Candied Tomatoes ★★

Pomodori canditi

Candied tomatoes can be used in several ways: as decoration, as a flavoring, to replace fresh tomatoes, or as a preserve to accompany a dish. They also look very attractive and keep for a reasonable length of time.

Makes one 8 oz. (250 g) jar
Preparation time: 10 minutes
Cooking time: 2 hours

Ingredients
2 lb. (1 kg) cherry tomatoes
Zest of 1 orange
Zest of 1 lemon
1 tablespoon thyme
1 tablespoon oregano
1 tablespoon sugar
5 tablespoons (75 ml) olive oil, plus more for the jar
Salt, pepper

Wash the tomatoes and sprinkle over all the remaining ingredients (1, 2, 3). Spread them on a baking sheet lined with parchment paper and leave them to become candied in the oven for 2 hours at 200°F (100°C) (4).
Place in the preserving jar and cover completely with oil. They will keep in the refrigerator for 10 days. Sterilize the jars first–in the oven or by boiling in water–to preserve the candied tomatoes longer.

Tomato-based sauces

Tomato-based sauces have become the symbol of popular Italian cooking. They accompany all sorts of dishes: pasta, gnocchi, polenta, bread (either toasted or plain).

To prepare these tomato-based sauces, use fresh tomatoes in summer and canned in winter. The latter have the advantage of being picked when ripe and immediately put into cans. Good-quality brands of canned tomatoes are generally the sweetest and most flavorsome. It is only in summer, and particularly in August and September, that you can make the sauces with really red, ripe tomatoes purchased from a market.

Choose tomatoes canned in tomato juice rather than water as the latter are generally acidic. To prepare a coulis, just mix with a stick blender. You can determine the consistency of the coulis by controlling the speed and time of mixing.

As regards the cooking of the tomato sauce, the result will be very different if the tomato is cooked for just a few minutes, to evaporate the juice, or for more than 2 hours. In the first case, you'll get a fresh, light sauce. In the second, you will have what is called a *stracotto*, a thicker, more concentrated, and flavorsome sauce.

Tomato and Basil Sauce ★

Pomodoro e basilico

This is the simplest, most classic of tomato sauces, prepared in 20 minutes with fresh or canned tomatoes.

Serves 4
Preparation time: 10 minutes
Cooking time: 15 minutes

Ingredients
2 ½ lb. (1.2 kg) ripe tomatoes or 2 ½ cups (14 oz./400 g) canned, peeled tomatoes
1 clove garlic
A few basil leaves
4 tablespoons (60 ml) olive oil
Salt

Wash the tomatoes, peel them (with a serrated vegetable peeler or by immersing them in boiling water for a few seconds, then in cold water); remove the stalk and core (remove the seeds too, if you wish).
Crush the garlic. Cook the tomatoes for 15 minutes in a saucepan with the garlic, chopped basil, and olive oil, season with salt.
Press through a sieve or vegetable mill (or not, if you prefer a more rustic sauce).
Serve this sauce with a dish of pasta and add plenty of grated Parmesan.

● Chef's note
For some dishes, such as gnocchi or fresh egg pasta, replace the olive oil with butter as a very good alternative.

Variations
· **Marinara sauce:** replace the basil with chopped parsley.

· **Arrabbiata sauce:** cook with garlic and finely chopped dried Thai/bird (bird's eye) chili; replace the basil with chopped parsley at the end of the cooking time.

· **Pizzaiola sauce:** replace the basil with chopped parsley and oregano.

Uncooked Tomato Sauce ★

Salsa crudaiola

This is a sauce for the summer, using raw tomatoes.
The higher the quality of the tomatoes, the better the sauce
will be.

Serves 4
Preparation time: 10 minutes

Ingredients
1 ⅓ lb. (600 g) ripe tomatoes
1 clove garlic, crushed
A few basil leaves, finely chopped
4 tablespoons (60 ml) olive oil
Salt
1 chili (optional)

Wash the tomatoes and peel them (with a serrated vegetable
peeler or by immersing them in boiling water for a few
seconds, then in cold water) (1). Remove the stalk and core
(remove the seeds too, if you wish).
Dice or cut the tomatoes into quarters and place them in
a large bowl. Add the garlic (2) and basil, then season with
salt and the chili if using it.
Serve this sauce with a dish of pasta and add plenty
of grated Parmesan.
You can also use this sauce to accompany cold pasta, fish,
and grilled meat, or spread on slices of toasted bread to
make *bruschette*.

Recipe idea
Bruschette and *Crostini* >> p. 300

Tomato Sauce ★

Sugo di pomodoro

A recipe for tomato sauce that is a little more complex.
The vegetables give additional flavor to the tomatoes.

Serves 4
Preparation time: 15 minutes
Cooking time: 30 minutes

Ingredients
2 lb. (1 kg) ripe tomatoes or 2 ½ cups (14 oz./400 g) canned,
   peeled tomatoes
1 onion
1 carrot
1 stick celery
4 tablespoons (60 ml) olive oil
A few basil leaves
Salt

If you use fresh tomatoes, wash and peel them (with a
serrated vegetable peeler or by immersing them in boiling
water for a few seconds, then in cold water)(1). Remove
the stalk and core (remove the seeds too if you wish).
Peel the vegetables and chop finely (2, 3) and brown them
in a saucepan with the olive oil (4). Add the tomatoes,
cut into pieces, and a few chopped basil leaves (5).
Season with salt and leave to cook for 30 minutes. Press
through a sieve or a vegetable mill (6) (or not, if you prefer
a more rustic sauce).
Serve this sauce with a dish of pasta and add plenty of
grated Parmesan.

● **Chef's note**
*If the sauce seems too acidic, add a pinch of baking soda or a tea-
spoon of sugar.*

Neapolitan Tomato Sauce ★

Sugo di pomodoro alla napoletana

This is one of the world's best-loved sauces.
The tomatoes are simply enhanced with a chopped onion
(for added sweetness) and a few basil leaves.

Serves 4
Preparation time: 10 minutes
Cooking time: 30 minutes

Ingredients
2 lb. (1 kg) ripe tomatoes or 2 ½ cups (14 oz./400 g) canned,
  peeled tomatoes
1 onion
1 tablespoon olive oil
A few basil leaves
A few parsley leaves
Salt

If you use fresh tomatoes, wash and peel them (with a
serrated vegetable peeler or by immersing them in boiling
water for a few seconds, then in cold water), and remove
the stalk and core (remove the seeds too if you wish) (1).
Chop the onion (2), and brown it in a saucepan with the olive
oil. Add the tomatoes, cut into pieces, and a few chopped
basil and parsley leaves (3).
Season with salt and leave to cook for 30 minutes. Press
through a sieve or vegetable mill (4, 5) (or not, if you prefer
a more rustic sauce).
Serve this sauce with a dish of pasta.

Bolognese Sauce ★ ★

Ragù alla bolognese

Bolognese sauce, commonly called *"ragù"*, is certainly one of the best known in the world, along with Neapolitan and tomato sauce.

In Italy, there are countless versions of this sauce, with each region, each province, and each family having its own authentic recipe.

The *ragù* recipe was patented in 1982 at the Chamber of Commerce in Bologna to protect its authenticity.

Serves 6
Preparation time: 50 minutes
Cooking time: 3 hours

Ingredients

8 oz. (300 g) chopped beef brisket (a piece of beef that is rich in fat is required to make the sauce unctuous)
5 oz. (150 g) pancetta
1 onion (4 oz./120 g approximately)
1 carrot (3 oz./80 g approximately)
1 stick celery (2 oz./60g approximately)
½ cup (125 ml) red or dry white wine (a Sangiovese would be ideal)
½ cup (125 ml) beef stock
4 teaspoons (20 g) tomato paste
5 tablespoons tomato coulis (see p. 44, 47)
1 cup (250 ml) whole milk
Salt, pepper

Chop the pancetta and brown in a saucepan over medium heat for 15 minutes (1).
Wash and peel the vegetables, chop them, add to the pancetta (2), and soften until they become translucent. Increase the heat to maximum then add the chopped meat and brown it well (this is critical to obtain a really tasty *ragù*) (3).
Deglaze with the wine (4), let evaporate. Meanwhile, in another saucepan, put the stock on to heat and dilute the tomato paste and coulis in it. Pour this mixture over the meat and vegetables. Season with salt, pepper, and let simmer. When the sauce begins to dry out, gradually stir in the milk.
Simmer for at least 3 hours, until the sauce has thickened substantially (5).
Serve with egg tagliatelle and grated Parmesan or in a baked lasagna.

● Chef's note

This sauce can be kept in the refrigerator for several days. It is important to cool it down very quickly once cooked, to prevent it from becoming acidic. It is also very suitable for freezing.

Variations

· You can serve the Bolognese sauce with peas added to the sauce toward the end of the cooking process, or cooked separately.

· It is becoming more and more common to prepare a "light" Bolognese sauce by replacing the brisket with lean ground beef.

· *Ragù* is the perfect way to use up remnants of leftover meat, most commonly pork, veal, chicken, and sometimes mutton; it should always be ground.
Each meat will transmit its characteristic flavor to the sauce.

· The quantity of tomato sauce varies depending on the recipe; as there is not very much in this recipe, you could increase the amount to suit your taste.

· The recipe from Bologna specifies moistening with whole milk; you can replace the milk with additional beef stock. This will make the sauce less rich.

· The pancetta can also be replaced by ¼ stick (1 oz./30 g) of butter or 2 tablespoons of olive oil.

· Bolognese sauce traditionally accompanies egg tagliatelle, another specialty typical of Bologna.
However, all over the world, Bolognese sauce is served with spaghetti, the pasta shape typical of southern Italy. This is because Italian regional cuisine is frequently misinterpreted outside Italy.

Dried pasta

Pasta made from durum wheat flour

The first "dry" (dried) pasta manufactured in Italy seems to date from the time of the Etruscans, as evidenced by the frescoes in the funeral chapel of Cerveteri (fourth century BCE). Originally, pasta (*lagan*) was cooked in the oven, but it was only from the Middle Ages that it began to be boiled in water. This method of cooking gave the pasta the texture and flavor we appreciate today.

It was also during the Middle Ages that the first artisans appeared in Italy who produced pasta in volume: first in Palermo, then in Naples and Genoa and, a century later, in Puglia and Tuscany. For a long time, pasta production was linked to these port cities as they benefited from natural ventilation that allowed pasta to dry slowly, and therefore to be kept longer. The degree of cooking varied through the centuries. Initially, it was served very well cooked as an accompaniment to meat. Pasta as a separate dish in its own right was consumed more and more al dente from the seventeenth century onward. In the nineteenth century, it found its ideal ally in tomato sauce.

Dried pasta is prepared from durum wheat flour and water and is mainly produced industrially. It is manufactured with an extrusion machine that pushes the dough through a bronze mold to create the desired pasta shape. This technique produces a pasta with a rough surface that "holds" the sauce. The higher the quality of the flour and water, the better the pasta. The dimensions and the quality of the bronze molds, as well as a long, natural drying time also contribute to the quality. For industrial or artisanal pasta, instructions for longer cooking times indicate a high-quality product.

Pasta shapes and sizes

Dried pasta can be divided into seven sub-categories:
- **Long, cylindrical, and compact** (different diameters): vermicelli, spaghettini, spaghetti, etc.
- **Long, cylindrical, and hollow**: *bucatini,* ziti, etc.
- **Long, rectangular or flattened**: linguine, fettuccine, tagliatelle, *trenette, bavette, tagliolini,* etc.
- **Long, wide**: *pappardelle,* lasagna, *reginette,* etc.
- **Short, smooth**: farfalle, fusilli, penne lisce, *eliche, paccheri,* etc.
- **Short, ridged**: rigatoni, penne rigate, *sedanini, tortiglioni,* etc.
- **Small, soup pasta shapes**: *avena, risi, stelline,* etc.

There are also many special pastas on the market; in addition to durum wheat flour, they can contain other flours to enhance them, such as chestnut, quinoa, spelt, etc., and/or colorants and natural aromas (cuttlefish, truffle, chili, and so on).

Equally worth a mention are dietetic pastas, where some ingredients are replaced for people who are gluten intolerant or require low-salt products.

Advice on cooking pasta successfully

1. Choose the shape of the pasta to complement the sauce it is accompanying. For example, spaghetti goes well with just oil or butter; *pappardelle* combines well with Bolognese sauce, and short pasta such as rigatoni is very well adapted for cooking in the oven.

2. Cook the pasta in a large saucepan with plenty of water. Allow 4 cups (1 liter) of water for every 4 oz. (110 g) of pasta and 2 teaspoons (10 g) of salt per liter. Never use less than 4 quarts (4 liters). The salt is added to the water only when it reaches boiling point to avoid slowing the process down. The pasta is immersed in the boiling water and the cooking time is calculated from the moment the water comes back to a boil.

3. Pasta should be stirred two or three times during cooking; this prevents it from sticking together, or to the bottom of the saucepan, and ensures it cooks evenly. Immerse the pasta in the water, wait 30 seconds after the boiling resumes, then give the pasta a first stir. Give it a second stir midway through and a third if the cooking time is long.

4. Only add a little oil to the water prior to cooking lasagna (the strips are wide, and tend to stick together on the surface). Avoid adding oil to the cooking water of other pasta to prevent a film of grease forming that will stop the sauce from clinging to it.

5. Cook pasta al dente: it will be more digestible and have more flavor. If it is to go in the oven, drain a few minutes before the cooking time is completed.

6. Drain the pasta through a colander. Season and serve immediately.

7. The best way to dress the pasta is to heat it through in a skillet with the sauce a few minutes before serving. This allows you to reheat and mix them together evenly. The pasta is drained and immediately added to the skillet with the sauce already hot. It is not necessary to cook the pasta that is to be reheated for less time (very al dente) because the additional heating is very rapid, providing the pasta used is of good quality.
Today, a new way to cook pasta has evolved in Italian cooking: a technique called *risottata*, meaning to cook the pasta in the manner of a risotto. The pasta is cooked in a skillet with the sauce by adding a ladle of water whenever necessary, until the pasta is al dente. This process allows the pasta to become completely impregnated with the flavors of the sauce.

8. Always reserve a little of the pasta cooking water to dilute the sauce so that it combines better with the pasta, particularly if the sauce seems slightly dry.

9. Use leftover pasta to make a gratin in the oven with a little Parmesan, tomato sauce, and/or béchamel. You can even make *timballi*: pasta pies (with puff pastry or flaky pie dough), to which you can also add béchamel, tomato sauce, and Parmesan. Other additions could be a little diced charcuterie (sausage, mortadella, ham, etc.) and/or various cheeses (*scamorza*, fontina, mozzarella, etc.). You can also make a pasta omelet.

10. Use the cooking juices from meat, fish, and vegetables for seasoning pasta; they make quick and economical sauces.

Traditional sauces

Garlic, Olive Oil, and Chili Sauce ★

Aglio, olio e peperoncino

This is every Italian's "midnight" spaghetti sauce. All Italians have cooked *pasta aglio e olio* in an emergency at least once in their lives!

Serves 4
Preparation time: 10 minutes
Cooking time: 10 minutes + pasta cooking time

Ingredients
2 cloves garlic
Generous ¾ cup (200 ml) olive oil
1 hot red chili (fresh or dry)
Salt, pepper

To serve with 1 lb. (500 g) spaghetti, spaghettini, or vermicelli.

Split the chili in two and seed it (1). Naturally, the more finely the chili is chopped, the more it will release its flavor and strength.
Peel and chop the garlic, then soften with the olive oil and chili in a skillet (2). Be careful not to color the garlic.
Cook the pasta, drain, and reheat in the very hot sauce with 2 tablespoons of the cooking water (3). Serve immediately.

● **Chef's note**
Don't remove the seeds if you want a more fiery sauce.

Pea and Ham Sauce ★

Piselli e prosciutto

This is a typical canteen recipe, and very popular with children.

Serves 4
Preparation time: 10 minutes
Cooking time: 10 minutes + pasta cooking time

Ingredients
2 cups (10 oz./300 g) shelled peas
3 oz. (80 g) cooked ham
1 onion
⅓ stick (1 ½ oz./40 g) butter
1 cup (250 ml) heavy cream
Salt, pepper

To serve with 1 lb. (500 g) farfalle, penne, or fusilli.

Peel the onion and chop it finely, soften in a skillet with the butter (1). As soon as the onion is translucent, add the peas (2) and 2 tablespoons of water. Season with salt. Cook for about 10 minutes.
Cut the ham into small dice and add with the cream (3) and some freshly ground black pepper. Cook for 1 minute and turn off the heat.
Cook the pasta, drain, and reheat in a skillet with the sauce and 2 tablespoons of the cooking water.
Serve immediately.

● Chef's note
In Italy, the peas and ham are often replaced by smoked salmon. You can also replace the cream with mascarpone.

1 2 3 4

Seafood Sauce ★★

Scoglio

Scoglio literally means pasta "of the rocks." It is also known as "pirate's" or "buccaneer's" sauce. The key is to include a minimum of four different seafoods. Pasta *al scoglio* can be prepared either *rosse* (red, with tomato) or *bianche* (white, without tomato).

Serves 4
Preparation time: 40 minutes
Soaking time: 1 hour
Cooking time: 10 minutes + pasta cooking time

Ingredients
10 oz. (400 g) clams (tellins/cockles/razor clams)
10 oz. (400 g) mussels
4 squid
4 langoustines
3 cloves garlic
1 shallot
1 chili
2 ½ cups (¾ lb./400 g) ripe cherry tomatoes
6 tablespoons (90 ml) olive oil
6 tablespoons (90 ml) white wine
1 tablespoon tomato paste
2 tablespoons chopped parsley
Salt

To serve with 1 lb. (500 g) spaghetti, spaghettini, *paccheri*, or linguine.

Put the clams in a bowl of cold salted water for 1 hour. Stir from time to time to make the sand sink to the bottom. Clean the mussels and rinse with large amounts of water. Cut up the squid.

Crush the garlic cloves separately. Chop the shallot. Finely chop the chili. Cut the tomatoes in two.
Heat 1 tablespoon of the olive oil in a skillet and let the mussels cook with one of the crushed cloves of garlic and 2 tablespoons of the white wine over a high heat (1).
When the shellfish have completely opened, keep them warm, and strain the cooking juices (2). Repeat the same process for the clams.
In the skillet, heat 1 tablespoon of olive oil, and quickly fry the squid with the remaining garlic. Deglaze with 2 tablespoons of white wine.
In another skillet, brown the langoustines with 1 tablespoon of olive oil (3). Remove the langoustines and keep warm. In the same pan, soften the shallot and chili with 2 tablespoons olive oil.
Add the tomatoes (4) and the tomato paste diluted with 2 tablespoons of water and let cook for a few minutes.
Cook the pasta very al dente and reserve some of the cooking water. Add the pasta to the pan with the tomato sauce. Add the strained shellfish cooking juices, the mussels and clams, and a little of the reserved pasta cooking water. Cook for 2 minutes. Add the langoustines and the squid and mix. Sprinkle with chopped parsley and serve very hot.

Carrettiera Sauce (version 1) ★

This recipe is the version by Ada Boni (author of the *Talismano della Felicità* or "The Talisman of Happiness"), a renowned Italian cookery reference book, first published in 1929.

Serves 4
Preparation time: 10 minutes
Cooking time: 10 minutes + pasta cooking time

Ingredients
6 oz. (180 g) pancetta
Scant ½ cup (100 ml) olive oil
½ cup (3 ½ oz./100 g) grated pecorino cheese
Chopped parsley
Salt, pepper

To serve with 1 lb. (500 g) spaghetti, spaghettini, or vermicelli.

Cut the pancetta into matchsticks and fry in a skillet with the olive oil until golden brown (1).
Cook the pasta al dente, drain, and reheat in the skillet with the pancetta; add the pecorino.
Season with very little salt and pepper to taste (2).
Sprinkle with the chopped parsley and serve immediately.

⬤ **Did you know?**
Carrettiera sauce is named for the "cart-drivers," who formerly carried goods and people across the country, and who would no doubt have appreciated this simple, tasty dish at the end of a long day.

Carrettiera Sauce (version 2) ★

A modern version of the recipe is made throughout Italy today.

Serves 4
Preparation time: 10 minutes
Cooking time: 10 minutes + pasta cooking time

Ingredients
⅓ cup (3 oz./80 g) tuna in oil
⅓ cup (1 oz./30 g) dried porcini
1 clove garlic
Scant ½ cup (100 ml) olive oil
Scant ½ cup (100 ml) tomato sauce
Chopped parsley
Salt, pepper

To serve with 1 lb. (500 g) spaghetti, penne, fusilli, or *bucatini.*

Soak the porcini for about 15 minutes in lukewarm water to rehydrate, and then squeeze out the water.
Slice the garlic and soften in a skillet with the olive oil and the porcini (1) for 1 minute, then add the tuna (2) and the tomato sauce (3). Season with salt and pepper and cook for 5 minutes.
Cook the pasta al dente, drain; reheat in the sauce. Sprinkle with chopped parsley and serve immediately.

Woodland Sauce ★

Boscaiola

This is a sauce "of the earth" rather than "of the sea" (see p. 171). It is simple, tasty, and prepared with mushrooms.

Serves 4
Preparation time: 20 minutes
Cooking time: 15 minutes + pasta cooking time

Ingredients
2 ½ oz. (70 g) *Speck* or smoked ham
1 lb. (500 g) button mushrooms or fresh porcini
1 onion
1 clove garlic
10 oz. (300 g) peeled tomatoes
3 tablespoons (45 ml) olive oil
3 ½ tablespoons (50 ml) white wine
1 tablespoon pine nuts
2 tablespoons chopped parsley
Scant ½ cup (100 ml) whipping cream
Salt, pepper

To serve with 1 lb. (500 g) penne, *bucatini*, spaghetti, tagliatelle, or gnocchi.

Clean the mushrooms and rinse them quickly under cold water, then slice them. Chop the onion and garlic. Crush or chop the tomatoes.
Fry the mushrooms in a skillet with 2 tablespoons of the olive oil, the onion, and garlic (1). Deglaze with the white wine. When it has evaporated, add the tomatoes, season with salt and pepper. Cover and cook for 15 minutes over low heat. Slice the *Speck* or smoked ham, and brown gently in another pan with 1 tablespoon of oil and the pine nuts (2).
As soon as the sauce is ready, add the speck (3), parsley, and the cream.
Cook the pasta al dente, drain, and heat it through in the pan with the sauce. Serve immediately.

Fresh pasta

Fresh pasta

The origins of pasta date back 7,000 years, to the early days of agriculture, when cereal grains were crushed and kneaded with water to be cooked in sheets on a hot stone. This practice is still used today in the Maghreb, where it is known as *trid*, and throughout Asia for making sheets of rice. In Italy, three categories of cereal-based preparations derive from this original method: bread, "*puls*" (a typical Roman preparation based on semolina, spelt, and water, the ancestor of polenta), and pasta. It is very difficult to trace the history of pasta. We have no evidence of its consumption by Etruscans, Romans, or Greeks, despite various—more or less feasible—interpretations found in the works of Apicius or Caton. The practice of stuffing pasta only gained momentum during the Middle Ages. To begin with, this consisted of baking tartlets made with pasta dough and various fillings. From these origins, ravioli, tortellini, and others gradually evolved. Pasta spread through France during the sixteenth century as a result of Catherine de Medici's marriage to Henry II.

Pasta "in sheets" and pasta "in strands"

Pasta, as we know it today, first appeared in the Middle Ages. Writing in 1154, al-Idrissi, geographer to Roger II of Sicily, described a food for the first time that was based on flour and water and cut into strands, which he named "*itriyah*." This was prepared in the city of Trabia in Sicily from where, following its apparent success, it was exported all around the Mediterranean. In 1279 in Genoa, the notary Ugolino Scappi mentioned a barrel of "macaroni" in the inventory of a deceased person!

Two different ways of preparing pasta spread through Italy: egg pasta produced "in sheets" emerged in the central regions, and dried durum wheat (semolina) dough, made "in strands," developed in the South, a major cultivation area of durum wheat. The first method became the tradition in the Po plain, notably in Bologna. The second spread throughout Italy from Sicily to port cities such as Palermo, Genoa, and Naples where, thanks to the favorable climate, it could be dried easily.

Fresh pasta and stuffed pasta

Pasta known as "fresh" is usually made with bread flour (soft wheat) and eggs, produced primarily by artisanal means. In some regions, the eggs are replaced by water or wine. Stuffed pasta also belongs to this category; a stuffing of meat, fish, vegetables, or cheese is enclosed within a wrapping of dough.

There is a multitude of different-shaped pasta, both stuffed and unstuffed, as well as more than 300 recognized names, including *tagliolini*, tagliatelle, *pappardelle*, lasagna, cannelloni, ravioli, tortellini, *cappelletti*, orecchiette, *malloreddus*, *pici*, *trofie*, and many more. Pasta names are specific to their shape, and also to the composition of the dough: traditionally there is no such thing as linguine containing egg or tagliatelle without egg.

Pasta dough

The recipe for pasta dough varies according to the region where it is made: in the Abruzzi, pasta called "guitar" spaghetti is made with durum wheat flour, water, and eggs (see p. 326) and in Lombardy there is a pasta called *pizzoccheri* (see p. 217) made with buckwheat flour.

Flavoring ingredients and/or colorants such as olive oil, cuttlefish, herbs, spinach, cocoa, etc. can be added to the pasta, and different mixes of flour can also be used (see table, p. 79). Pasta dough can be made by hand or with an electric mixer.

Portions

For two people, 1 cup (3 ½ oz./100 g) of bread flour and 1 egg will provide average-size portions of pasta. For pasta made with durum wheat flour, 1 cup (3 ½ oz./100 g) of durum wheat flour and 3 ½ tablespoons (50 ml) water are needed per person. Egg-based pasta tends to double in volume during cooking. Individual portion size should always relate to the composition of the meal, depending on whether it is the main dish or accompanying other foods.

For stuffed pasta or pasta prepared in the oven, allow half the above quantities per person.

Cooking

Handmade pasta only needs cooking for 1 to 2 minutes; stuffed pasta will require 4 to 5 minutes. The cooking time will also vary depending on the thickness of the dough, whether it is stuffed or not, and on the date of production. It is always best to try the pasta as it is cooking to determine when it is ready. Dried pasta made with durum wheat flour requires a slightly longer cooking time (8 to 15 minutes, depending on how long it has dried for). Use 4 cups (1 liter) of water for every 3 ½ oz. (100 g) of pasta and 2 teaspoons (10 g salt) per liter of water.

Storing fresh pasta

Approximately 1 hour after making fresh pasta, it will become a little brittle. Remove it from the dryer (if using) and place on a dry cloth. You can keep fresh egg pasta, well covered in plastic wrap, for 3 to 5 days in the refrigerator and up to 3 months in the freezer. Pasta made without egg and cut a little thicker will keep at room temperature for 1 week once it has dried.

Stuffed pasta will only keep for 2 days in the refrigerator, whereas it will keep for 3 months in the freezer.

Pasta Dough ★

Here is the basic recipe for fresh pasta dough made with eggs. All the different pasta shapes can be cut from rolled-out sheets of this dough. Flavorings and/or colorings of your choice can be added to this basic dough, as shown in the table on page 79.

Serves 4
Preparation time: 20 minutes
Resting time: 30 minutes

Ingredients
2 cups (7 oz./200 g) bread flour
2 medium eggs (1 ²/₃ oz.-2 oz./53 g-63 g each)

Weigh and sift the flour onto a smooth surface, preferably wooden, or into a bowl. Make a well in the center of the flour and break the whole eggs into it (with any additional colorings or flavorings). Whisk the eggs lightly and gradually incorporate them into the flour using your fingers or a fork. Be careful that they do not spill out onto the surface. When all the flour is incorporated, knead the mixture by hand as firmly as possible until it forms a smooth ball. Let rest for 30 minutes, covered in plastic wrap.

To roll the dough by hand.
Place the dough on a smooth, floured surface, preferably made of wood. Roll the dough from the center outward using a wooden rolling pin. Turn the dough by 90 degrees, and turn it over, frequently. Flour the work surface if there is a risk of the dough sticking (but not too much as the dough can crack). Continue until you have a very thin, evenly rolled sheet that you can almost see through. You can then cut it into the shapes required.

To roll the dough with a pasta machine.
Divide the dough into several pieces and pass them through the pasta machine, decreasing the thickness with each roll. For the first and second rolls, pass the dough through twice on the same setting. Cut the dough to the required shape.

Tagliatelle ★

The word *tagliatella* comes from the verb *tagliare* meaning "to cut" in Italian. The precise width for Bolognese tagliatelle is ¹/₃ in. (8 mm).

Serves 4
Preparation time: 20 minutes
Drying time: 15 minutes
Cooking time: 2 minutes

Ingredients
10 oz. (300 g) pasta dough (basic recipe, see left)

To cut the dough by hand.
Place the sheets of pasta on the counter and roll them up lengthwise. Cut these rolls with a knife at ¹/₃ in. (8 mm) intervals to make tagliatelle. Unroll each one and sprinkle it with flour. Hang the tagliatelle on a drying rack or place on a floured dish towel to dry.

To cut the dough with a pasta machine.
When the sheets have dried a little (10 to 15 minutes) and become slightly brittle, cut them into tagliatelle or tagliolini using the appropriate attachment on the pasta machine. Sprinkle the pasta strands with flour and hang on a drying rack or place on a floured dish towel to dry.

Cook the tagliatelle for 1 to 2 minutes in a large quantity of boiling water, then drain.

● Chef's note
The ideal accompaniment for tagliatelle is ragù (Bolognese sauce), in keeping with Bolognese tradition (see p. 52). You can also prepare pappardelle by cutting the dough by hand to a width of about 1 in. (2.5–3 cm).

● Did you know?
A strand of tagliatelle, made of gold and with its correct measurements codified, is displayed in a case at Bologna's Chamber of Commerce.

http://flamm.fr/ic02

Stuffed pasta

Ravioli ★★

Ravioli are stuffed pasta that are cooked throughout Italy. Each region, each village, each family has its own recipe for dough, stuffing, and sauce. Ravioli are usually square but can be round, triangular, half-moon, or another shape. They will each have a different name depending on their shape and the stuffing.

Serves 6
Preparation time: 1 hour
Cooking time: 4-5 minutes

Ingredients
10 oz. (300 g) pasta dough (basic recipe, see p. 69)

Stuffing
1 cup (7 oz./200 g) cooked spinach, well drained and chopped
1 cup (7 oz./200 g) ricotta
1 egg
⅓ cup (2 oz./50 g) grated Parmesan cheese
Nutmeg, grated
Salt, pepper

Make the ravioli stuffing.
In a bowl, quickly incorporate the spinach with the rest of the ingredients until you have an evenly mixed stuffing.

Prepare the pasta.
Take a sheet of dough (1), cut it into four rectangular strips approximately 6 × 20 in. (15 × 50 cm).
Place the stuffing on one half of the dough in equally spaced and sized mounds with a spoon or a pastry bag, keeping a straight line (2).
Fold the other half of the dough over the stuffing.
Gently press all around each mound of stuffing to eliminate any air bubbles and make a perfect seal between the two sheets of pasta (3).

Using a dough cutter, first cut lengthwise, ensuring that there is a double layer of pasta the whole length (4). Then cut in between the ravioli to seal and separate them (5). Place them individually on a lightly floured dish towel. Cook the ravioli for 4 to 5 minutes in a large quantity of boiling water (6) and remove them with a slotted spoon.

● **Chef's notes**
To shape fresh pasta, you can buy "pasta cutters" (non-sharp, serrated cookie cutters), and also many other cutters of different shapes and sizes, as well as preformed ravioli molds.
However the dough cutter (see p. 168) allows you to vary the shape with a single instrument and gives the ravioli a more "home-made" character. It is also the perfect tool for sealing the ravioli.
You can use a glass to cut out round ravioli, and the other cutters to make different shapes. Use these cutters upside down (the blunt side) to press the dough down firmly and seal the edges well. Place something over the sharp side to protect your hand.
If there are no air bubbles inside the ravioli and the edges are clean and well sealed, there will be no risk of them opening and the stuffing escaping while cooking.
Always prepare a firm stuffing; you should be able to form it into balls that hold their own shape.

❙ **Recipe idea**
Piedmontese Ravioli with a Veal Stuffing ›› p. 196

http://flamm.fr/ic03

Fresh pasta

Tortellini ★ ★ ★

The recipe for tortellini was registered by Dotta Confraternita del Tortellino (The Tortellini Brotherhood), and by the Italian Academy of Cooking, at Bologna's Chamber of Commerce, in 1974. The recipe is given here as faithfully as possible. Tortellini differ slightly from cappelletti and *anolini* in their shape and their stuffing.

Serves 6-8
Preparation time: 1 hour 30 minutes
Cooking time: 4-5 minutes

Ingredients
10 oz. (300 g) pasta dough (basic recipe, see p. 69)

Stuffing
3 oz. (100 g) pork loin
3 oz. (100 g) mortadella (from Bologna, if possible)
3 oz. (100 g) raw ham, finely sliced
2 teaspoons (10 g) butter
1 clove garlic unpeeled, left whole
1 sprig of rosemary
1 egg
1 cup (5 oz./150 g) grated Parmesan (*stravecchio* if possible–aged for 30 months)
½ teaspoon grated nutmeg
Salt, white pepper
Beef stock (see p. 93) or capon stock

Cut the pork loin into cubes. Brown for a few minutes (1) in the butter with the garlic and rosemary (2). Let cool.
Finely chop the pork, the mortadella, and the ham in a food processor (3).
Add the egg, Parmesan, and nutmeg to the mixture, then season with salt and pepper (4).
Roll out sheets of the dough, cut out disks of 1 ½ in. (4 cm) in diameter or squares of 1 ¾ to 2 in. (4.5 to 5 cm) (5).
Place a small mound of stuffing in the middle of each disk or square (6).

http://flamm.fr/ic04

5

6

7

Fold the tortellini firmly in two **(7)**, then fold them in two again by wrapping them around your finger **(8)**. Press the two ends together and pinch firmly to seal **(9)**. Place the tortellini on a dry, floured dish towel **(10)**. Cook them al dente (4 to 5 minutes) in the stock **(11)** and serve.

● Chef's note
Tortellini are also often cooked in boiling salted water and served with a cream sauce.
Serves 4: stir 1 ½ tablespoons (10 g flour) into ¾ tablespoon (10 g) melted butter, add 1 cup (250 ml) of whipping cream, with salt and pepper to taste. Mix together and simmer for a few minutes.

● Did you know?
Tortellini are traditionally served in a beef or capon broth, especially on Christmas Day.

Variations
You can make a lighter dish by replacing the pork in the stuffing with chicken or veal; the taste will be quite different. The cappelletti of Emilia Romagna are made with a "lean" stuffing exclusively made up of cheeses: 10 ½ oz. (300 g) ricotta, 10 ½ oz. (300 g) crescenza or Fossa cheese, 7 oz. (200 g) Parmesan, 2 egg yolks, nutmeg, a little lemon zest, and salt. Serve in a meat stock (see p. 93) or with melted butter.

Fresh pasta made from durum wheat flour

Most pasta made from durum wheat flour has been developed since the sixteenth century with the use of progressively sophisticated machinery. However, some short varieties of this type of pasta can be shaped by hand. This basic dough can also be used to make other shapes such as orecchiette, or *trofi*.

Farfalle ★

Serves 4
Preparation time: 40 minutes
Resting time: 30 minutes
Cooking time: 5-7 minutes

Ingredients
4 cups (14 oz./400 g) durum wheat flour
¾ teaspoon (4 g) salt
Scant 1 cup (200 ml) lukewarm water

Make a well in the flour on the work surface or in a bowl. Add the salt to the lukewarm water and pour it into the well; gradually stir it into the flour, being careful not to let it spill over. When all the flour is incorporated, knead the mixture by hand as firmly as possible until it forms a smooth ball (1). Let rest for 30 minutes, covered in plastic wrap.
Roll out the dough (2) and cut the sheets into strips of approximately 2 ½ in. (6 cm) with a serrated pasta cutter. Cut these strips in rectangles of 2 ½ × 1 in. (6 × 2.5 cm) with a non-serrated cutter (3) or with a knife. Pinch the rectangles of dough in the middle to make the butterfly shape (4). Cook them in salted boiling water (5 to 7 minutes) and serve them with cheese sauce (see p. 78) or another of your choice.

● **Did you know?**
Farfalle (meaning butterflies) are called strichetti *in Emilia-Romagna, where they are made with egg pasta with Parmesan and nutmeg added to it.*

http://flamm.fr/ic05

Cheese and Herb Sauce ★

Quattro formaggio e erbe aromatiche

Serves 4
Preparation time: 10 minutes

Ingredients
1 lb. (450 g) of mixed cheeses, e.g. 5 oz. (150 g) Gorgonzola,
  5 oz. (150 g) *Taleggio*, and 5 oz. (150 g) Gruyère
Scant 1 cup (200 ml) whipping cream
¼ stick (1 oz./30 g) butter
Salt, pepper
1 cup (5 oz./150 g) grated Parmesan
10 sprigs chervil, finely chopped
10 strands chives, finely chopped
²/₃ cup (3 oz./80 g) crushed pistachios

Put the selected cheese in a saucepan with the whipping
cream and butter over low heat until just melted; remove
from the heat and season with salt and pepper.
When the pasta is cooked, mix it into the sauce, and heat
through gently.
Serve directly onto hot plates and sprinkle with Parmesan.
Decorate with the finely chopped herbs and the pistachios.

Butter and Sage Sauce ★

Burro e salvia

This sauce is very quick to prepare and is a classic in Italy.
It complements homemade pasta very well, especially ravioli
(see p. 70) and potato gnocchi (see p. 83).

Serves 4
Preparation time: 5 minutes

Ingredients
1 stick (4 oz./100 g) butter
10-15 fresh sage leaves, chopped
Salt
Grated Parmesan

Melt the butter over low heat in a saucepan with the chopped
sage; season with salt.
Serve with the Parmesan.

Advice on making fresh pasta

Pasta dough should not be particularly pliant but it should be
very smooth. To prepare it, use 1 egg to 1 cup (3 oz./100 g) flour.
However, medium eggs vary from 1 ²/₃ oz. to 2 ¼ oz. (53 g to 63 g)
and the water content of flour can also vary (depending on the
ambient humidity and according to its freshness).
It may be necessary to take a few precautions: if your dough does
not hold together, even after thorough kneading, it needs more
water; add very little water at a time to be sure not to exceed what
is strictly necessary. If the dough sticks to your hands and is difficult to knead, it needs more flour; add very little flour at a time.

• The most suitable surface for pasta making is a pinewood board
oiled with cooking oil (olive, sunflower, etc.), and then dried well.

• When you roll out the sheet of dough, rotate it and turn it over
regularly to ensure that it does not stick to the counter or board.
Also be aware that pasta dries quickly. To roll it out easily, work
quickly, adding as little flour as possible.

• While shaping pasta, always keep the piece of dough not being
used covered in plastic wrap; this will prevent the formation of a
crust on the surface of the dough.

• If you roll out the dough using a pasta machine, it is important
to put the dough through all the settings so that the rolling is
gradual. This helps prevent the dough breaking or tearing.

Various pasta doughs

You can vary pasta by adding colors, flavorings, or different flours to the basic dough.

Doughs	Bread flour	Other flours	Eggs	Water	Other ingredients	Salt
Egg	4 cups (14 oz./400 g)		4			
Durum wheat		4 cups (14 oz./400 g) durum wheat flour	0	Scant 1 cup (200 ml)		1 pinch
Egg and mixed flour	2 cups (7 oz./200 g)	2 cups (7 oz./200 g) durum wheat flour	4			
Egg and water (or other liquids)	3 ½ cups (12 oz./350 g)		From 0 to 3, proportionate to the amount of water used*	From 2 cups (200 ml) to 2 tablespoons	Water, wine, beer, milk, vegetable juice, etc.	
Whole-wheat flour	2 cups (7 oz./200 g)	2 cups (7 oz./200 g) whole-wheat flour	4			
Chestnut flour	3 cups (10 ½ oz./300 g)	1 cup (3 ½ oz./100 g) chestnut flour	2	2 ½ cups (600 ml)		
Buckwheat flour	1 cup (3 ½ oz./100 g)	3 cups (10 ½ oz./300 g) buckwheat flour	0	Scant 1 cup (200 ml)		1 pinch
Colored with wet ingredient (spinach, tomato, nettles, beets, etc.)	2 ½ cups (9 oz./250 g)		2		2–3 tablespoons (1 oz./30 g) puree	
Flavored (coffee, cocoa, herbs, spices)	3 ½–4 cups (12–14 oz./360–390 g)		4		1 ½–6 tablespoons (1/3–1 1/3 oz./ 10–40 g) powder or finely chopped herbs	
Black ink	4 cups (14 oz./400 g)		4		½ tablespoon (8 ml) cuttlefish ink	

* The fewer eggs you use, the more water you will need, and vice versa.

Gnocchi

Gnocchi

There are several theories for the origin of the word "gnocchi." These include a link to *nocchio*, the Italian name for a knot in wood, and to *Knöchel*, a Middle High German word for knuckle. It may also come from the Lombard *knohha*, which refers to any spherical dough shape. In the Middle Ages, gnocchi were prepared with different semolina flours, water, and eggs. Some, based on bread crumbs, milk, cheese, and ground almonds, were known as *zanzarelli*. It was only in 1700, with the introduction of the potato to Europe, that potato-based gnocchi became widespread. Today the term still covers several variations.

Potato gnocchi are mostly found in the North of Italy and Lazio; in the extreme North, gnocchi are made of bread (*canederli*), whereas toward the South, they are mainly prepared with flour or wheat semolina. There are many other traditional ways of making gnocchi: from vegetables, fish, corn flour, buckwheat flour, or cheese.

Potato gnocchi

These are the best-known gnocchi. They belong to the traditional cooking of the Veneto, Emilia, and Lazio regions. It is mainly the accompanying sauces that bring variety to gnocchi. Factory-made gnocchi have nothing in common with homemade ones.

Prepared by hand with good-quality potatoes, homemade gnocchi are soft, fluffy, and light. The choice of the potato is of prime importance. It must be a dry, floury variety, suitable for making puree, e.g. Russet, King Edward, or Maris Piper. Gnocchi dough should contain the least possible moisture, so cook the potatoes in their skins to prevent them absorbing water.

Finally, it is important to add only a small amount of flour to the potato, otherwise the gnocchi will become solid and indigestible. There are several methods for giving gnocchi the characteristic shape that enables the sauce to cling to them in the best way.

Colored gnocchi

To make colored and/or flavored gnocchi, you can mix different ingredients with the potatoes. Increase the amount of flour a little from 1 to 2 tablespoons (10 to 20 g), depending on the consistency of the vegetables added.

• **Green gnocchi:** add 2 ¾ cups (1 lb./500 g) of cooked, well-drained chopped spinach (or nettles) to the basic recipe.
• **Orange gnocchi:** add a puree prepared with 2 ¼ cups (12 oz./400 g) of cooked, well-drained carrots to the basic recipe.
• **Black gnocchi:** add 1 ¾ tablespoons (25 ml) of cuttlefish ink to the basic recipe.
• **Other variations:** you can add saffron, or purees made from beets, chestnuts, plums, etc. to the basic recipe.

Storing fresh gnocchi

To keep homemade gnocchi for a few days, cook them in water, drain, then mix them with a little sunflower oil to prevent them from sticking together.

They can then be kept for 2 days in the refrigerator or 3 months in the freezer. When you wish to serve them, immerse them in boiling water as for fresh gnocchi; they will lose their oil as they reheat.

You can also bake them in the oven with a Bolognese sauce and Parmesan (*gnocchi pasticciati*). In this case, place them directly in a gratin dish and do not add any oil.

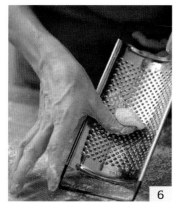

Potato Gnocchi ★★

Gnocchi di patate

Serves 6
Preparation time: 1 hour
Resting time: 30 minutes
Cooking time: 1-2 minutes

Ingredients

1 lb. 5 oz. (600 g) floury potatoes (e.g. Russet,
    King Edward, Maris Piper)
1 heaping cup (4 oz./120 g), approximately, flour
Salt

Wash the potatoes and cook them unpeeled in salted water.
Once cooked, remove the skins and press them through a
potato ricer or coarse sieve (1). Let cool, add a pinch of salt
and the flour a little at a time. As soon as the dough is firm
enough to shape (2), stop adding the flour. The quantity of
flour varies according to the quality of the potatoes.
Make several long rolls with the dough ⅔ in. to 1 in. (2 to
3 cm) in diameter and cut into ⅔ in. to 1 in. (2 to 3 cm) pieces
(3). Flour them lightly. Quickly roll them on a fork (4), on
a ribbed, wooden gnocchi shaper (5), or on the back of a
Parmesan grater (6), so as to create a small hollow on one
side and a well-defined ridge on the other.
Roll them lightly again in flour. Arrange them on floured
boards or trays (7).
Leave to stand for 30 minutes.
Drop the gnocchi, one by one, into a large quantity
of lightly salted boiling water (too much salt will break up
the gnocchi).
Lift them out with a slotted spoon as they rise to the surface.
Serve with the sauce of your choice: butter and sage (p. 78),
tomato and basil (p. 47), Bolognese (p. 52), cheese and herb
(p. 78), etc.

● Chef's note
A dish of gnocchi without sauce contains fewer than 350 calories.

http://flamm.fr/ic06

Gnocchi *alla Romana* ★

They might be called gnocchi *alla Romana* (in the Roman style), but this recipe is widespread throughout Italy. The simplicity of the recipe has contributed to its success. It is a baked gratin of semolina gnocchi that can be prepared in advance.

Serves 6
Preparation time: 30 minutes
Cooking time: 40 minutes

Ingredients
4 ¼ cups (1 liter) milk
3 cups (8 oz./250 g) medium-fine semolina
2 eggs
5 tablespoons (2 ½ oz./70 g) butter
⅔ cup (4 oz./120 g) grated Parmesan (Parmigiano Reggiano
  or Grana Padano if possible)
Salt

Preheat the oven to 350°F (180°C).
Bring the milk to a boil, add a pinch of salt. Remove
the saucepan from the heat and slowly pour in the semolina,
whisking well to avoid lumps forming (1). Cook for
10 minutes mixing continuously.
Remove from the heat and stir in the eggs, 3 ½ tablespoons
(1 ¾ oz./50 g) of the butter (2) and ⅓ cup (2 ½ oz./70 g) of
the Parmesan.
Turn out the mixture onto a wet surface (marble is ideal) (3)
and spread with a spatula to a thickness of ½ in. (1 cm) (4).
Let cool, then cut out rounds using a glass or cookie cutter (5).
Butter a baking dish and cover the base with a layer of the
rounds (6), interspersed with the cutting-out leftovers. Cover
evenly with the rest of the gnocchi, slightly overlapping.
Dot with the remaining butter, and sprinkle on the
remaining Parmesan (7). Bake for 30 minutes.
Serve very hot.

● Chef's notes
You can add vegetable puree to the basic recipe to make colored gnocchi and you can replace the Parmesan with other cheeses (Gorgonzola, for example).
You can also put cooked vegetables (asparagus tips) or herbs on the gnocchi before finally sprinkling them with the cheese prior to baking.

5

6

7

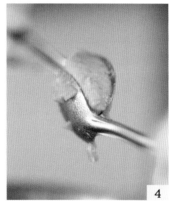

Pumpkin Gnocchi ★★

Gnocchi di zucca

Gnocchi can be prepared with different sorts of vegetables: carrots, zucchini, eggplants, etc.

Serves 6
Preparation time: 50 minutes
Cooking time: 30 minutes

Ingredients
2 lb. (1 kg) pumpkin
2 cups (6 oz./200 g) flour
1 egg
1 stick (4 oz./120 g) butter
2 sage leaves, chopped
½ cup (3 oz./80 g) grated Parmesan
Salt

Preheat the oven to 350°F (180°C).
Cut the pumpkin into quarters, and roast for approximately 30 minutes. Remove the flesh using a spoon (1) and crush it with a fork.
Make a well in the flour and place the pumpkin flesh in the middle with the egg and salt, stir thoroughly until evenly mixed (2). The quantity of flour varies depending on the consistency of the pumpkin. Stop adding it when the dough is firm enough to shape.
Shape the gnocchi using two spoons (3, 4) and immerse them in a large quantity of lightly salted boiling water (5). Remove them with a slotted spoon as soon as they rise to the surface.

Melt the butter with the sage in a saucepan and add this sauce to the gnocchi, sprinkle with Parmesan, and serve hot. You can replace the Parmesan with grated smoked ricotta or add meat stock to the gnocchi to flavor them.

● Did you know?
Pumpkin gnocchi belong mainly to the culinary tradition of Lombardy and Friuli. Every year, the last Friday of the Verona Carnival is led by "Papa Gnocchi," who carries a giant fork topped with gnocchi. This is in honor of Tomasso da Vico, who is said to have donated the ingredients for gnocchi to the starving citizens of Verona after a terrible famine in 1531. Gnocchi is handed out to Veronese citizens at the festival to this day.

Risotto

Risotto

The cultivation of rice appears to have been introduced into Italy in the fourteenth century, mainly in the Milan area, where it was a means of exploiting the marshlands.

Today, Italy is the principal European producer of rice, and exports varieties intended for making risotto worldwide. Appearing in recipe books dating back to the sixteenth century, risotto became established during the seventeenth century, particularly saffron risotto, always with reference to an original recipe from the North of Italy.

Advice on making a successful risotto

Choice of saucepan

Choose a heavy-bottom pan as it will be a good conductor of heat. The ideal is copper–stainless steel or plain stainless steel. The pan should not be too deep or too wide and should hold the finished risotto without it overflowing (beware, rice increases its volume two and a half times during cooking).

In Italy there are pans designed exclusively for cooking risotto: they have a single handle and a very rounded bottom (see pp. 92–93 and p. 169).

The rice is cooked uncovered, except when resting at the end of the cooking time.

Choice of rice

The choice of rice depends on the length of time the grains can withstand high heat and steam while cooking without falling apart, and on its starch content, the binding agent which gives risotto its creamy character.

Several varieties of rice grown in Italy meet these criteria; they have large grains and a high starch content. These "japonica" varieties are known by the following names: *carnaroli* (grown primarily in Piedmont), *nano vialone* (Veneto), and *arborio* (Po valley).

Risotto rice should never be rinsed, as this would remove all the starch.

Allow 2 to 2 ½ oz. (65 to 80 g) of rice per person, depending on the volume of the other ingredients.

Toasting process and choice of cooking fat

First of all the grains of rice need to be toasted in fat over a steady heat. Using a wooden spoon, stir the grains of rice vigorously around the bottom of the pan to color and heat them evenly. You need just enough cooking fat to coat all the grains of rice equally—no more, no less (¾ tablespoon/10 g per portion, approx-

imately). Once the grains are very hot and cease sliding across the bottom of the pan, the toasting process is complete.

This step allows the surface of the rice grains to withstand the cooking process better and to release their starch in order to bind with the other ingredients.

The choice of cooking fat (butter, olive oil, or other) is always a matter of debate in Italy. Being a northern Italian dish, rice is more likely to have been cooked in butter originally. Ideally your choice should complement your risotto's additional ingredients, and may also be guided by your dietary requirements.

Soffritto

Once the fat has melted, and before adding the rice, chopped or sliced vegetables are usually browned in the bottom of the pan. This process is called *soffritto*.

Traditionally the vegetables selected are onion, carrot, and celery, chopped together, or onion, shallot, leek, garlic, and parsley. The *soffritto* base should be chosen to complement the other risotto ingredients.

Wine and stock

Once the toasting is completed, the pan is deglazed with alcohol. This will help to dilute the residual juices and give acidity to the finished dish. You can use white or red wine or another alcohol, or vinegar, depending on the risotto's ingredients.

Once the alcohol has completely evaporated, the stock is added, allowing the real cooking of the risotto to begin. This step is also open to debate: some people add all the stock at once and never stir, others add a little at a time, stirring frequently. These different methods influence the final result. The perfect risotto varies from one region to another, just like the methods for making it.

The following is a reliable method: begin by adding 1 or 2 ladles of stock without completely covering the rice. Only add more (1 ladle at a time) when the first addition has almost entirely evaporated.

The choice of stock is also of fundamental importance, since it will permeate the rice with its flavor. A stock made from vegetables, poultry, beef, fish, or shellfish can be used. Some people even opt for a stock of salted water. It can also be worth preparing stock from the trimmings of the ingredients used in the recipe, for example a stock made with asparagus stalks for asparagus risotto, or with the bones from filleting the fish for a fish risotto. The important thing is to consider well in advance what will complement the other ingredients. The use of stock cubes is strictly prohibited when making risotto, unless you want a "stock cube" risotto!

As a general rule for cooking risotto, use twice the volume of liquid to the initial volume of rice. However, this rule can vary depending on the cooking method, the temperature, the amount of stirring, the quality of rice, and the nature of the other ingredients.

Always use hot stock, keeping it simmering in a separate pan throughout the cooking time, and also during the meal, for moistening the risotto again for second helpings.

Time and cooking method

The cooking time varies depending on the rice chosen (see the packet instructions) and the method of cooking. In general 16 to 18 minutes will be the maximum cooking time.

The creaminess of the finished risotto also varies, depending on the techniques used. The more it is stirred, the more the rice will release its starch. Make sure, however, that you do not break the grains of rice by stirring too vigorously at this stage.

Cooking over low heat allows you to stir less often; the grains of rice will be nicely al dente and well separated, but the risotto will be less creamy. If cooking over higher heat, you will need to stir more frequently and the result will be thick and creamy, but the grains may be broken and less well separated. The success of a risotto is a question of balance.

Ingredients

The cooking time of each ingredient depends on when they are added to the rice. Stir in the ingredients that take longest to cook (pumpkin, artichokes, meat, etc.) at the beginning of the cooking process. Those that cook more rapidly (for example, leaf vegetables) or very fast (langoustines, scallops, etc.) should be added midway or toward the end. Ingredients that take a long time to cook may also require precooking. Some ingredients can also be cooked separately and added just before serving.

Whether the ingredients are cut into small or large pieces depends on whether you want them to be integral with the rice or the dominant feature of the recipe.

Mantecatura

The *mantecatura* is the final stage of preparing risotto and gives it its typical character.

Once the rice is cooked, check the seasoning, and allow the remaining liquid to evaporate. Remove from the heat. Add the butter and stir it in gently.

Add the grated Parmesan or other cheese and mix briefly, making sure you do not break the rice grains, which will by now be very fragile. Traditionally, a slotted spoon is used, as this makes less impact on the grains of rice.

In some regions of Italy, they prefer to serve a more fluid risotto known as *all'onda* (literally "wavy"). In this case, the butter and cheese will need adding before the rice has absorbed all the liquid. As a general rule, when the *mantecatura* is completed, the rice should be slightly more liquid than you want to serve it, then left covered to rest for 2 minutes.

Serving

As the saying goes: "Risotto never waits for the guest, it is the guest who waits for the risotto," which neatly sums it up, because it is a dish that cannot be prepared in advance. Once it has rested for 2 minutes, the risotto should be served immediately, otherwise it will cease to be creamy very quickly and become a compact mass.

It is possible to offer a second helping (though it will never be as good as the first) by adding a little hot stock to the remaining risotto and mixing it in gently.

To achieve the best results, do not attempt to make risotto in large quantities (no more than eight portions at the same time). A restaurant that serves a good risotto is easily recognized: it will state on the menu that, if ordering the risotto, you must expect a wait of around 20 minutes.

To speed up the process, it is possible to prepare all the ingredients in advance, ready to begin cooking the risotto shortly before you wish to serve it.

Risotto with Sparkling Wine ★★

Risotto allo spumante

Serves 6
Preparation time: 20 minutes
Cooking time: 20 minutes
Preparation and cooking time for the stock: 2 hours 10 minutes

Ingredients

For 8 cups (2 liters) meat stock
2 lb. (1 kg), approximately, stewing beef or 1 medium chicken
10 cups (2.5 liters) water
1 carrot
1 stick celery
1 onion
1 leek
1 sprig of parsley
1 clove
1 bay leaf

Risotto
2 ⅓ cups (1 lb./500 g) rice (*carnaroli* or *arborio*)
1 onion (or 4 shallots), chopped
⅔ stick (3 oz./80 g) butter
2 tablespoons olive oil
2 cups (500 ml) Prosecco or spumante wine
⅓ cup (1 ¾ oz./50 g) grated Parmesan
Salt

Prepare the meat stock.
Place the beef or chicken in a pan with 10 cups (2.5 liters) of cold water, the carrot, celery, onion, leek, parsley, clove, bay leaf, and a pinch of salt.
Simmer for 2 hours, strain, and return to low heat.

Make the risotto.
Soften the onion in a heavy-bottom pan with 4 tablespoons (2 oz./50 g) of the butter and the olive oil, without letting it color.
As soon as the onion is translucent, add the rice and toast it (1), by vigorously stirring the grains around the bottom of the pan. Deglaze with 1 ½ cups (375 ml) of the wine (2).
Once the alcohol is completely evaporated, add the stock one ladle at a time (3), without covering the rice completely. Stir well with each addition of stock to distribute it evenly through the rice.
Allow a cooking time of 16 to 18 minutes. Check the seasoning.

3

Once the rice is cooked, add the rest of the wine. Mix well. Remove from the heat and let rest for 2 minutes.
Stir in the rest of the butter and the Parmesan. Stir again (see *mantecatura*, p. 91) and serve immediately.

● Chef's notes

This is a classic, chic risotto recipe. You can make it with all sorts of wines that will lend their particular color and flavor to the risotto.
The best-known variation is risotto with Barolo, the delicious Piedmontese red wine.

❙ Recipe ideas

Risotto *alla Milanese* >> p. 214
Risotto with White Truffles from Alba >> p. 199

http://flamm.fr/ic07

Spring Risotto ★

Risotto primavera

Serves 6
Preparation time: 40 minutes
Cooking time: 20 minutes
Preparation and cooking time for the stock:
  50 minutes

Ingredients
Vegetables
16 asparagus spears
2 artichokes
1 leek
1 potato
A few sprigs of parsley
5 basil leaves
1 stick celery
2/3 cup (3 ½ oz./100 g) shelled peas
½ stick (2 oz./50 g) butter
2 tablespoons olive oil

1 ⅓ cups (10 oz./280 g) rice (*carnaroli* or *arborio*)
2 cups (500 ml) white wine

½ cup (3-4 oz./100 g) grated Parmesan
Salt, pepper

For 4 cups (1 liter) vegetable stock
3 ½ oz. (100 g) Swiss chard
1 carrot
1 stick celery
1 tomato
1 clove garlic
1 onion, peeled and chopped
2 teaspoons (10 g) salt

Prepare the vegetable stock.
Heat 6 cups (1.5 liters) of water in a large saucepan with the
Swiss chard, carrot, celery, tomato, garlic, onion, and salt.
Simmer for 40 minutes. Strain and replace over low heat.

Prepare the vegetables.
Clean the asparagus spears and artichokes. Separate the
tips from the asparagus stems. Cut the tips of asparagus in
two and slice the stems. Slice the artichokes and leek very
thinly. Cut the potato into small dice. Chop the parsley, basil,
and celery.
Blanch the peas, asparagus, and artichokes by immersing
them in salted boiling water: cook the peas for 3 minutes,

the asparagus stems and artichokes for 1 minute, and the
asparagus tips for 30 seconds. Make sure there is plenty
of water and that it does not go off the boil.
Drain the vegetables and immerse them in cold water with ice
cubes added. Once they have cooled completely, dry them.

Make the risotto.
Soften the chopped leek and celery in a heavy-bottom
pan with ¼ stick (1 oz./25 g) of the butter and the olive oil,
without coloring them (1). Once they are translucent, add the
potato cubes and the rice. Toast them, vigorously stirring the
rice grains and potato cubes around the bottom of the pan.
Deglaze with the wine (2). After evaporation, add the stock
one ladle at a time, without covering the rice completely.
Mix well with each addition of stock to distribute it evenly
through the rice. Add the rest of the vegetables (3). Allow
a cooking time of 16 to 18 minutes. Season with salt and
pepper. Remove from the heat and let rest for 2 minutes.
Stir in the rest of the butter and the Parmesan cheese and
mix together gently. Then add the parsley and basil. Serve
immediately.

● **Chef's note**

*This risotto recipe can be made with different vegetables and
herbs that will transmit their flavor and color to it.*

Shrimp, Zucchini, and Lemon Risotto ★★

Risotto gamberi, zucchine e limone

Serves 4
Preparation time: 30 minutes
Cooking time: 20 minutes
Preparation and cooking time for the stock: 30 minutes

Ingredients
1 ½ cups (10 oz./300 g) raw shrimp
7 oz. (200 g) zucchini
1 onion
1 clove garlic
4 tablespoons (60 ml) olive oil
1 ⅓ cups (10 oz./280 g) rice (*carnaroli* or *arborio*)
Juice and zest of ½ a lemon
½ cup (120 ml) white wine
Salt, pepper

Shellfish stock
Shells and heads of the shrimp
1 stick celery
1 onion
1 carrot
A few parsley leaves
1 bay leaf
Zest of ¼ of a lemon
1 teaspoon fennel seeds
Scant ¼ cup (50 ml) brandy
1 teaspoon (5 g) salt

Shell the shrimp **(1)**, reserving the shells. Keep the shrimp meat on one side.

Prepare the shellfish stock.
Put the shrimp heads and shells in a pan with 6 cups (1.5 liters) of cold water, the celery, onion, carrot, parsley, bay leaf, lemon zest, fennel seeds, brandy, and salt **(2)**. Simmer for 20 minutes, strain, and return to a low heat.

Make the risotto.
Wash the zucchini, julienne half of them and chop the rest. Chop the onion and garlic.
Soften the onion in a heavy-bottom pan with the olive oil, without coloring it.
Once the onion is translucent, add the garlic and the zucchini. Add the lemon juice and zest. One minute later, add the rice. Toast it by vigorously stirring the rice grains around the bottom of the pan.
Deglaze with the wine. After evaporation, add the fish stock one ladle at a time **(3)**, without covering the rice completely. Mix well with each addition of stock to distribute it evenly through the rice. Allow a cooking time of 16 to 18 minutes. Season with salt and pepper.
Add the zucchini and the shrimp 3 minutes before the end of the cooking time **(4)**. Remove from the heat, let rest for 2 minutes, and then serve immediately.

● **Chef's note**
Generally Parmesan and other dairy products are not added to risotto recipes based on fish, as its delicate flavor can be overwhelmed by the pronounced taste of cheese.

What to do with leftover risotto

You can vary many of the most traditional risotto recipes to use up leftovers, possibly with the addition of extra ingredients.

• **Rice omelet:** just add 1 or 2 beaten eggs and cook in a skillet. You can also add julienne vegetables, slices or pieces of charcuterie, cheese, etc.

• **Rice cakes:** heat a knob of butter and 1 tablespoon of olive oil in a skillet and add the rice, flattening it down well. Let cook for 5 minutes. Turn over with the help of a plate or lid and cook the other side for a further 5 minutes.

• **Rice meatballs:** add ground meat, a spoonful of flour, and an egg. Shape the meatballs, dip them in bread crumbs, and cook in a skillet.

• *Suppli* or *arancini*: add an egg to risotto, shape into balls. Slip a teaspoon of tomato sauce or Bolognese sauce into the center with a few cubes of soft cheese (mozzarella, *scamorza*, fontina, etc.). Close up the balls firmly, dip them in flour, then beaten egg, and lastly in bread crumbs, before frying them (see deep-fried rice balls, p. 418).

• *Timballo*: butter an ovenproof dish and create alternate layers of risotto and cheese and/or tomato sauce or Bolognese sauce. You can also include layers of fresh tomato, charcuterie, ground meat, etc. Finish with a layer of rice, sprinkle with grated Parmesan, and dot with butter. Bake for 30 minutes at 400°F (200°C).

Polenta

Polenta

Polenta is a staple of the traditional food of northeast Italy. Originally it was a peasant gruel made from a base of chickpeas, beans, or buckwheat.

Corn arrived in Europe from America in the sixteenth century and lent itself well to this method of preparing food. Both its easy cultivation and its high yield helped to stem famine, particularly in Trentino and Friuli. In these regions it is still called "*Grano Turco*" (Turkish grain), because corn was imported from Turkey in quantity during the seventeenth century.

Different types of polenta

• **Yellow polenta:** prepared with yellow corn flour, this is the classic polenta. It adapts well to all sorts of recipes.

• **White polenta:** prepared with white corn flour, this is the finest polenta. It is served with delicate foods such as fish.

• *Taragna* **polenta:** prepared with buckwheat flour. This is more rustic and quite rich. It is accompanied by very simple sauces based on anchovies or cheese.

• **Chickpea or bean polenta:** polenta is still prepared from these ingredients in the South of Italy.

• **Chestnut polenta:** prepared with chestnut flour, in the Tuscan tradition.

Firm or soft?

There are several ways to prepare polenta: firm or soft, cooked and served immediately, cut into slices and then fried, broiled, or poached. It can also be baked in the oven as a gratin with other ingredients added to it (cheese, butter, tomato sauce, meat, etc.)

The different-sized particles of the grain in the polenta flour naturally produce varying results. A fine-grained flour will result in a creamier polenta, but it is more difficult to make without lumps. With a thicker flour, it is easier to avoid lumps, but the polenta will be more rustic.

Polenta prepared with corn flour requires a long cooking time and needs to be stirred continually. These days, it is easy to find pre-cooked polenta flour commercially, which saves a great deal of time (it takes 5 minutes rather than 45 to 60 minutes). The results obtained from such products are perfectly acceptable.

Hardware

Traditionally, polenta is cooked in a wide pan made from beaten copper known as a "*paiolo*," but you can now find *paioli* made from cast iron, aluminum with a nonstick lining, or from soapstone. There are even *paioli* available that have an integral electric whisk. Once cooked, the polenta can be poured onto a wooden board, allowed to cool, and then cut up with a cotton thread or knife. The classic polenta board is round (facing page, photograph no. 3, and p. 169).

Advice on making polenta

• The quantities of polenta given are for 4 cups (1 liter) of water; however, depending on the type of flour, polenta may require more or less water.

• Add a tablespoon of olive oil to the water just after adding the flour. This will save you having to stir constantly.

• For a very fine polenta, you can avoid lumps by pouring the flour into the water before boiling point is reached.

• For preference, use a coarse-grained flour (*bramata*) for a firm polenta and a finer grained flour (*fioretto*) for a soft polenta.

• Always stir polenta in the same direction (as for mayonnaise, for example).

• The cooking time for polenta is very important: the longer it is cooked, the more flavorsome and digestible it will become.

• During the cooking process, air bubbles form inside the mass of polenta, these bubbles cause continuous eruptions, so be very careful that you do not get splashed and scalded.

• Keep 1 cup (250 ml) of boiling water to hand in case the polenta becomes too thick.

• You can cook the polenta in a pressure cooker. Once the flour and water are mixed, close the lid and cook for 20 minutes. Turn off the heat and reduce the pressure, then open the lid and stir vigorously before serving or pouring onto a polenta board.

• To avoid stirring continuously during the cooking process, you can cook the polenta in a bain-marie, but the cooking time will be longer.

Traditional Polenta ★★

Polenta tradizionale

Serves 4-6
Preparation time: 10 minutes
Cooking time: 45-60 minutes

Ingredients
4 cups (1 liter) water
1 tablespoon (15 g) salt
2 ½ cups (10 oz./300 g) white or yellow polenta flour for firm
  polenta
or
1 ½ cups (7 oz./200 g) white or yellow polenta flour for soft polenta

Boil the water in a saucepan. Add the salt, then pour in the flour,
mixing continuously with a whisk to prevent lumps forming (1).
Let simmer for 45 to 60 minutes, stirring continuously
(after the initial phase the whisk can be replaced by a
wooden spoon) (2). The polenta is cooked once it comes away
from the sides of the saucepan and forms a cohesive mass.
Spread it onto the polenta board and leave to firm up (3).
(White polenta flour has been used in these photographs.)

Quick Polenta ★

Polenta rapida

Serves 4-6
Preparation time: 10 minutes
Cooking time: 5 minutes

Ingredients
4 cups (1 liter) water
1 tablespoon (15 g) salt
2 ½ cups (10 oz./300 g) precooked polenta flour for firm polenta
or
1 ½ cups (7 oz./200 g) precooked polenta flour for soft polenta

Boil the water in a saucepan, add the salt, then remove from the heat. Pour in the flour, mixing continuously with a whisk to prevent lumps forming (1).
Replace over the heat and cook for a few moments (see the packet instructions), stirring continuously (2). The polenta is cooked once it comes away from the sides of the saucepan. Spread it onto the polenta board and leave to firm up (3). (Yellow polenta flour has been used in these photographs.)

Buckwheat Flour Polenta ★★

Polenta taragna

Serves 4-6
Preparation time: 10 minutes
Cooking time: 1 hour

Ingredients
4 cups (1 liter) water
1 tablespoon (15 g) salt
3 cups (10 oz./300 g) buckwheat flour
1 stick (4 oz./100 g) butter
1 ½ cups (6 oz./200 g) cheese: raclette or other quick melting
   variety (traditionally a cheese from the Valtellina called *bitto*
   is used)

Boil the water in a saucepan. Add the salt, then pour in the
flour, mixing continuously with a whisk to prevent lumps
forming (1).
Let simmer for 45 to 60 minutes, stirring continuously
(after the initial phase the whisk can be replaced by
a wooden spoon).
Add the butter and the cheese in small pieces and cook
for an additional 5 minutes (2, 3). Serve immediately on
warmed plates.

Chestnut Flour Polenta ★

Polenta alla farina di castagne

Serves 4-6
Preparation time: 10 minutes
Cooking time: 30 minutes

Ingredients
4 cups (1 liter) water
1 tablespoon (15 g) salt
1 tablespoon olive oil
3 cups (10 oz./300 g) chestnut flour

Boil the water in a saucepan. Add the salt and olive oil,
then pour in the flour, mixing continuously with a whisk
to prevent lumps forming (1).
Let simmer for about 30 minutes, stirring continuously
(after the initial phase the whisk can be replaced by
a wooden spoon) (2).
At the end of the cooking time, stir vigorously (3),
and immediately pour onto a polenta board to firm up.
Accompany with soft cheese, charcuterie, sausages,
herrings, or a meat- or mushroom-based sauce.

Different ways to serve polenta

Soft polenta is usually served directly from the saucepan onto plates with a sauce to accompany it.

Polenta prepared for dishes requiring a firmer texture is poured onto a polenta board, spread out, and left to firm up (allow approximately 30 minutes). It can then be cut into ½ in. to 1 in. (1 to 2 cm) slices, which can be served immediately or cooked a second time.

- **Broiled or grilled polenta** (*grigliata*) (1)
Place the slices of polenta under a broiler or on a lightly oiled, pre-heated ribbed grill pan. Cook for 2 minutes on each side until well browned.

- **Baked polenta** (*al forno*)
Place the slices of polenta on a sheet of parchment paper on a baking sheet. Bake at 450°F (250°C) until well browned (approximately 5 minutes).

- **Fried polenta** (*fritta*) (2)
Fry the slices of polenta in oil heated to 350°F/180°C. The slices are cooked as soon as they are well browned. Drain on paper towel. You can make polenta "fries" by cutting it into sticks rather than slices.

- **Polenta gnocchi** (*gnocchi di polenta*)
Immerse the polenta cut into dice in salted boiling water. As soon as the dice rise to the surface, drain them, and add butter and grated cheese (Parmesan or firmly set ricotta).

Suggested accompaniments

- **Shrimp (Friuli style):** Top soft polenta with shrimp sautéed in butter with garlic, parsley, and button mushrooms.

- **Sausage (Roman style):** soften onions with olive oil, chopped garlic, and parsley in a saucepan, then add the sausages and brown them. Deglaze with white wine and add tomato sauce. Cook for 15 minutes. Serve on soft polenta on warmed plates and sprinkle with grated pecorino.

- **Pancetta lardons:** create alternate layers of soft polenta, cheese, and bacon, lightly fried in a skillet with butter and sage.

- **Onion (Trentino style):** top grilled polenta with onions softened in a skillet with olive oil and rosemary, seasoned with salt and pepper.

- **Salt cod (Venetian style):** all recipes for preparing salt cod go well with polenta (see stockfish *alla Vicentina*, p. 249).

- **Quail polenta (Bergamo style):** cook the cleaned quail for 20 minutes in a skillet with butter and sage, serve them with their juices on top of soft polenta served on warm plates. You can also serve the polenta with kebabs of quail.

- **Beef or wild boar Bolognese sauce** (*ragù*): serve soft polenta on warmed plates topped with the sauce and grated Parmesan.

- **Gorgonzola (Milanese style):** pour half of the cooked polenta onto a polenta board, dot with butter and small cubes of Gorgonzola, cover with the rest of the polenta; cut into portions and serve immediately.

- **Polenta Como Valley style** (*uncia*): in a serving dish, create alternate layers of soft polenta with grated Parmesan, and onions lightly fried in a skillet with butter and sage.

- **Cheese polenta (specialty of Oropa in Piedmont and of the Val d'Aosta):** after cooking polenta for 30 minutes, add 8 oz. (250 g) cheese (a mixture of Gorgonzola, fontina, and Tomme) cut into small dice. Complete the cooking time and stir in about 1 stick (4 oz./115 g) of melted butter. Add another 3 ½ oz. (100 g) of cheese and mix in well. Remove from the heat and serve immediately.

- **Porcini:** fry sliced porcini in a skillet with olive oil, garlic, and parsley. Season with salt and pepper and deglaze with white wine. Serve on slices of grilled polenta.

Baked Polenta ★

Polenta pasticciata

Serves 8
Preparation time: 45 minutes
Cooking time: 30 minutes

Ingredients

10 oz. (300 g) ground beef
2 chipolata sausages
1 stick (4 oz./100 g) butter
1 onion
1 carrot
1 stick celery
½ cup (1 oz./30 g) dried porcini (soaked in water for 10 minutes)
3 ½ oz. (100 g) *guanciale* (cured pork cheek flavored with herbs)
1 cup (250 ml) white wine
1 ½ cups (8 oz./250 g) peeled tomatoes
4 oz. (100 g) raw ham
1 portion polenta cooled on a polenta board
1 ½ cups (7 oz./200 g) grated Gruyère
⅓ cup (2 oz./50 g) grated Parmesan
Salt

Fry the beef and the chipolatas in a saucepan with half the butter. Wash, peel, and chop all the vegetables except the tomatoes and add them to the pan with the rehydrated porcini and the *guanciale*.
Let soften, then deglaze with the wine. Add the tomatoes and a scant ½ cup (100 ml) water, season with salt, then leave this sauce to simmer for 15 minutes.
Cut the ham into strips.
In a buttered baking dish, create alternate layers of polenta and sauce (**1**). Sprinkle each layer with grated Gruyère cheese and ham (**2**).
Finish with a layer of polenta. Sprinkle over Parmesan cheese and dot with the remaining butter (**3**).
Bake for 30 minutes at 350°F (180°C).

● **Chef's note**
Another traditional, lighter version is to replace the sausage and beef with veal and the livers and hearts from chicken or other poultry.

● **Did you know?**
The literal translation of the Italian name of this dish is "messy polenta."

Deep-fried foods

Deep-fried foods

Italy has a range of traditional recipes for deep-fried foods, the components varying from one region to another. The use of certain ingredients such as meat, fish, and vegetables remains constant. There are also many recipes for deep-fried bread and pizza, as well as for sweet fritters.

Advice on preparing deep-fried foods

Different frying oils

Use an oil that will not exceed the critical temperature of its smoking point to avoid breaking down the fat molecules (pyrolysis). This phenomenon produces bad odors and transmits an unpleasant taste to foods, generating toxic substances.

Oils rich in polyunsaturated fats, which are unstable and become carcinogenic at high temperature, should therefore be avoided. In some countries, you are strongly advised not to use these oils for frying, especially sunflower oil.

The smoking point is therefore of fundamental importance when choosing a frying oil. It is different for each oil.

Olive oil is the most stable, containing natural antioxidants and only 10 percent polyunsaturated fats. It has a smoking point of 410°F/210°C. However, its flavor can be too pronounced for some foods and it has the disadvantage of being expensive.

The smoking point of sunflower oil is below 266°F/130°C (65 percent polyunsaturated fats); corn oil's smoking point is 320°F/160°C (60 percent polyunsaturated fats), and for peanut oil it is 356°F/180°C (30 percent polyunsaturated fats). There are also oils called "frying" oils that are processed to remain stable at a high temperature, in particular refined palm oil (464°F/240°C), which is widely used in the restaurant trade, and modified vegetable oil, generally composed of sunflower oil with fractionated vegetable oil added.

Lard is also very stable for frying (500°F/260°C) and therefore widely used (especially for pâtisserie).

Depending on the products to be fried, olive oil and peanut oil remain the best choice for domestic use. Clarified butter is an alternative.

Advice on more healthful ways of frying

Ideally, for health reasons, the oil in a fryer should be changed every time food is fried, or at least every other time.

Filter the oil after frying to eliminate the debris that might carbonize next time it is used (the oil used to cook fries will keep longer than oil used for frying foods coated in batter).

Keep the oil in a cool, dark place in a sealed container to prevent oxidation. Do not keep longer than 2 to 3 weeks.

To prevent the oil burning, always use in large quantities (at least three times the volume of the foods to be fried) and, once it has reached the desired temperature, do not hold it there for long with nothing cooking in it, just add a piece of bread if necessary. The temperature when frying at home should never exceed 350°F/180°C. There are several signs that indicate that frying oil is deteriorating: a dark color, an unpleasant smell and taste, smoking, persistent surface foam, and increased viscosity, all resulting in greasy food that does not drain well.

Temperatures for frying different categories of foods

The smaller the item of food to be fried, the higher the frying temperature needs to be.

Depending on the food, it varies between 280°F/140°C and 350°F/180°C. If the temperature is not high enough, the moisture in the food does not evaporate and the result will not be crisp. To achieve a good, crisp, non-greasy result, cook as few items as possible at the same time. The temperature chosen must remain constant.

350°F/180°C: small pieces of vegetables or fish, precooked foods, shrimp, offal, frozen foods;

320°F/160°C to 340°F/170°C: breaded meat and fish, cakes, vegetables;

300°F/150°C: large portions of chicken or rabbit, whole fish, and all foods that require a longer cooking time.

How to prepare the foods to be fried

The food should be dry and at room temperature before being fried. Avoid adding salt or spices as this can accelerate the deterioration of the oil and affect the adherence of any coating to the food. Once the food is drained, place immediately on paper towel, and do not cover. Serve immediately. You can keep the food that has been fried first in a warm oven with the door left open while you fry the remainder.

What equipment is needed?

An electric fryer is ideal for precise temperature control.

A large pan fitted with a basket also works well. To drain the fried food, it is best to use a slotted spoon that will not retain the oil as a sieve might. In the absence of an electric fryer, you can use an immersion or infrared thermometer.

How to avoid bad smells

Add apple slices, sprigs of fresh parsley, or coriander seeds to the frying oil, and change them regularly. This will diminish the odors.

Frying time

The time different foods take to cook depends on the nature and size of what you are frying. In general the food is ready when it turns a nice golden color and rises to the surface.

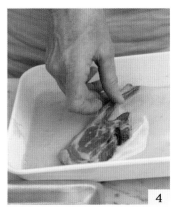

Selection of Deep-Fried Meats and Vegetables ★ ★

Fritto misto di terra

A mixed selection of deep-fried meats and vegetables is a traditional Piedmontese dish, prepared with a wide choice of foods "of the earth": meats, vegetables, and cakes. Similar versions are Bolognese *fritto misto*, with an even richer selection (cold meats, fruit, acacia flowers, etc.); Roman, with a more limited selection (mainly offal and artichokes); Milanese, based on boiled meats; and Ligurian, mainly composed of vegetables and fish.

Serves 6

Preparation time: 1 hour
Frying time: 25 minutes
Cooling time for the semolina: 1-2 hours

Ingredients

1 ²/₃ cups (400 ml) milk
Zest of 1 lemon
²/₃ cup (6 oz./160 g) sugar
1 cup (3 ½ oz./100 g) fine semolina
1 lb. (500 g) mixed vegetables (eggplant, zucchini, zucchini flowers, mushrooms, artichokes, cabbage, and broccoli)
1 lb. (500 g) assorted meat (veal sweetbreads, brains, veal escalope, calf's liver, sausages, poultry drumsticks, pork chops and spare ribs, lamb chops, and frogs' legs)
6 soft amaretti biscuits
1 apple, sliced
4 eggs
4 cups (8 oz./250 g) fresh bread crumbs
Sufficient quantity of olive oil or peanut oil for deep frying
Salt

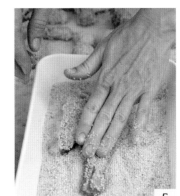

Prepare the semolina.
Bring the milk to a boil with the lemon zest and sugar. Pour in the semolina all at once (1), whisking continuously. Cook for a few minutes (2), then pour onto a flat surface or polenta board (3). Let cool, then cut into diamond-shaped lozenges.

Clean and cut up the vegetables.
Cut the meat into evenly sized pieces.
Dip all the ingredients, including the lozenges of semolina, amaretti biscuits, and pieces of apple into the beaten eggs (4), and then the bread crumbs (5).
Fry them in the oil at 330°F/165°C until they are golden brown (8 to 12 minutes for the meat, 3 minutes for vegetables, 2 minutes for the amaretti) (6).
Drain on paper towel and sprinkle with salt.
Serve immediately.

● Chef's note
To make a lighter coating, use beaten egg whites instead of whole eggs.

Selection of Deep-Fried Fish and Shellfish ★

Fritto misto di mare

Deep-fried fish is the most commonly found fried food in Italy, appearing on almost every restaurant menu. This dish can consist of just shellfish and mollusks (calamari and shrimp), or fish, known as "*paranza*," or a mixture of the two.

Serves 6
Preparation time: 30 minutes
Frying time: 12 minutes

Ingredients
1 ½ lb. (800 g) fish for frying (mullet, dabs, small mackerel, anchovy, etc.)
6 oz. (200 g) shrimp
6 oz. (200 g) calamari rings
2 tablespoons, approximately, flour or durum-wheat flour
Sufficient quantity of olive oil or peanut oil for deep frying
1 lemon
Salt

Wash the fish and shellfish and drain carefully. Dip them in a very small quantity of flour (1, 2). Shake them to eliminate the surplus and fry them in the oil at 350°F/180°C until they are well browned (2 minutes for shrimp, 4 minutes for the calamari and other small fish) (3). Drain on paper towel and sprinkle with salt (4).
Serve immediately with lemon wedges.

● Chef's notes
For a lighter result, use a minimal amount of flour. Put the ingredients in a bag with 1 tablespoon of flour, close the bag and shake. You can also shake the ingredients in a tamis or drum sieve, once they are floured, to remove any excess flour. The flour is only used to eliminate any trace of moisture on the surface of the ingredients.
You can sprinkle the fried foods with chopped parsley before serving.
You can also add scampi, small squid or cuttlefish, whole octopus (moscardini), and soft-shell crab.

Fried Mozzarella Sandwich ★

Mozzarella in carrozza

"Mozzarella in a carriage" is a Neapolitan dish created to use up mozzarella that is no longer completely fresh or moist.

Serves 4
Preparation time: 30 minutes
Resting time: 1 hour
Frying time: 5 minutes

Ingredients
8 oz. (250 g) mozzarella
8 slices soft white bread
2 eggs
2/3 cup (150 ml) milk
3 tablespoons flour
Sufficient quantity of olive oil or peanut oil for deep frying
Salt

Drain the mozzarella and leave it exposed to air, uncovered, for 1 hour.
Cut it into four slices approximately ½ in. (1 cm) thick.
Remove the crusts from the bread. Place the slices of cheese on half of the bread.
Cover with the remaining slices of bread and press down well before moistening the edges with water and flouring them to form a seal. This will prevent the mozzarella escaping during the frying process.
Beat the eggs with the milk. Dip each sandwich into the beaten egg, allowing them to soak up as much egg as possible (1). Let rest for a few minutes then fry in the oil at 350°F/180°C until they are well browned (2) (approximately 5 minutes). Drain on paper towel and sprinkle with salt (3). Serve immediately.

● Chef's notes
You can replace the soft white bread by one- or two-day-old slices from a rustic loaf. Add a fillet of anchovy in oil to the cheese.
Fried, breaded mozzarella is prepared by frying the slices of cheese dipped in egg and bread crumbs. They are then sprinkled with salt and oregano.

Deep-Fried Bread and Pizza ★

Figattole e pizzelle

Fried bread, pizza, and turnovers made from bread dough, with or without additional ingredients, are extremely tasty and ideal for serving with antipasti.

Serves 4
Preparation time: 20 minutes
Rising time: 2 hours
Frying time: 10-12 minutes

Ingredients
1 tablespoon (½ oz./15 g) fresh yeast
Scant ½ cup (100 ml) water
1 teaspoon brown sugar
1 ¾ cups (6 oz./180 g) all-purpose flour
Sufficient quantity of olive oil or peanut oil for deep frying
Salt

Deep-fried bread (*figattole*).
Dilute the yeast in the water with the sugar (1) and combine the flour with a pinch of salt. Mix well (2) and knead until you have a smooth ball. Let rise for 1 hour, covered with a dish towel (3).
Divide the dough into small pieces (4). Roll out the dough to a thickness of approximately ¼ in. (5 mm). Cut diamonds of approximately 5 in. (10 cm) and make an incision in the middle (5).
Fry at 340°F/170°C until they are a light golden brown (2 to 3 minutes).
Drain on paper towel and sprinkle with salt.
Serve these *figattole* very hot with charcuterie and cheese.

Deep-fried pizza (*pizzelle*).
To make fried pizza, shape the risen dough into small rounds.
Fry them (6), then top with a spoonful of tomato sauce, grated Parmesan, and basil leaves, or fillets of anchovy, capers, and oregano.

● Did you know?
Pizzelle, widely available as street food in southern Italy, appear in the 1954 film L'Oro di Napoli *(The Gold of Naples), directed by Vittorio de Sica and starring Sophia Loren.*

Sweet Fritters ★

Chiacchere

Serves 6
Preparation time: 20 minutes
Resting time: 30 minutes
Frying time: 4-6 minutes

Ingredients

3 cups (10 oz./300 g) cake flour
¼ cup (1 ¾ oz./50 g) superfine sugar
2 eggs
1 ½ tablespoons (20 ml) melted butter
1 vanilla bean or zest of 1 lemon
1 tablespoon alcohol (Marsala, sweet wine, grappa)
Sufficient quantity of lard for deep frying
1 tablespoon confectioners' sugar

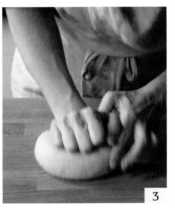

Mix the flour and superfine sugar, then add the eggs and the melted butter (1). Knead until you have a smooth dough (2, 3). Wrap in a dish towel and let rest for 30 minutes.
Using a rolling pin, roll out the dough to approximately ¹/₁₂ in. (2 mm) thick (4) and cut into strips, rectangles, or diamonds with a serrated pasta cutter (5).
Make two incisions in the middle of each shape (6).
Fry them in the lard at 350°F/180°C until lightly browned (about 2 minutes).
Drain on paper towel and serve them dusted with the confectioners' sugar.

● Did you know?

Very popular at Carnival time, these sweetened dough fritters are given different names in every region. Cenci (rags), chiacchiere (gossip), galani (ribbons), or bugie (lies) are among the most widely known.

Fish and shellfish

Whole fish

Italian fish restaurants often have a display of fresh fish at the entrance, where you can choose fish to be cooked to order for you. More and more fishmongers also have a small restaurant attached to their shop.

Fish served whole is still very widespread in Italy. It is the most rewarding method of cooking when it is very fresh.

Advice on preparing fish

A few precautions before cooking fish

Choose firm, gleaming fish with red gills; the eyes should be bright, round, and prominent. There should only be a faint smell of the sea.

Just before cooking a fish, rinse in fresh water, then dry it.

For cooking on a barbecue or in a salt crust, leave the scales on the fish.

For roasting fish that weigh more than 1 ½ lb. (700 g), make incisions diagonally through the skin on both sides so that the inside can cook more effectively.

It is best to keep fish the shortest time possible as it loses its freshness very quickly. However, you can keep a whole fresh fish in the fridge to cook the next day if it is cleaned, rinsed, and drained, then wrapped in paper towel and placed on a stainless steel or plastic tray.

If you wish to cook a whole fish that has been frozen, defrost it completely and rinse thoroughly before cooking.

Season well

To enhance the flavor of fish cooked in the oven or on the barbecue, you can marinate it beforehand with your choice of flavorings (olive oil with bay leaves, wild fennel, rosemary and garlic, onions, etc.). When you cook it, you can add a few vegetables (potatoes, tomatoes, artichokes, fennel, mushrooms, etc.) as an accompaniment. For baked fish, you can also add some shellfish and/or crustaceans.

To concentrate the flavors, you can also enclose the fish in an envelope of parchment paper or foil, with the selected flavorings and vegetables.

To enhance the taste of fish cooked in steam, or poached, flavor the cooking water with a strip of lemon zest, a carrot, an onion, a stick of celery, parsley, garlic, bay leaf, salt, and white wine.

Monitor the cooking

When you poach a whole fish it should be placed in a pan of cold water with the selected flavorings and cooked gently on low heat, as it can easily fall apart during this method of cooking.

A small fish is cooked as soon as the water reaches boiling point; otherwise, allow 10 minutes per 1 lb. (500g). The best way to accompany poached fish is with a simple mayonnaise.

The fish's eyes are a means of judging the degree of cooking: they turn completely white and opaque when it is fully cooked.

Fish Baked in Salt ★★

Pesce al sale

This recipe particularly highlights the delicate taste of the fish. The salt forms a crust that encases the fish and seals in all its flavor until the moment of serving.

Serves 4
Preparation time: 20 minutes
Cooking time: 45 minutes

Ingredients
1 fish approximately 2 ¾ lb. (1.2 kg) (bass, sea bream, red porgy, snapper, etc.)
5 ½ lb. (2.5 kg) kosher salt
Olive oil
Lemon

For cooking in a salt crust, the fish should be cleaned without removing its scales.

Preheat the oven to 400°F (200°C).

Spread a thick layer of salt over the base of an ovenproof dish.

Place the fish on it and cover it with a second layer about 1 in. (2 cm) thick (1), well pressed down (2). Bake for 45 minutes: allow 30 minutes for a 1 lb. (500 g) fish and 1 hour for a 3 lb. (1.5 kg) fish. To serve, remove as much of the salt as possible (3) and allow guests to help themselves to olive oil and lemon.

● Chef's note
You can flavor the fish prior to baking by slipping any combination of the following into its belly cavity: rosemary, bay, garlic, parsley, citrus zest, etc.

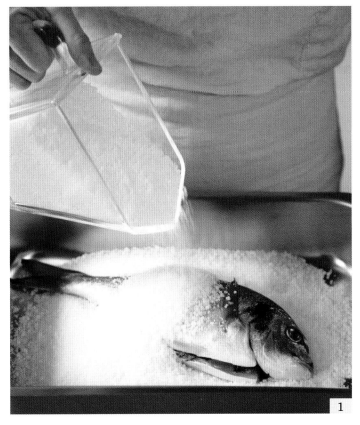

Fish *all'Acqua Pazza* ★★

Pesce all'acqua pazza

Fish cooked in *acqua pazza*, meaning "crazy water," is a typically southern Italian recipe. The fish is cooked in a broth scented with various flavorings and tomatoes. This is a very simple recipe particularly used for a fish called *pezzogna* (porgy or red sea bream in English), but one that also works well for cooking other fish.

Serves 4
Preparation time: 30 minutes
Cooking time: 20 minutes

Ingredients
1 fish approximately 3 lb. (1.5 kg) (red mullet, sea bream, umbra, bass, etc.)
2 cloves garlic
1 stick celery
1 carrot
2/3 cup (150 ml) olive oil
1 cup (250 ml) white wine
10 oz. (300 g) cherry tomatoes, cut into quarters
1 red chili
4 sprigs of parsley
Salt

Place the cleaned fish in a medium-size pan (1) with all the ingredients and 2 glasses of water.
Cook over moderate heat and remove as soon as the fish is cooked (about 20 minutes from the moment the water reaches boiling point) (2), and serve with the cooking juices and the tomatoes. The fish is cooked when the eyeballs turn completely white.

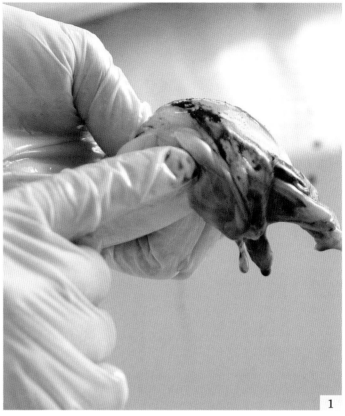

Mollusks, shellfish, and crustaceans

Cleaning cuttlefish, extracting the ink

Separate the head with tentacles attached from the body. Remove the membrane that envelops the body and the transparent, quill-like cartilage. Open the cuttlefish out flat and clean the inside, making sure not to break the ink sac. You'll recognize this sac by its mother-of-pearl color **(1)**. Separate it and set aside in a small glass dish. Rinse the body and place it on paper towel. Cut off the tentacles just below the eyes using scissors **(2)**; remove the beak (mouth) made of cartilage that is found in the middle of the tentacles **(3)**; rinse everything well.

http://flamm.fr/ic08

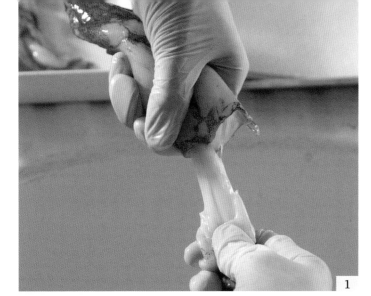

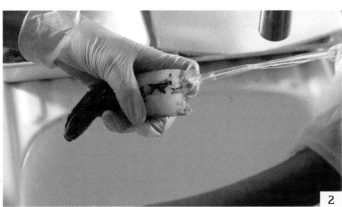

Cleaning calamari

Cleaning calamari, squid, and baby squid is the same as for the cuttlefish. Separate the body from the head and tentacles (1). Empty the squid and remove the quill (2). The ink found in calamari is not particularly tasty but you can keep the calamari tubes for stuffing. Rinse them and remove the membrane (3).
Cut off the tentacles just below the eyes (4). Rinse everything well.

Cleaning sea urchins and extracting the tongues

Turn over the sea urchin and using scissors cut the entire perimeter around the small opening to create a hat shape, allowing you to open it up by a third (1). Using a spoon, gently retrieve the tongue (orange/yellow) (2) and place it in a small dish (3). (Be careful the tongues do not come into contact with fresh water, as there is a risk of them dissolving.) Discard the rest of the sea urchin.

Cleaning octopus

Turn the body inside out, rinse, then turn back to its initial position. Remove the eyes with scissors just above the tentacles and cut off the beak that is found in the middle of them; rinse and wipe dry with paper towel. The cleaning process is the same for *moscardini*, baby octopus that are recognizable by a single row of suction cups on their tentacles instead of the two rows that octopuses have.

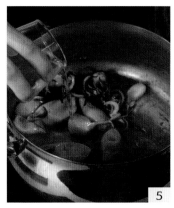

Mussel and Squid Stew with Tomato ★

Zuppetta di cozze

Zuppetta is a recipe based on shellfish and crustaceans, which is presented like a fish soup, but with much less juice, and is served with slices of toasted bread.

Serves 4
Preparation time: 30 minutes
Cooking time: 25 minutes

Ingredients
8 slices rustic bread
Generous measure of olive oil
2 lb. (1 kg) mussels
1 lb. (400 g) squid (cleaned weight)
1 cup (250 ml) white wine
4 cloves garlic
1 red chili
1 lb. (400 g) canned, peeled tomatoes
Parsley
Salt

Brush the slices of bread generously with olive oil and toast under a broiler or on a ribbed grill pan.
Clean the mussels and squid. Place the mussels in a saucepan and simmer with 1 or 2 tablespoons of olive oil and 2/3 of the white wine (1) until their shells have all fully opened (approximately 10 minutes).
Keep them warm. Strain the juice through a fine mesh sieve (2, 3).
In another saucepan, fry the unpeeled garlic with the olive oil and crumbled chili (4).
Add the squid, lightly brown, and deglaze with the remaining white wine (5). Once the wine evaporates, add the peeled tomatoes (6) and the chopped parsley; season with salt.
Simmer for 5 minutes. Stir in the mussels and their strained juices (7).
Serve with the slices of toast. Decorate with a few sprigs of parsley (8).

● Chef's note
You can add extra shellfish (clams, etc.) and/or crustaceans (shrimp, prawns, scampi, etc.) to the stew. Also try the version without tomato sauce (in bianco in Italian).

Seafood Salad ★

Insalata di mare

Serves 4
Preparation time: 40 minutes
Cooking time: 30 minutes

Ingredients

14 oz. (400 g) mussels (shell on)
3 ½ oz. (100 g) clams (shell on)
7 oz. (200 g) squid
4 shrimp
4 prawns
Olive oil
3 cloves garlic
Generous bunch of parsley
1 carrot
3 sticks celery
1 lemon
1 bay leaf
½ cup (3 ½ oz./100 g) cooked haricot beans (optional)
Salt, freshly ground pepper

Clean the shellfish. Crush one of the cloves of garlic. Tip the mussels and clams into a saucepan over high heat with a tablespoon of olive oil, the crushed garlic, and a sprig of the parsley, until the shells have all opened fully. Leave to cool. Wash and peel the vegetables. Clean the squid.
Bring 8 cups (2 liters) of water to a boil with the carrot, 1 stick of the celery, 1 strip of lemon zest, the bay leaf, a second clove of garlic, and 1 sprig of parsley. Simmer for 10 minutes (1). Add the squid, shrimp, and prawns. After 1 minute, remove the crustaceans and drain them; remove and drain the squid after 2 more minutes.
Prepare a lemon dressing with olive oil, salt, pepper, and lemon juice.
Chop the parsley with the remaining clove of garlic. Remove the shells from three quarters of the mussels and clams and place them all in a bowl (setting aside a few in their shells for decoration). Pour over a little of the dressing (2). Peel the shrimp and prawns, de-vein them, and cut them in two lengthwise. Add them to the salad bowl. Cut the squid into strips (if they are small, you can leave them whole) and add them, with their tentacles, to the other seafood (3). If using, add the beans too. Season everything with the rest of the dressing, the chopped garlic and parsley, salt and pepper (4). Mix well. Decorate with the remaining shellfish in their shells.
Serve cold with slices of toasted bread.

1

2

3

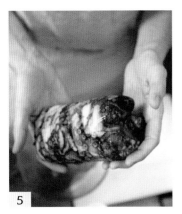
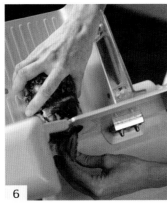

Octopus Carpaccio ★★★

Carpaccio di polpo

Serves 4
Preparation time: 30 minutes
Cooking time: 1 hour
Cooling time: 24 hours minimum

Ingredients
2 ½–3 lb. (1.2 kg) octopus
1 stick celery
1 carrot
1 onion
4 juniper berries
7 peppercorns
4 bay leaves
Sprigs of thyme
Chopped parsley
1 clove garlic

Lemon dressing
Olive oil
Juice of 1 lemon
Salt, pepper

Equipment
1 cork stopper and 1 small weight (optional)
1 plastic bottle

Wash and peel the vegetables. Clean and rinse the octopus thoroughly under running water. Heat a saucepan of water with the celery, carrot, onion, and juniper berries, peppercorns, and bay leaves. If you wish, you can add a cork to the water, as this purportedly makes the octopus more tender. When the water boils, slowly and gradually add the octopus and cook for 1 hour (1).

Remove the octopus and let drain. Cut a plastic bottle in two and keep the lower part; make small holes in the base. Push the octopus down inside the bottle, interspersed with sprigs of thyme (2). Press down well with a glass (3), for example, and place a small weight on top. Secure the whole thing with elastic bands (4) or string to keep it tight. Stand the bottle in a small dish in the coldest part of the refrigerator for 24 hours minimum. At the end of this time, remove the octopus from the bottle (5) and slice as finely as for dried sausage (using a meat slicer, if available) (6). Finely chop the parsley and garlic. Spread the octopus slices on a plate and season with the chopped parsley and garlic, lemon dressing (see p. 128), and freshly ground pepper.

● **Chef's note**
The cooking time for the octopus is approximately 1 hour for 2 lb. (1 kg). If the octopus is very big, beat it prior to cooking with a meat tenderizer or, better still, freeze it for 24 hours.

Langoustine Carpaccio ★

Carpaccio di scampi

Serves 4
Preparation time: 20 minutes

Ingredients
1 lb. (600 g) langoustines
Generous quantity of olive oil
Juice of 1 lemon
1 stick celery
Pink salt
White pepper

Peel the langoustine tails and remove the heads (1). Place the tails on an oiled plate, cover with plastic wrap, and flatten gently with a meat tenderizer (2). Place in the refrigerator.
Prepare the lemon dressing by mixing the lemon juice with a little salt and the olive oil (3). Just before serving, pour the dressing over the langoustines.
Cut the celery into very thin julienne and immerse in a bowl of iced water for a few minutes (to make them curl and to prevent them from wilting). Add a few grinds of white pepper and the well-drained celery (4).
Serve immediately.

Winkles *alla Diavola* ★

Lumachine di mare alla diavola

Serves 4
Preparation time: 20 minutes
Maceration time: 1 hour
Cooking time: 30 minutes

Ingredients
1 lb. (500 g) winkles
¾ lb. (400 g) peeled tomatoes
10 sprigs of parsley
3 cloves garlic
1 or 2 red chilies (to taste)
2 tablespoons olive oil
1 tablespoon chopped thyme
½ cup (120 ml) white wine
Salt

Rinse the winkles thoroughly. Leave them covered in salt water for 1 hour.
Coarsely chop the tomatoes. Wash and chop the parsley. Peel and chop the garlic. Seed and chop the chili then soften it in a little olive oil with the garlic, three quarters of the parsley, and all of the thyme (1). Add the drained winkles (2), cook for 5 minutes, and deglaze with the white wine. Once the wine has evaporated, add the tomatoes and cook for 30 minutes (3). Sprinkle over the remaining chopped parsley. Serve with toasted bread and pass round pins for extracting the winkles.

134

 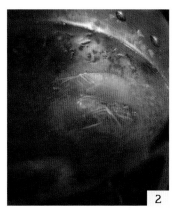 

Fish Soup ★★★

Zuppa di pesce

In Italy, fish soup is generally prepared with a mixture of fish, shellfish, mollusks, and crustaceans. Ideally small rock fish (unusable in any other recipe) are used.
Avoid oily fish (anchovies, sardines, mackerel, skipjack tuna, etc.) and fatty fish (salmon).

Serves 6
Preparation time: 1 hour
Cooking time: 1 hour

Ingredients

Fish soup

2 lb. (1 kg) cleaned weight mixed fish (scorpion fish, red mullet, white bream, monkfish, sting fish, hake, John Dory, sole, etc.)
10 oz. (300 g) shrimp and/or prawns and/or langoustines
2 lb. (1 kg) squid
7 oz. (200 g) mussels
7 oz. (200 g) clams and/or razor clams
1 stick celery
1 carrot
1 onion
5 tablespoons olive oil
2 cloves garlic, peeled
1 bay leaf
5 sprigs of parsley
1 tablespoon chopped thyme
¾ cup (200 ml) white wine
4 ripe tomatoes or canned, peeled tomatoes
Salt

12 small slices toasted bread
1 clove garlic

Wash, peel, and chop the celery, carrot, and onion. Brown in a saucepan with 2 tablespoons of the olive oil. Add 1 clove of garlic, the bay leaf, 1 or 2 sprigs of parsley, and the thyme. Deglaze with ½ cup (150 ml) white wine and let evaporate. Cut the tomatoes into quarters and add to the pan (1) with 6 cups (1.5 liters) of water and a pinch of salt. Bring to a boil and add the well-rinsed fish. Cook for 1 hour.
Add the crustaceans (shrimp, etc.) to the broth for a few minutes (2), then remove and shell some of them. Set the tails aside and put the shells back in the broth. When the cooking process is complete, pass the soup through a coarse mesh sieve or vegetable mill; to both blend and strain it (3). Chop the parsley and the second clove of garlic.
Clean and cut up the squid if they are big, or leave whole. Heat 1 tablespoon of olive oil in a pan. Add the parsley, garlic, and squid, and brown (4). The squid release a lot of water at first. Once it has evaporated, deglaze with ¼ cup (50 ml) wine and cook for 5 minutes.
In another saucepan, heat the shellfish with a tablespoon of olive oil (5) until they have all fully opened.
Strain the juices and add them to the soup. Put a few aside in their shells for decoration and shell the remainder.
Divide all the seafood between hot plates. Pour over the fish broth and decorate with the whole crustaceans and shellfish and the toasted bread, rubbed with garlic.
Drizzle over the remaining tablespoon of olive oil and serve.

Scaloppine

Scaloppine and *piccatas*

Veal is an essential component of traditional Italian cuisine. The best universally known recipes are for scaloppine (escalopes) and *piccatas*. These two cuts of meat are very similar and are cut from the top of the leg or from the rump. Scaloppine are cut thinly (from ¼ in. to ½ in./5 to 10 mm), whereas *piccatas* are cut slightly thicker and three times smaller than a scaloppine. It is common practice to beat these pieces with a meat tenderizer to flatten and tenderize them.

Scaloppine are flatter than *piccatas*. Generally one scaloppine or three *piccatas* are served per person.

● Chef's notes

Veal of good quality should be very pale and slightly pinkish in color.

It is important to cook all the scaloppine at the same time in the skillet, otherwise it is necessary to replace the butter each time a new piece of meat is cooked.

Although scaloppine are traditionally prepared from veal, you can also use pork, poultry (turkey or chicken), or beef.

1

Scaloppine with Lemon ★

Scaloppine al limone

Serves 4
Preparation time: 10 minutes
Cooking time: 10 minutes

Ingredients

4 veal scaloppine or 12 *piccatas* approximately
  1 lb. (500 g) in total
½ cup (2 oz./50 g) flour
¾ stick (3 oz./80 g) butter
1 tablespoon olive oil
1 lemon
1 chicken stock cube
A few sprigs of parsley
4 slices of lemon
Salt, pepper

Cover the scaloppine with plastic wrap and flatten with a tenderizer, mallet, or rolling pin (1). Make a few small cuts around the edges to prevent them curling up while cooking (2). Dip them in the flour (3) and sprinkle with a little salt.

Heat up the butter with the oil in a skillet. Cook the scaloppine for 2 minutes on each side. Pour over the juice of the lemon **(4)**, then remove the scaloppine from the pan. Replace the skillet over the heat and add a ladle of chicken stock made up from the cube (in the absence of stock, use water) to dilute the juices on the base of the pan **(5)**. Add a knob of butter, the chopped parsley, and the slices of lemon. Return the scaloppine to the pan to finish cooking in this sauce (approximately 2 minutes).
Spoon the sauce over the scaloppine and serve.

● Chef's note

You can serve scaloppine and piccatas with salad leaves, fries, mashed potatoes, beans, green beans, spinach, polenta, etc.

Variations
· **Scaloppine with Marsala**: prepare the meat as in the recipe above, but replace the lemon with Marsala and do not add parsley.

· **Scaloppine with white wine**: replace the Marsala with a good white wine.

· **Scaloppine Pavarotti with balsamic vinegar**: prepare the scaloppine as in the recipe above, but replace the stock with balsamic vinegar. Do not add lemon juice.

· **Scaloppine with Gorgonzola**: prepare the scaloppine as in the recipe above, but replace the lemon with grappa. Add ⅔ cup (5 oz./150 g) diced Gorgonzola at the same time as the stock. Do not use parsley.

· **Scaloppine *pizzaiola***: heat the olive oil with a clove of chopped garlic. Add the scaloppine and color them well on both sides. Add 1 tablespoon capers and 1 tablespoon black olives. Add 14 oz. (400 g) crushed tomatoes and 1 teaspoon oregano. Season with salt and pepper and cook for 7 to 8 minutes over medium heat. Turn off the heat and place thinly sliced mozzarella on top of the scaloppine. Cover and wait until the cheese has melted slightly. Serve immediately.

Saltimbocca ⋆

Saltimbocca is one of the signature dishes of Roman cooking. It is prepared with very thin scaloppine cut from a leg of veal that are covered with ham and sage and held together with a toothpick. It is a dish that's easy and quick to cook.

Serves 4
Preparation time: 10 minutes
Cooking time: 20 minutes

Ingredients
12 oz. (300 g) veal scaloppine
4 oz. (120 g) dry-cure ham
2/3 stick (3 oz./80 g) butter
8 fresh sage leaves
½ cup (100 ml) white wine (ideally Vino dei Castelli Romani)
Salt, pepper

Flatten the scaloppine finely in such a way as to give you approximately 5 in. (10 cm) squares (1).
Season lightly with salt and pepper.
Place a slice of ham and a sage leaf on each one (2), fixing them in place with a toothpick (3).
Heat half the butter in a skillet and brown them for 2 minutes on each side, beginning with the ham side down (be careful that the ham does not cook too fast, it can become very dry) (4).
Deglaze with the white wine and finish cooking. Remove the saltimbocca and keep warm. Dilute the juices on the base of the pan with 2 tablespoons of water and add the rest of the butter to bind the sauce.
Serve the saltimbocca coated with the sauce.

● Chef's notes
You can accompany the saltimbocca with green beans, peas, spinach, potatoes, etc.
Saltimbocca is often confused with involtini: *these are scaloppine rolled around a stuffing, usually made with cheese.*

● Did you know?
Saltimbocca literally means "jumps in the mouth" in Italian, because the dish is regarded as so tasty.

Cutlets *alla Milanese* ★ ★ ★

Cotoletta alla milanese

Cutlets *alla Milanese* is the signature dish of the capital of Lombardy. This original recipe, using a thick cutlet of veal cooked on the bone, is relatively unknown. A simplified recipe, prepared with a thinner, crisper escalope, is much more famous, and is sometimes called "elephant's ear."

Serves 4
Preparation time: 20 minutes
Cooking time: 15 minutes

Ingredients
4 veal cutlets on the bone (see Advice on preparing meat
   alla Milanese, p. 143), approximately 1 in. (2 cm) thick
1 ¾ sticks (7 oz./200 g) butter
1 egg
1 cup (2 oz./60 g) fresh bread crumbs
Salt, pepper

Make a few cuts around the edge of the cutlets to prevent them curling while cooking.
Trim the end of the bone so that it is visible, but taking care it does not become detached from the rest of the meat.
Prepare the clarified butter: melt the diced butter in a saucepan on low heat. Skim off any foam that forms on the surface, then leave it to settle for a few minutes. Transfer all the clear fat that has risen to the top to a container, using a spoon. Discard the milky residue in the bottom of the saucepan.
Beat the egg in a bowl with a little pepper. Spread the bread crumbs on a plate. Dip the cutlets in egg (1), then in bread crumbs (2).
Heat the clarified butter in a skillet (3) and fry the cutlets for 2 minutes on each side (4).
Sprinkle with salt and moisten them with the buttery cooking juices. Serve immediately.

● Chef's note
You can prepare the clarified butter in advance and keep it in the refrigerator for several months in a hermetically sealed container. Butter that has been clarified can be heated to a high temperature (350°F/180°C) without risk of burning.

● Did you know?
This recipe appeared on the menu of an official lunch for the clerics of the church of Saint-Ambroise in 1134, under the name of Lombos cum Panitio (rib chops in bread crumbs). It also featured in works by fifteenth-century chef Martino da Como.

Variations

· **Bolognese**: cook the scaloppine *alla Milanese* as in the recipe on the facing page.
Put it in the oven at 390°F (210°C) for 4 minutes, covered with a slice of ham and a few shavings of Parmesan. Serve coated with a hot tomato sauce.

· **Valdostana**: make a horizontal slit in the side to form a pocket and slip a thin slice of fontina (or other quick-melting cheese) into it, with perhaps a few thin slices of white truffle. Close and lightly flatten with a weight.
Dip the cutlet in flour (especially the edge with the pocket in order to seal it), then in egg, then in bread crumbs. Cook as in the recipe opposite.

· **Modenese**: fry slices of onion in a knob of butter with some diced pancetta. Add the breaded cutlets and color them well on both sides.
Deglaze with white wine, let evaporate, and add 4 cups (1 liter) of stock, then 1 cup (100 g) of crushed tomato. Season with salt and pepper. Turn the cutlets and leave to cook, covered, for 10 minutes more on medium heat.

● Did you know?

Although you can often find scaloppine and cutlets alla Milanese *accompanied by spaghetti with tomato sauce or tagliatelle in Italian restaurants, especially in other countries, this is not an Italian custom at all. In Italy, you would find the dish served with fries, salads, green vegetables, jacket potatoes, etc.*

Advice on preparing meat *alla Milanese*

· Cutlets for cooking *alla Milanese* are traditionally veal loin chops (recognizable by their small T-shaped central bone). For scaloppine *alla Milanese*, however, the meat is taken from the veal cushion or the rump.

· In most recipes *alla Milanese*, there is a step for flattening and tenderizing the meat as much as possible by "beating" it. Only beat meat thinly for preparing scaloppine; they can be flattened to the size of a plate. The loin, on the other hand, is a very tender cut of meat that does not lend itself to this practice.

· The method of cooking is crucial when preparing meat *alla Milanese*. It must be cooked evenly, and quickly, and be nicely crisp. To achieve this, cook the meat in very hot fat to color it rapidly. Clarified butter is best for this, because it can be heated to a high temperature.
In place of clarified butter, you can use browned butter with a spoonful of olive oil added (this will allow it to be heated to a higher temperature). You can also use sunflower oil, but the flavor will be less good. You are strongly advised not to use olive oil on its own as it will transmit too strong a flavor to the meat.

· In several recipes for cooking meat *alla Milanese*, it is recommended that you dip it in flour before dipping in the beaten egg to encourage the egg to adhere better. This is true when the meat is cold, but when heated the flour tends to make the egg and bread crumb coating come away from the meat. Avoid adding salt to the egg as this draws the moisture from the meat and also has the effect of making the coating fall off.

· Certain recipes suggest adding Parmesan to the bread crumbs.

· Meat cooked *alla Milanese* can also be served cold (often in a sandwich with a lettuce leaf and a little mayonnaise). For this, the scaloppine should be well drained on paper towel after frying.

· To make the cutlets easier to eat, the bone can be wrapped in foil or parchment paper.

· Always cook meat from room temperature. You will achieve better results as it will be less likely to shrink.

Ice cream and sorbets

Ice cream and sorbets

Italians have greatly contributed to ice cream's fame and popularity. In the sixteenth century, the Florentine architect Bernardo Buontalenti was the originator of a recipe for sorbet served at the table of the Medicis. It was, in fact, Catherine de Medici, wife of Henri II, who introduced this delicacy to the French court. Perfected in England by Charles I's pastry chefs, ice cream also enjoyed great success in seventeenth-century Paris.
At the end of the eighteenth century, Italian immigrants opened the first ice-cream parlors in the United States. The success of this dessert prompted William Young to invent the first ice-cream maker in 1800.
Ices (or ice creams) differ from sorbets and granitas because they contain eggs, milk, and cream.

Advice on making ice cream and sorbets

When making ice cream or sorbets, it needs to be remembered that the chilling process diminishes the flavor. For the same reason, the proportion of sugar needs be higher than for desserts served at room temperature.
The use of an ice-cream maker or churn is ideal. However, it is possible to prepare ice creams or sorbets without this type of device: place in the freezer and stir every 30 minutes until the solidifying process is complete, or leave to freeze in ice-cream trays and mix in a food processor just before serving.

Ice cream

Vanilla Ice Cream ★

Gelato alla crema

Serves 4
Preparation time: 20 minutes
Chilling time: 2 hours

Ingredients
1 cup (250 ml) milk
1 cup (250 ml) whipping cream
½ vanilla bean (or 1 teaspoon vanilla extract) or zest of ½ lemon
4 egg yolks
¾ cup (5 ¼ oz./150 g) granulated sugar

Equipment
1 kitchen thermometer
1 ice-cream maker or 1 ice-cream churn (optional, see advice on the left)

Heat the milk and the cream in a saucepan. Cut the vanilla bean in two lengthwise, scrape out the seeds, and add them to the milk mixture (1). Beat the egg yolks with the sugar until thick and pale (2) and pour the hot milk and cream over them (3). Mix well. Return the mixture to the saucepan and heat to 185°F (80°C), stirring continuously, for 2 minutes without letting it boil. Remove from the heat and stir thoroughly. Leave to chill in the refrigerator for approximately 2 hours.
Stir again, and then pour into the ice-cream maker (4) and follow the manufacturer's directions for the freezing time (5). Ice cream should be stored at -0.4°F (-18°C).

● Chef's notes
Depending on how creamy you wish the ice cream to be, you can increase the quantity of milk and decrease the quantity of cream in the same proportions or vice versa. With 1 ²/₃ cups (400 ml) of milk and ½ cup (100 ml) of cream, you will have a lighter but less creamy ice cream.
You can add various ingredients to vary the flavor of the ice cream: chopped hazelnuts or hazelnut paste, powdered coffee, chocolate chips for stracciatella; *amarena Fabbri (wild cherries in syrup) with their juice for an* amarena *ice cream; pistachio paste; fruit purees, etc.*

Sorbets

Lemon Sorbet ★

Sorbetto al limone

Serves 4
Preparation time: 20 minutes
Chilling time: 2 hours

Ingredients
1 cup (250 ml) lemon juice (or orange or clementine juice, etc.)
Zest of ½ lemon
1 cup (7 oz./200 g) granulated sugar
1 egg white, beaten until stiff with 2 tablespoons sugar

Equipment
1 ice-cream maker or 1 ice-cream churn (or see advice p. 146)

Mix the strained lemon juice or that of another citrus fruit with the zest (1) and sugar (2). Make sure the sugar dissolves and chill the mixture in the refrigerator for approximately 2 hours.
Pour the mixture into an ice-cream maker and switch it on. When the mixture begins to solidify, add the whisked egg white and sugar (3), then continue churning until fully frozen. Keep it in an ice tray in the freezer.

● Chef's notes
Traditionally, citrus fruit, apple, kiwi, melon, and watermelon sorbets are made with water and red berry, banana, peach, and apricot sorbets are made with milk. You can add whisked egg white or whipped cream to the mixture to make a lighter, creamier sorbet that will melt less rapidly.
You can serve lemon sorbet in hollowed-out citrus fruits that have been well chilled.

● Did you know?
In Italy, lemon sorbet is traditionally served in a glass with a splash of vodka as a digestif, after a meal of fish.

Strawberry Sorbet ★

Sorbetto alla fragola

Serves 4
Preparation time: 20 minutes
Chilling time: 2 hours

Ingredients
1 cup (7 oz./200 g) superfine sugar
Scant 1 cup (200 ml) milk
2 ½ cups (14 oz./400 g) ripe strawberries (or peaches, apricots, bananas, etc.)
1 egg white, stiffly beaten

Equipment
1 ice-cream maker or 1 ice-cream churn (or see advice p. 146)

Add the sugar to the milk and heat until dissolved. Chill. Wash the strawberries, remove the stalks, and puree them in a blender. Sieve to remove some of the pips. Mix the strawberries with the chilled milk. Refrigerate for approximately 2 hours.
Pour the mixture into an ice-cream maker and switch on. When the mixture begins to solidify, add the egg white and continue churning until fully frozen.
Keep in an ice tray in the freezer.

● Chef's notes
You can add a few finely chopped basil leaves to the mixture to give it a fresh and original flavor, or drizzle over some balsamic vinegar reduction (see p. 153) when serving.
To make an alcohol-based sorbet, mix 2 cups (14 oz./400 g) of sugar with 1 ⅔ cups (400 ml) of water and put it into an ice-cream maker or churn. Once the mixture begins to solidify, add 8 tablespoons of the desired alcohol (rum, Grand Marnier, Cointreau, vodka, etc.) and 1 egg white beaten with 2 tablespoons of sugar until stiff.

Almond Granita ★

Granita di mandorla

Serves 6
Preparation time: 15 minutes
Chilling time: 2 hours

Ingredients
1 ⅔ cups (12 oz./300 g) almond paste
½ cup (3 oz./100 g) granulated sugar
4 cups (1 liter) lukewarm mineral water
2 tablespoons (10 g) ground almonds

Equipment
1 ice-cream maker or 1 ice-cream churn (or see advice p. 146)

Dissolve the almond paste and sugar in the lukewarm water (1).
Add the ground almonds (2), mix with a stick blender, and churn in the ice-cream maker (3) according to the manufacturer's directions. Serve immediately for the best result (4).
You can keep the granita in the freezer, but bear in mind that it will tend to harden.

● Did you know?
Granita is very popular in Sicily, where homemade versions with different flavors are found everywhere: coffee, lemon, mint, fig, blackberry, watermelon, etc.
The Sicilians have it for breakfast with a sweet brioche and sometimes with whipped cream too.

1 2
3 4

Ice cream and sorbets

1

2

3

4

Coffee *Semifreddo* ★ ★ ★

Semifreddo al caffe

Semifreddi are frozen desserts presented as individual portions or as cakes. They consist mainly of pastry cream, with added whipped cream and Italian meringue.

Serves 8
Preparation time: 45 minutes
Chilling time: 6 hours

Ingredients
For 1 cup (7 oz./200 g) pastry cream
Scant ½ cup (100 ml) milk
1 egg yolk
¼ cup (2 oz./50 g) granulated sugar
1 tablespoon flour
1 teaspoon cornstarch
20 drops coffee extract
1 tablespoon rum
½ cup (3 oz./80 g) hazelnut paste

For ½ cup (3 ½ oz./100 g) Italian meringue
2 egg whites
1/3 cup (2 oz./60 g) granulated sugar

2/3 cup (170 ml) whipping cream
¼ cup (1 oz./30 g) confectioners' sugar

Equipment
1 kitchen thermometer

Prepare the pastry cream.
Heat the milk to boiling point. Whisk the egg yolk with the sugar until thick and pale; add the sifted flour and cornstarch. Whisk together well. Add the hot milk gradually to this mixture, stirring continuously. Return to the heat and boil for 1 minute. Remove from the heat and leave to cool, stirring from time to time, to avoid a skin forming on the surface.

Make the Italian meringue.
Whisk the egg whites with 1 2/3 tablespoons (20 g) sugar. Heat 3 1/3 tablespoons (40 g) of sugar with 2 teaspoons (10 ml) of water in a saucepan and stir until the sugar is completely dissolved and small bubbles form on the surface; the syrup should reach 239°F (115°C). Pour the syrup slowly onto the beaten egg whites (1), whisking continuously until quite cold.

Assemble the dish.
Place the whipping cream with the confectioners' sugar in a chilled bowl and whisk until stiff.
Add the coffee extract, rum, and hazelnut paste to the pastry cream and mix.
Gently fold in the Italian meringue using a spatula (2, 3). Next, add the whipped cream in the same way, taking care that the mixture does not begin to collapse.
Pour the mixture into individual ramekins (4), or into a metal container. Freeze for 6 hours.
To unmold, just moisten the outside of the molds with a damp cloth and turn out. Decorate with chocolate chips and powdered coffee.

Balsamic Vinegar Reduction ★

Salsa di aceto balsamico

Preparation time: 5 minutes
Cooking time: 30 minutes

Ingredients
1 cup (250 ml) balsamic vinegar from Modena (PGI)
1/3 cup (2 oz./60 g) granulated sugar
1 cup (250 ml) red wine

Put the balsamic vinegar, granulated sugar, and red wine in a saucepan, then reduce the liquid by half over a low heat (approximately 30 minutes).

⬤ **Chef's note**
This unusual sauce goes very well with ice creams and sorbets, especially vanilla ice cream and strawberry sorbet.

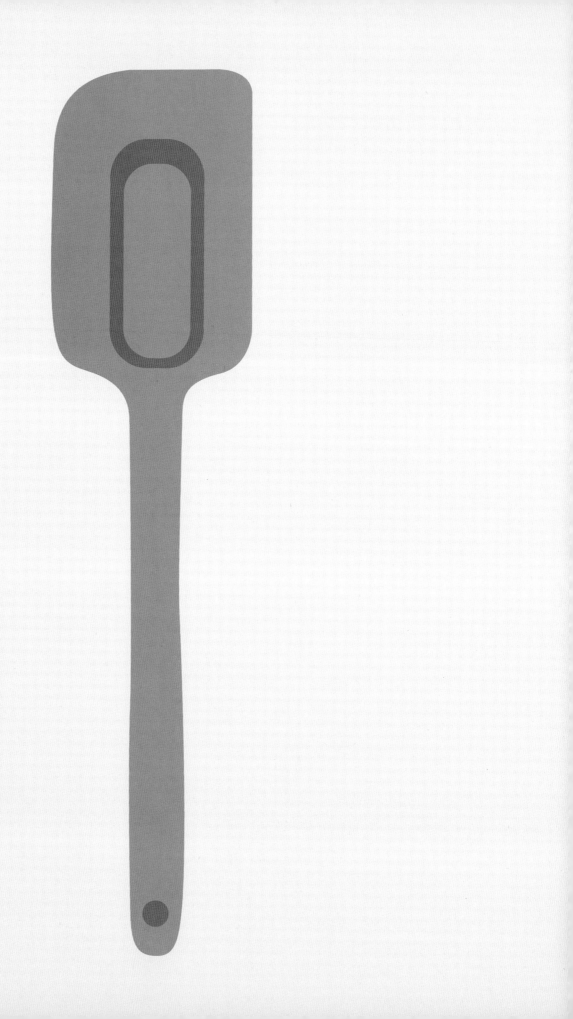

Practical
Guide

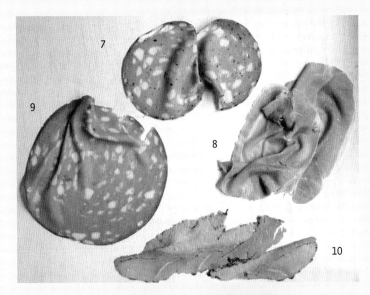

Charcuterie

Salumi

Charcuterie is mainly prepared by processing pork (but beef, poultry, and other meat can also be used). It can be prepared from whole pieces of meat, or ground meat with flavorings added, and then put into natural or artificial casings. The charcuterie is then seasoned, salted, sometimes smoked, and finally cooked or left to age.

Hams and *bresaola*
1. Smoked ham *Speck*
2. Air-dried salted beef *Bresaola della Valtellina*
3. Parma ham *Prosciutto di Parma*
4. Air-dried salted horse meat *Bresaola equina*
5. Vecchio Sauris ham *Prosciutto Vecchio Sauris*
6. Sardinian ham with black pepper *Prosciutto sardo al pepe*

Cooked hams, *mortadella, zampone,* and *cotechino*
7. Black truffle mortadella *Mortadella al tartufo nero*
8. Cooked ham *Prosciutto cotto*
9. Bologna mortadella *Mortadella Bologna*
10. Ham with herbs *Prosciutto cotto alle erbe*

Salamis, *coppa*
11. Salami with fennel and chili *Ventricina*
12. Salami with fennel *Finocchiona*
13. Abruzzo salami *Salame abruzzese*
14. Felino salami *Salame Felino*
15. Coppa
16. Pressed chili salami *Spianata calabrese*
17. Cacciatorino

Bacon and lards
18. Cured pork cheek *Guanciale*
19. Aged Colonnata lard *Lardo di Colonnata*
20. Aged Arnad lard with herbs *Lardo di Arnad*
21. Rolled pancetta *Pancetta arrotolata*

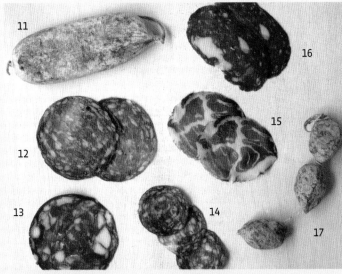

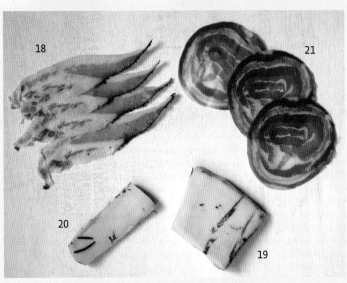

Cheeses

Formaggi

In Italy there are more than 400 different cheeses, of which 45 have Protected Designation of Origin (PDO) status (*Denominazione di Origine Protetta* in Italian, or *DOP*). These are mainly cheeses produced from cow milk and sheep milk. There are very few goat milk cheeses but, in southern Italy, buffalo milk cheese (Mozzarella di Bufala Campana) is very common.

Parmesan—Parmigiano Reggiano (PDO): Unpressed hard cheese prepared with raw, heat-treated cow milk, free of all additives and preservatives. On average 88 lb. (40 kg) of Parmesan is obtained from 1,162 pints (550 liters) of milk. Once the curds have formed, the whole cheese is plunged in brine before an aging period of 12–36 months or longer.

It is generally accepted that Parmesan reaches full maturation after approximately 24 months, when its intense citrus flavors and grainy structure have fully developed. Used in various forms in cooking—grated, shaved, in chunks—it is also completely soluble. Three main levels of maturity exist to correspond with Parmesan's different uses: 18 months, 22 months, and 30 months.

Parmesan
Parmigiano Reggiano

Mozzarella di Bufala Campana (PDO): fresh spun paste (*pasta filata*) cheese, prepared from whole buffalo milk. Once the milk has been heated and curds have formed, they are spun with the addition of boiling water to give the cheese its characteristic ball or braid shape. It can then be smoked by traditional, natural methods. It has a porcelain whiteness and delicate flavor, with a fresh, yeasty aroma when cut.

Gorgonzola (PDO): soft, uncooked blue-veined cheese. It is developed from whole, pasteurized cow milk with added lactic ferments and selected mold strains that give it its characteristic marbling. There are two kinds available: mild and strong. Mild is creamy and soft, very tasty, subtly piquant, and aged 2 months, minimum. Strong is firm enough to cut into portions, distinctly marbled, has a strong, tangy flavor, and is aged 3 months, minimum.

Ricotta: Ricotta is not a cheese in the true sense. It is made from the whey produced after milk is curdled and strained during cheese production. The milk can be cow, buffalo, sheep, or goat. The whey is reheated to produce ricotta. It contains less fat than any other cheese but it is still flavorsome and lends itself to many recipes, both savory and sweet.

Burrata: traditional cow milk cheese from Puglia, produced from raw or pasteurized milk. It is a spun paste cheese, shaped into balls weighing about 9 oz. (250 g). Each ball is filled with fresh cream mixed with shreds of spun paste, a filling known as *stracciatella*.

Scamorza: traditional, raw cow milk cheese from Campania. It is a spun paste, medium-hard cheese made in the shape of a pear, weighing approximately 14 oz. (400 g). It is aged for a fortnight, then may be smoked or left plain.

Stracchino: soft cow milk cheese with no rind, traditionally from the Lombardy region, and more recently from Tuscany. *Stracchino* is aged for about twenty days; when not aged it is known as *cresenza*.

Mascarpone: fresh creamy cheese, traditionally from Lombardy, that owes its great popularity to tiramisu, of which it is the main ingredient. It is made exclusively from fresh cream and has a particularly delicate flavor, although it is somewhat calorific.

Primosale: fresh ewe milk cheese, called tuma, that has been salted for one month, traditionally from Sicily. When aged for an additional four months it becomes known as pecorino.

Raschera: a round or square, medium-hard, pressed cheese weighing about 17 lb. (8 kg). It can be from mountain pastures or from the plains and is typical of the Cuneo area in Piedmont. It is a cow milk cheese to which ewe or goat milk may be added to enrich the flavor. It is aged for one month.

Spun paste cheeses

Smoked mozzarella
Mozzarella affumicata

Burrata

Braided mozzarella
Mozzarella treccia

Baby mozzarella
Mozzarella bocconcini

Scamorza
and smoked *scamorza*
Scamorza e affumicata

Fresh cheeses

Sheep milk ricotta for grating
Ricotta pecorina

Stracchino

Fresh buffalo milk ricotta
Ricotta fresca di bufala

Mascarpone

Fresh cow milk ricotta
Ricotta fresca di mucca

Robiola di Roccaverano

Semi-fresh
cheeses

Raschera

Gorgonzola

Provolone

Primosale

Goat milk Taleggio
Stracco

Taleggio

Asiago

Pasta

Plain or stuffed fresh pasta made from bread (soft wheat) flour

1. *Reginette*
2. Lasagna
3. *Pici*
4. Tortellini
5. Tagliatelle
6. Cappelletti
7. *Maltagliati*
8. *Tagliolini*
9. Ravioli
10. *Pansotti*
11. *Pappardelle*
12. *Agnolotti del Plin*
13. *Quadrucci*

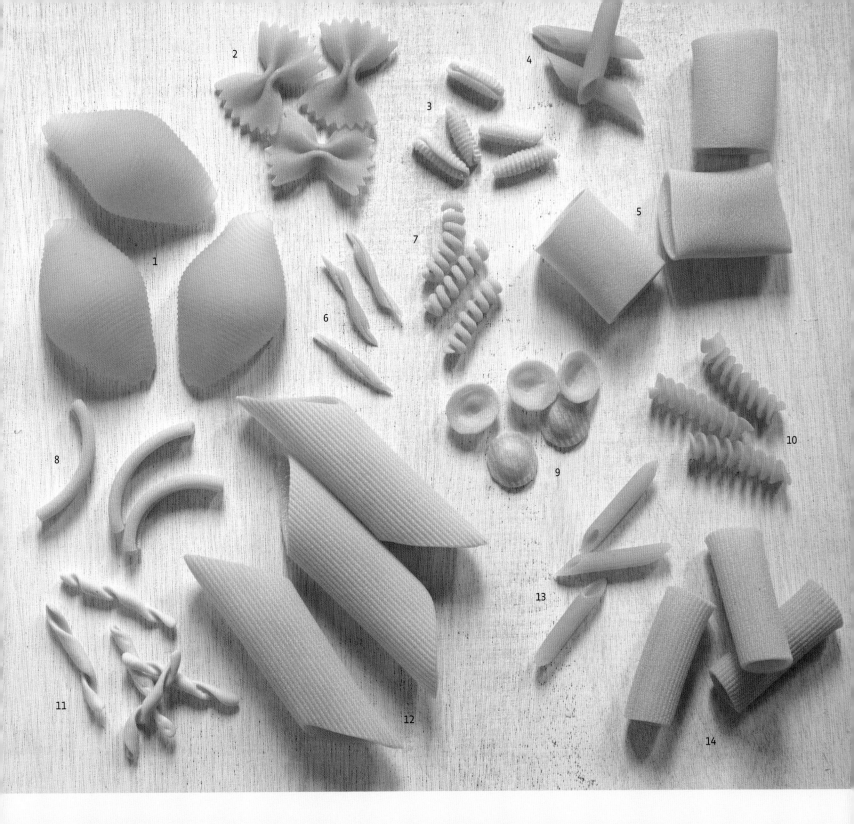

Short dried pasta made from durum wheat flour

1. *Conchiglioni*
2. Farfalle
3. *Gnocchetti sardi*
4. Penne
5. *Paccheri*
6. *Trofie*
7. Fusilli *bucati*
8. *Caserecce*
9. Orecchiette
10. Fusilli
11. *Fileja*
12. *Pennoni*
13. Penne *mezzane*
14. Rigatoni

Long and small dried pasta made from durum wheat flour

Long pasta
1. *Bigoli*
2. *Ziti*
3. *Bucatini*
4. Spaghetti
5. Vermicelli
6. *Mafalde*
7. Linguine
8. Fettuccine
9. *Trenette*

Small pasta
10. *Alfabeto*
11. *Lumachine*
12. *Risi*
13. *Filini*
14. *Stelline*
15. *Ditalini rigati*

Matching pasta with sauces

Matching the various pasta shapes with a multitude of sauces is an art. There are no strict rules; everyone acts according to their own taste. However, there are a few major principles:

Fresh stuffed pasta: given the richness of the stuffing, very simple, delicate sauces are the best match (butter and sage, cream and butter, olive oil and Parmesan).

Thin pasta (*tagliolini*, linguine, *capellini*, etc.): these do not stand up to very rich sauces, which risk masking their flavor.

Pasta made of durum wheat flour: with a less pronounced flavor, this type of pasta is easier to match than fresh egg pasta.

Small pasta (*risi, stelline, tempestine, ruote* [cartwheels] etc.): these are generally used to give body to soups and broths or prepared with butter and Parmesan for young children.

It is therefore important to select suitable pasta for the sauce you wish to prepare.

PASTA	Bucatini	Caserecce	Farfalle	Fusilli *lunghi*	Linguine	Orechiette	Paccheri	Penne	Rigatoni	Spaghetti	Tagliatelle	Ziti
Amatriciana	*								*	*		
Arrabbiata				*			*	*	*			
Baked		*		*			*	*	*			*
Bolognese								*	*	*	*	*
Carbonara	*			*					*	*		
Carrettiera		*		*			*	*	*		*	*
Cuttlefish ink										*		
Garlic, oil, and chili					*					*		
Ham and pea				*			*	*	*		*	*
Marinara								*		*		
Meatballs			*	*			*		*	*	*	*
Mussel/clam							*			*		
Napoletana		*		*		*	*	*	*	*	*	*
Norcina		*		*						*	*	
Norma	*	*	*	*		*	*	*	*	*		*
Pesto			*	*		*				*		
Puttanesca	*	*							*	*		
Seafood							*			*		
Sea urchin										*		
Spiny lobster	*						*			*	*	
Swordfish	*		*				*			*		
Woodland		*	*	*					*	*	*	

Rice

Riso

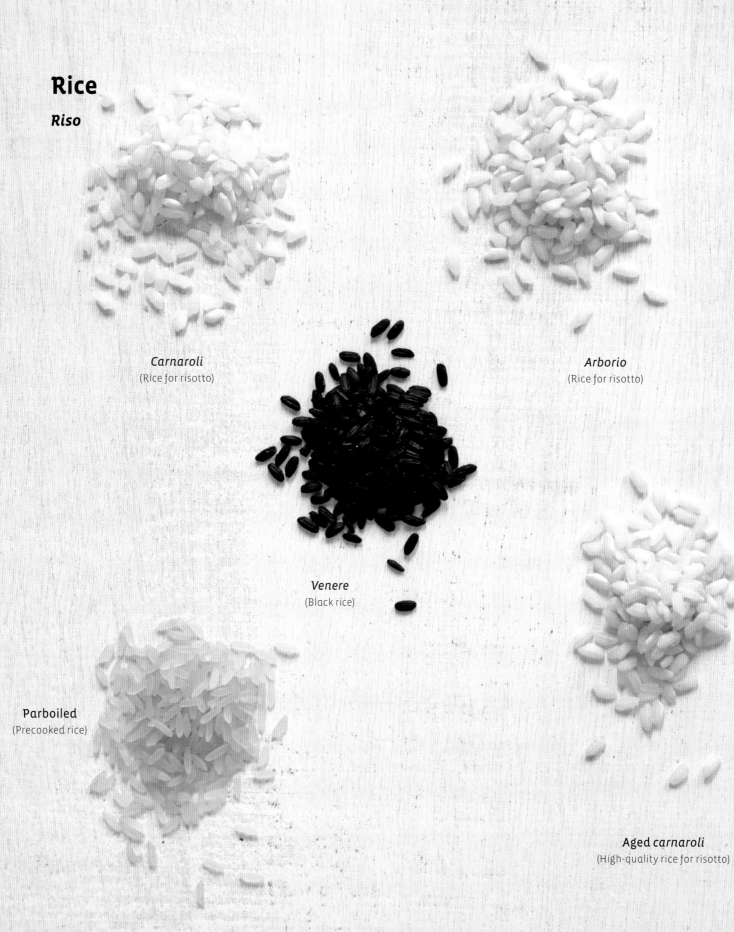

Carnaroli
(Rice for risotto)

Arborio
(Rice for risotto)

Venere
(Black rice)

Parboiled
(Precooked rice)

Aged *carnaroli*
(High-quality rice for risotto)

Olive oil

Olio d'oliva

Olive oil is the fat content of olives extracted in an oil mill.

There are several categories of olive oil but extra virgin olive oil is the most common commercially. It is extracted by mechanical process (not chemical) and from the first pressing of the olives. The best olive oils, those that retain most of their nutritional characteristics, are extracted by cold pressing. The temperature during the extraction stage does not exceed 80°F (27°C). On tasting, olive oils can have different flavors: fruity, flowery, pungent, bitter, green, ripe, full, sweet, astringent, and/or acid.

It is important to know how to read the label, especially concerning the product's origin.
The packaging is often misleading. Ensure that the place where the olives originated and even the variety is clearly marked. None of the other details, i.e. where they were bottled, distributed, the packaging (brand, photos, colors, designs), or the place of sale are proof of the real provenance of the olives.
Look for a reference to the product's country of origin and a possible protected designation (see p. 174) (*DOP* [PDO], *IGP* [PGI], SLOW FOOD). The absence of a reference indicates a blended oil of unspecified origin.

Guide to using olive oil in the kitchen:
Smoking point: 410°F (210°C) (the best frying oil)
4 cups (1 liter) of olive oil = 2 lb. (910 g)
Storage: Store the oil in a cool place, protected from light, in stainless steel or smoked glass containers. Consume within 12 to 18 months following production (see date on the packaging).

Designation of Italian olive oils

Name	Designation	Geographic Area
Alto Crotonese	PDO	Calabria
Aprutino Pescarese	PDO	Abruzzo
Brisighella	PDO	Emilia-Romagna
Bruzio	PDO	Calabria
Canino	PDO	Lazio
Cartoceto	PDO	Umbria
Chianti Classico	PDO	Tuscany
Cilento	PDO	Campania
Collina di Brindisi	PDO	Puglia
Colline di Romagna	PDO	Emilia-Romagna
Colline Pontine	PDO	Lazio
Colline Salernitane	PDO	Campania
Colline Teatine	PDO	Abruzzo
Dauno	PDO	Puglia
Garda	PDO	Lombardy Trentino-Veneto
Irpinia-Colline dell'Ufita	PDO	Campania
Laghi Lombardi	PDO	Lombardy
Lametia	PDO	Calabria
Lucca	PDO	Tuscany
Molise	PDO	Molise
Monte Etna	PDO	Sicily
Monte Iblei	PDO	Sicily
Penisola Sorrentina	PDO	Puglia
Pretuziano delle Colline	PDO	Abruzzo
Riviera Ligure	PDO	Liguria
Sardegna	PDO	Sardinia
Seggiano	PDO	Tuscany
Tergeste	PDO	Friuli-Venezia Giulia
Terra d'Otranto	PDO	Puglia
Terra di Bari	PDO	Puglia
Earth Aurunche	PDO	Campania
Terre Tarentine	PDO	Puglia
Toscano	PDO	Tuscany
Tuscia	PDO	Lazio
Umbria	PDO	Umbria
Val di Mazara	PDO	Sicily
Valdemone	PDO	Sicily
Valle del Belice	PDO	Sicily
Valli Trapanesi	PDO	Sicily
Veneto Valpolicella	PDO	Veneto
Vulture	PDO	Basilicata

Kitchen
equipment

Pasta "guitar"

Pasta machine

Double pasta cutter

Dough/pasta cutter

Serrated
cookie cutter

Gnocchi shaper

Rolling pin

Larding needle

Trussing needle

Meat tenderizer

Ice-cream scoop

Pasta tongs

Polenta board

Truffle mandolin

Parmesan knife

Cylindrical molds for Sicilian cannoli

Garlic press

Pandoro mold

Copper pan for risotto

Pizza shovel

Pasta skillet

Refractory stone

Map of Italian regions

Val d'Aosta

Trentino-Alto Adige

Friuli-Venezia Giulia

Lombardy

Veneto

Piedmont

Emilia-Romagna

Liguria

Tuscany

Marche

Umbria

Abruzzo

Lazio

Molise

Campania

Puglia

Basilicata

Sardinia

Calabria

Sicily

Structure of an Italian meal

A full Italian meal consists of eight courses: *aperitivo, antipasto, primo, secondo, contorno, dolce, frutta,* and *caffè.*

Aperitivo (aperitif)
This is the moment for a drink: a glass of wine, a spirit or cocktail, or a drink without alcohol (in Italy, there are several alcohol-free beverages, designed as aperitifs, which resemble cocktails based on vermouth and alcoholic bitters). Aperitifs are always accompanied by a few appetizers, all served in very small portions (savory petits fours, salted nuts, cheeses, charcuterie, vegetables, sauces, breads, pasta, etc.). The aperitif hour can turn into a veritable meal of appetizers. In local cafés it is a very convivial time of day.

Antipasto (appetizer)
This is the dish that introduces the meal. Served in smaller portions than the main dish, it can include charcuterie, vegetables, fish and meat, etc.

Primo (first course)
Pasta, risotto, soups, polenta are all first courses. This is the dish served before the main course. It can also be served in greater quantity as a main course if it is substantial and nutritious.

Secondo (second course)
The main dish (*piatto forte*), or highlight of the meal, as defined in Italian. It is prepared with meat or fish accompanied by a *contorno* (side dish).

Contorno (accompaniment)
This is the accompaniment to the *secondo*, prepared with vegetables, pulses, potatoes, or polenta. In Italy, traditionally pasta or rice are never served as *contorno*, though there is a single exception: osso buco is served with saffron risotto *alla Milanese*.

Dolce, frutta, and caffè (dessert, fruit, and coffee)
A traditional meal finishes with a dessert, followed by fresh fruit, and the not-to-be-missed *caffè ristretto*! Cheese at the end of a meal has become more or less obsolete in Italy.

Meals of this complexity are not prepared at home every day. They are reserved for formal celebrations. At such events, numerous hot and cold starters can follow the aperitif, then two *primi*, several *secondi* with their *contorni*, cheese, dessert, fruit, and coffee with a digestif (grappa, limoncello, sweet wine, *amaro*, etc.). Everyday meals usually consist of a *primo* followed by a *secondo* with *contorno* or, more often these days, just a single dish! Another special feature of the Italian meal that is quite widespread is the clear distinction between dishes "of the earth" and dishes "of the sea." Often meals both in the home and in restaurants are based on this distinction, by linking together either dishes based on meat, cheese, and vegetables, or fish, shellfish, and vegetables. Both may be offered at formal celebrations.

Italian regional specialties

Piedmont and Val d'Aosta
Amaretti cookies: small, round, slightly bitter cookies made of sweet and bitter almonds that can be crisp or soft.

Amaretto di Saronno: liqueur, 28% alcohol by volume, produced from almonds and herbs, originating in the town of Saronno, in northwest Italy.

Biova: bread rolls weighing 3 oz. to 1 lb. (100 to 500 g), with a very crisp crust and very little crumb that are the perfect accompaniment for Piedmontese dishes.

Chocolate gianduja: a chocolate mixture containing cocoa and hazelnuts. This is the basis for different Piedmontese products such as *gianduiotti* (small, trapezoid-shaped chocolates) or rum-flavored *cuneesi* (*gianduja* and rum chocolates).

Fassone: a breed of cattle native to Piedmont, characterized by a high meat yield when slaughtered, but also by the excellent quality of its milk, making it exceptionally productive. Protected geographic status (*IGP*/PGI) (see p. 174) is currently being sought for Fassone.

Grissini: long, thin, crisp breadsticks of different sizes that can be plain or flavored with olive oil, olives, rosemary, chili, etc.

Salsa rubra: a typical Piedmontese sauce derived from a traditional sauce called *bagnet rosso*, resembling American ketchup. It is mainly served with boiled and roasted meats.

Savoyard cookies: soft with an elongated shape, made from an egg-raised dough. An essential ingredient for the preparation of tiramisu and *zuppa inglese*.

Tajarin: very thin tagliatelle, approximately 1/8 in. (3 mm) wide, made of egg pasta with added Parmesan. They are mostly served with roasted meat juices (*al brucio*), with butter and sage, or in a more luxurious manner with white truffle.

White truffle of Alba: white truffle, *magnatum pico,* light ocher color, 4–8 in. (10–20 cm) in diameter. They can be picked during October and November.

Lombardy

Luganega: very long sausage prepared with both the fat and lean meat from shoulder of pork, fresh or cured, known mainly for accompanying polenta or risotto *alla luganega*.

Mostarda di Cremona: preserve made with whole or pieces of candied fruits (apple, pear, cherry, pumpkin, fig, and orange peel), macerated in a sugar- and mustard-based juice. It is mainly served with boiled and roasted meats.

Panettone and colomba: large brioche made with flour, eggs, butter, sugar, and yeast, to which pieces of candied fruit and raisins are added. Panettones are dome-shaped and prepared for Christmas, while *colombe* are dove-shaped and prepared for Easter. There are, however, several variations of the original recipe: chocolate, limoncello, sabayon, and others.

Rosetta o michetta: a small hollow roll in the shape of a flower, domed in the center. It is used to accompany meals, but more especially for making *panini*.

Veneto, Trentino-Alto Adige, and Friuli-Venezia Giulia

Baicoli: small, lightly sugared cookies that look more like thin slices of toasted bread for accompanying cream desserts and sweet wines at the end of a meal.

Pandoro: cake made of yeast-raised dough, typical of Verona, in the form of a dome with an eight-pointed star base. It is prepared especially at Christmas.

Pinza: sweet bread made with honey, prepared traditionally at Easter.

Liguria

Baci: small cakes made of ground almonds and hazelnuts shaped into two half-spheres sandwiched together with chocolate cream. *Baci* means "kisses" in Italian and the chocolates are presented wrapped in a "love note."

Biscotti del Lagaccio: rusks flavored with aniseed, typical of the Genoa region.

Gamberi rossi di Sanremo: medium-size shrimp of a bright red color when raw, whose flesh is very tasty and can be eaten uncooked. They are fished in both east and west Liguria.

Salsa di noci: sauce of walnuts, garlic, bread crumbs, and olive oil that accompanies borage ravioli, typical of the west coast of Liguria.

Taggiasche olives: small, very fragrant olives cultivated around Taggia. They form the basis of different recipes such as rabbit San Remo, or olive paste.

Emilia-Romagna and Marche
Traditional balsamic vinegar, a little-known treasure

Aceto balsamico tradizionale di Modena and **Aceto balsamico tradizionale di Reggio Emilia**: balsamic vinegar is traditionally prepared from unfermented white grape must that is cooked until it is reduced by 30 to 70 percent (depending on the year). The must is then filtered, cooled, and placed in barrels to age.

For a minimum of 12 years the must is transferred to increasingly smaller barrels of different wood (oak, chestnut, cherry, etc.) each time it is reduced. An extraordinary 220 lb. (100 kg) of grape must is needed to obtain a maximum of 2 quarts (2 liters) of vinegar. Twelve years is the minimum aging period for traditional aged balsamic vinegar and 25 years minimum for the *extravecchio* (extra mature) that is put into numbered bottles.

The bottles (designed by the automobile designer Giorgetto Giugiaro) are the same for all the vinegars, as established by the Consortium for Traditional Balsamic Vinegar (Consorzio dell'Aceto Balsamico Tradizionale). Each producer has his own label and a sticker, stating 12 or 25 years aging for the *Modena*, colored silver or gold for the *Reggio Emilia*.

There are different sorts of vinegars bearing the designation "balsamic" available commercially. In addition to the traditional, there is balsamic vinegar PGI: vinegar of quality but not aged, identifiable by a sticker. There are, above all, a multitude of other products that are just imitations.

How to recognize a traditional balsamic vinegar?

The bottle is numbered and bears the PDO sticker; the price is high (between €70 and €150 [$95–$200/£55–£120]); and the bottle is small and never contains more than 3 1/3 fl. oz. (100 ml).

All the houses producing traditional balsamic vinegar follow a centuries-old tradition, and not for anything in the world would they produce a vinegar of lesser quality than their competitors. That is why, at this level of excellence, they are worth their weight in gold! Keep this precious liquid at room temperature and away from products that might contaminate its aroma.

The simplest way to recognize the quality of balsamic vinegar from Modena PGI is to look on the label for the percentages of wine must and vinegar in the product: the more must it contains, the better the quality. For a manufactured product, the components are always given in descending order in the list of ingredients, according to the proportion present in the product.

Amarena Fabbri: this Italian specialty has created a world-famous brand name. Black cherries are candied in a fragrant syrup that gives the recipe its character and sold in white glass jars with a distinctive blue pattern. They are served with ice cream and desserts.

Coppia ferrarese: bread made from two pieces of twisted dough attached centrally, thus forming an "X." The weight of each loaf can vary from 3 to 9 oz. (80 to 250 g). A golden color with pale marbling, it has an intense, appetizing aroma.

Zampone and cotechino: prepared with the meat of boned-out pig's feet and other fat meat including the fat found under the skin. The meat and fat is seasoned with a mixture of spices, including cloves, cinnamon, pepper, nutmeg, thyme, and bay. For *zampone*, the boned-out pig's foot is filled with this mixture and cooked. For *cotechino*, natural casing is used.

Tuscany and Umbria

Bistecca alla fiorentina (Florentine rib of beef): usually a rib of Chianina beef (from the Chiana Valley), taken from a mature animal and aged for a minimum of 20 days. It is then cut as a "T" bone with the fillet on one side and the sirloin on the other. It is cooked upright in a wood-fired oven or over a wood fire for 15 minutes plus 5 minutes per side and served simply with salt, olive oil, and perhaps a little pepper.

Brigidini: crisp cookies flavored with aniseed.

Cinta Senese: typically Italian breed of pig, black with a "belt" (*cinta*) of white.

Copate: round cake, typical of Siena, made of honey and almonds sandwiched between two "communion" wafers.

Ricciarelli: diamond-shaped cookies, made of almond paste, candied fruit, and vanilla.

Sotto ranno olives: very mild in flavor, almost sweet; prepared in a solution of ashes and water.

Tartufo di Norcia/Tartufo di Spoleto: *Melanosporum vittadini*, a variety of black truffle of very high quality.

Lazio, Abruzzo, and Molise

Olive di Gaeta: large, pinkish olives prepared in brine or from which oil of the same name is extracted.

Porchetta: this method of preparing pork is found in several regions of Central Italy. Once the hams and shoulders have been removed for making charcuterie, the pork is cleaned out and stuffed with a large quantity of spices, fennel, and garlic as well as the chopped offal. It is then closed up and cooked slowly on a spit over a wood fire. It is usually served sliced, in sandwiches sold on the streets by the local *porchettari*.

Zafferano dell'Aquila: a well-known saffron from Abruzzo that carries PDO status.

Campania

Colatura di Cetara: amber, liquid sauce obtained by maturing anchovies in oak casks with sea salt. This condiment is used for seasoning both pasta and vegetables.

Limoncello: alcohol made from lemons (traditionally those of the Amalfi coast and Sorrento), usually served chilled at the end of meals.

Sfogliatelle: shell-shaped cakes of puff pastry stuffed with ricotta cheese and flavored with citrus and vanilla.

Puglia and Basilicata

Castagnedde: cakes shaped as chestnuts, made of almond paste flavored with vanilla and lemon, and covered with chocolate.

Lampascioni: small, wild hyacinth bulbs that resemble little onions and have a slightly bitter taste. They are often preserved in oil with aromatic herbs.

Miele di fichi: honey obtained from cooking very ripe figs and used to sweeten the local desserts.

Peperone di Senise: sweet red peppers dried in the sun and threaded on strings. They are then fried or used for flavoring different dishes and preserves. They are called *cruschi* (crunchy) locally.

Calabria

Bergamotto: citrus fruit widely found in this region used in cake making and perfumery.

Nduja: soft sausage paste made of pork meat and chilies.

Sicily

Bottarga di tonno: preserve made with dried tuna roe.

Capperi di Pantelleria: capers of high quality, like those from the Aeolian islands. Capers are classified as very small (*puntine*), normal, and large. The latter are the fruit of the caper plant that can be preserved in vinegar (*cucunci*).

Cioccolato di Modica: chocolate made from cocoa and unrefined sugar.

Cubbaita: soft nougat covered with sesame seeds.

Frutta di Martorana: small cakes in the shape of fruit, made of almond paste.

Ossa di Cristo morto: small cakes flavored with cloves.

Pistacchi di Bronte: this pistachio nut from the Catania region is the most famous in the world. It is used for making Sicilian pistachio pesto, pistachio ice cream, and other delicacies.

Zibibbo: grapes with a very high sugar content from which *passito* wine and raisins are produced.

___

Sardinia

Fregola: small pasta balls made from durum wheat flour that are baked in the oven after shaping. They are traditionally accompanied by a sauce of littleneck clams (*arselle*).

Mirto: myrtle is a very perfumed plant that produces almost black berries. It is used in Sardinia for flavoring different recipes and for making an alcohol of the same name.

Pane carasau or carta musica: sheets of bread made of durum wheat flour, without yeast. Traditionally cooked in a bread oven, it is served as bread or seasoned with olive oil (*pane guttiau*), or prepared as a kind of lasagna (*pane frattau*). It was the bread traditionally taken to the fields by shepherds because it kept well.

Porcheddu: suckling pig seasoned with herbs (mint, rosemary, myrtle, bay, sage, etc.) and traditionally cooked over a wood fire in a hole dug in the earth (*carraxiu*).

Presidio Slow Food products

The Slow Food movement (Presidio Slow Food) is an international association created in Bra (Piedmont) in 1986. Founded by Carlo Petrini, it is designed as a response to the exponential spread of fast food, and to the frenetic pace of life that erodes the quality of food culture everywhere. Slow Food wants to restore the value of mealtimes and wine and food traditions around the world. The association is involved in defending biodiversity and people's rights to food sovereignty by fighting against the globalization of taste, mass agriculture, and genetic manipulation.

Slow Food has introduced two additional designations independent of community laws: the Presidio (195 products) and the Arca del Gusto (412 products). Their vocation is to retrieve and save small productions threatened by large-scale industrialization, globalization, and ecological degradation.

Protected product designations

PDO (*DOP*): 154 products of Protected Designation of Origin (*Denominazione d'Origine Protetta*). Their characteristics are strictly linked to their area of production for its geographical factors and local knowledge.

PGI (*IGP*): 95 products of Protected Geographical Indication (*Indicazione Geografica Protetta*). Their characteristics relate directly to a specific geographical area of production.

TSG (*STG*): 2 Italian products are Traditional Specialty Guaranteed (*Specialità Tradizionale Garantita*). Their characteristics relate specifically to traditional methods of production.

Products with protected designation of origin

AGRICULTURAL PRODUCTS

Name	Description	Geographic Area	Designation
Aglio Bianco Polesano	Polesano white garlic	Veneto	PDO
Amarene Brusche di Modena	Amarena cherries from Modena	Emilia-Romagna	PGI
L'Arancia Rossa di Sicilia	Blood oranges from Sicily	Sicily	PGI
Asparago Bianco di Bassano	White asparagus from Bassano	Veneto	PDO
Basilico Genovese	Basil from Genoa	Liguria	PDO
Bergamotto di Reggio Calabria	Bergamot from Calabria	Calabria	PDO
Cappero di Pantelleria	Capers from Pantelleria	Sicily	PGI
Carciofo Romanesco del Lazio	Romanesco artichokes from Lazio	Lazio	PGI
Carciofo Spinoso di Sardegna	Spiky artichokes from Sardinia	Sardinia	PDO
Castagna Cuneo	Chestnuts from Cuneo	Piedmont	PGI
Castagna del Monte Amiata	Chestnuts from Monte Amiata	Tuscany	PGI
Cipolla Rossa di Tropea	Red onions from Tropea	Calabria	PGI
Fagiolo di Lamon della Vallata Bellunese	Marbled red Lamon bean from Vallata Bellunese	Veneto	PGI
Fagiolo di Sorana	Beans from Sorana	Tuscany	PGI
Farro della Garfagnana	Farro wheat from Garfagnana	Tuscany	PGI
Fico Bianco del Cilento	White figs from Cilento	Campania	PDO
Fungo di Borgotaro	Porcini from Borgotaro	Emilia-Romagna	PGI
Lenticchia di Castelluccio di Norcia	Lentils from Castelluccio	Umbria	PGI
Limone Costa d'Amalfi	Lemons from Costa Almalfi	Campania	PGI
Limone di Sorrento	Lemons from Sorrento	Campania	PGI
Liquirizia di Calabria	Licorice from Calabria	Calabria	PDO
Marrone del Mugello	Chestnuts from Mugello	Tuscany	PGI
Mela Alto Adige	Apples from Alto Adige	Trentino-Alto Adige	PGI
Mela di Valtellina	Apples from Valtellina	Lombardy	PGI
Melannurca Campana	Annurca apples from Campania	Campania	PGI
Mela Val di Non	Apples from the Val di Non	Trentino	PDO
Nocciola del Piemonte	Hazelnuts from Piedmont	Piedmont	PGI
Oliva Ascolana del Piceno	Olives from Ascoli Piceno	Marche	PDO
Peperone di Senise	Peppers from Senise	Basilicata	PGI
Pistacchio Verde di Bronte	Green pistachios from Bronte	Sicily	PDO
Pomodorino del Piennolo del Vesuvio	Vine tomato clusters from Vesuvius	Campania	PDO
Pomodoro di Pachino	Tomatoes from Pachino	Sicily	PGI
Pomodoro San Marzano dell'Agro Sarnese-Nocerino	San Marzano tomatoes from Agro Sarnese-Nocerino	Campania	PDO
Radicchio di Chioggia	Radicchio from Chioggia	Veneto	PGI
Radicchio Rosso di Treviso	Red chicory from Treviso	Veneto	PGI
Radicchio Variegato di Castelfranco	Variegated chicory from Castelfranco	Veneto	PGI
Riso del Delta del Po	Rice from the Po delta	Veneto, Emilia-Romagna	PGI
Riso di Baraggia Biellese e Vercellese	Rice from Barraggia in the Biella and Vercelli provinces	Piedmont	PDO
Riso Nano Vialone Veronese	Nano Vialone rice from Verona	Veneto	PGI
Zafferano dell'Aquila	Saffron from Aquila	Abruzzo	PDO
Zafferano di San Gimignano	Saffron from San Gimignano	Tuscany	PDO
Zafferano di Sardegna	Saffron from Sardinia	Sardinia	PDO

CHEESE AND DAIRY PRODUCTS

Name	Description	Geographic Area	Designation
Asiago	Medium-hard cow milk cheese aged 6 months to 2 years	Veneto-Trentino	PDO
Caciocavallo Silano	Spun paste and medium-hard cow milk cheese aged 2 months to 2 years	Puglia	PDO
Canestrato	Mixed milk hard cheese (cow, goat, sheep) pressed fresh, or aged	Puglia, Basilicata	PDO
Castelmagno	Uncooked blue veined cow milk cheese aged 2 to 5 months	Piedmont	PDO
Fiore Sardo	Hard, uncooked sheep milk cheese aged minimum 2 months	Sardinia	PDO
Fontina	Half-cooked cow milk cheese aged 3 to 5 months	Val d'Aosta	PDO
Formaggio di Fossa	Uncooked sheep milk cheese aged 3 months in natural caves	Emilia-Romagna, Marche	PDO
Gorgonzola	Creamy blue-veined cow milk cheese	Lombardy, Piedmont	PDO
Grana Padano	Hard, cooked cow milk cheese aged minimum 10 months	Lombardy, Piedmont, Emilia-Romagna, Veneto, Trentino	PDO
Montasio	Hard, cooked cow milk cheese semi-aged 3 to 18 months	Friuli-Venezia Giulia, Veneto	PDO
Mozzarella	Fresh spun paste cow milk cheese	National production	TSG
Mozzarella di Bufala Campana	Fresh spun paste buffalo milk cheese	Campania, Lazio, Puglia, Molise	PDO
Parmigiano Reggiano	Hard, cooked cow milk cheese aged 12 to 36 months	Emilia-Romagna, Lombardy	PDO
Pecorino Romano	Hard, cooked ewe milk cheese aged 5 to 8 months	Lazio, Tuscany, Sardinia	PDO
Pecorino Sardo	Hard, semi-cooked ewe milk cheese aged minimum 20 months	Sardinia	PDO
Pecorino Toscano	Soft or medium-hard sheep milk cheese with different aging times	Tuscany, Umbria, Lazio	PDO
Provolone Valpadana	Spun paste cow milk cheese aged minimum 3 months	Emilia-Romagna, Lombardy, Veneto, Trentino	PDO
Ricotta di Bufala Campana	Dairy product obtained by cooking the whey of buffalo milk	Campania, Lazio, Puglia, Molise	PDO
Ricotta Romana	Dairy product obtained by cooking the whey of cow milk	Lazio	PDO
Robiola di Roccaverano	Fresh, uncooked cow milk cheese	Piedmont	PDO
Squacquerone di Romagna	Fresh, soft cow milk cheese	Emilia-Romagna	PDO
Taleggio	Soft, semi-mature cow milk cheese aged 40 days	Lombardy, Piedmont, Veneto	PDO
Toma Piemontese	Cow milk cheese aged 15 to 60 days	Piedmont	PDO
Valtellina Casera	Cooked cow milk cheese aged 70 days	Lombardy	PDO

MEAT PRODUCTS AND CHARCUTERIE

Name	Description	Geographic Area	Designation
Abbacchio Romano	Roman lamb	Lazio	PGI
Agnello di Sardegna	Lamb from Sardinia	Sardinia	PGI
Bresaola della Valtellina	Air-dried salted beef, aged for 2–3 months	Lombardy	PGI
Capocollo di Calabria	Capocollo from Calabria	Calabria	PDO
Cinta Senese	Cinta Senese breed of pig	Tuscany	PDO
Coppa di Parma	Coppa from Parma	Emilia-Romagna, Lombardy	PGI
Cotechino Modena	Cotechino from Modena	Emilia-Romagna, Lombardy, Veneto	PGI
Culatello di Zibello	Aged, cured pork	Emilia-Romagna	PDO
Lardo di Colonnata	Lard from Colonnata	Tuscany	PGI
Mortadella Bologna	Lightly smoked sausage	Emilia-Romagna, Lombardy, Veneto, Trentino, Piedmont, Marche, Lazio, Tuscany	PGI
Pancetta Piacentina	Pancetta from Piacenza	Emilia-Romagna	PDO
Porchetta di Ariccia	Roast sucking pig from Ariccia	Lazio	PGI
Prosciutto di Modena	Ham from Modena	Emilia-Romagna	PDO
Prosciutto di Norcia	Ham from Norcia	Umbria	PGI
Prosciutto di Parma	Parma ham	Emilia-Romagna	PDO
Prosciutto di San Daniele	Ham from San Daniele	Friuli-Venezia Giulia	PDO
Prosciutto Toscano	Tuscan ham	Tuscany	PDO
Prosciutto Veneto Berico-Euganeo	Ham from the Veneto	Veneto	PDO
Salame Cremona	Salami from Cremona	Emilia-Romagna, Lombardy, Veneto, Piedmont	PGI
Salame Felino	Felino salami	National production	PGI
Salame d'Oca di Mortara	Goose salami from Mortara	Lombardy	PGI
Salamini Italiani alla Cacciatora	Italian hunter's sausage	National production	PDO
Soppressata di Calabria	Pressed sausage from Calabria	Calabria	PDO
Soprèssa Vicentina	Sausage from Vicenza	Veneto	PDO
Speck dell'Alto Adige	Smoked ham from Alto Adige	Trentino-Alto Adige	PGI
Val d'Aosta Jambon de Bosses	Bosses ham from the Val d'Aosta	Val d'Aosta	PDO
Val d'Aosta Lardo d'Arnad	Arnad lard from the Val d'Aosta	Val d'Aosta	PDO
Vitellone Bianco dell'Appenino Centrale	White veal from the Central Apennines	Emilia-Romagna, Marche, Tuscany, Abruzzo, Molise, Campania, Lazio, Umbria	PGI
Zampone Modena	Boned and stuffed pig's trotter	Emilia-Romagna, Lombardy, Veneto	PGI

FISH

Name	Description	Geographic Area	Designation
Acciughe sotto Sale del Mar Ligure	Anchovies in salt from the Ligurian Sea	Liguria	PGI
Tinca Gobba Dorata del Pianalto di Poirino	Golden hump tench from Pianalto di Poirino	Piedmont	PDO
Trote del Trentino	Trout from Trentino	Trentino-Alto Adige	PGI

BAKED PRODUCTS AND PASTRIES

Name	Description	Geographic Area	Designation
Coppia Ferrarese	Coppia bread from Ferrara	Emilia-Romagna	PGI
Focaccia di Recco con Formaggio	Cheese focaccia from Recco	Liguria	PDO
Pane di Altamura	Bread from Altamura	Puglia	PDO
Pane di Matera	Bread from Matera	Basilicata	PGI
Pizza Napoletana	Neapolitan pizza	National production	TSG
Ricciarelli di Siena	Almond cookies from Siena	Tuscany	PGI

OTHER PRODUCTS

Name	Description	Geographic Area	Designation
Aceto Balsamico di Modena	Balsamic vinegar from Modena	Emilia-Romagna	PGI
Aceto Balsamico Tradizionale di Modena	Traditional balsamic vinegar from Modena	Emilia-Romagna	PDO
Aceto Balsamico Tradizionale di Reggio Emilia	Balsamic vinegar from Reggio Emilia	Emilia-Romagna	PDO
Pasta di Gragnano	Pasta from Gragnano	Campania	PDO
Sale Marino di Trapani	Sea salt from Trapani	Sicily	PDO

Dandelion
Catalogna

Spinach
Spinaci

Green beans
Fagiolini

Wild asparagus
Asparagi selvatici

Beans
Fave

Trumpet zucchini
Zucchine trombette

Romanesco cabbage
Cavolo "mappa" romano

Celery
Sedano

Arugula
Rucola

Mild dwarf peppers
Friggitelli

Vegetables

San Marzano tomato
Pomodoro San Marzano

Radicchio (red chicory) from Treviso
Radicchio Trevisano

Yellow onion
Cipolla gialla

Chili
Peperoncini

Beef tomato
Pomodoro cuore di bue

Artichoke
Carciofo

Red onion from Tropea
Cipolla di Tropea

Vegetables

Olives and capers

Black olives from Gaeta
Oliva nera di Gaeta

**Mild green olives
cured in lime**
*Oliva verde dolce
alla calce*

Soft Ascolana olives
Oliva Ascolana tenera

Capers in vinegar
Capperi sott'aceto

Capers in salt from Pantelleria
Capperi sotto sale di Pantelleria

Green olives from Cerignola
Olive verdi di Cerignola

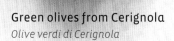

Caper berries
Frutti del cappero "cucunci"

Taggiasche olives
Olive taggiasche

Herbs

Thyme
Timo

Mint
Menta

Rosemary
Rosmarino

Bay
Alloro

Oregano
Origano

Marjoram
Maggiorana

Flat-leaf parsley
Prezzemolo

Sage
Salvia

Basil
Basilico

Spices

Dried Thai/bird (bird's eye) chilies
Peperoncini secchi

Wild fennel
Finocchietto

Cumin
Coumino

Aniseed
Anice

Cinnamon
Cannella

Nutmeg
Noce moscata

Mace
Macis

Juniper
Bacche di ginepro

Saffron
Zafferano

Vanilla
Vaniglia

Cloves
Chiodi di garofano

Black pepper
Pepe nero

Recipes

Piedmont
Val d'Aosta

Enrico Crippa

For me, Piedmont is a land blessed by the gods, a region abounding in produce of the finest quality. First of all, there is the white truffle of Alba, the town where my restaurant–Piazza Duomo–is located. Then there is the Fassone breed of cattle that is native to Piedmont, Sambucana lamb, and round Gentile hazelnuts, not to mention the excellent wines and cheeses: a veritable godsend for those in the same profession as me.

Gastronomy is an integral part of discovering the Piedmontese region. Wine and food tourism is a growing phenomenon, and through our cuisine we offer an additional way of accessing the beauty of our region.

However, though it is connected to the local area, my cuisine is contemporary, light, and very personal in style. I favor a balance between modernity and tradition. A chef must not limit himself to cooking alone, but must be sensitive to the art in all its aspects, paying special attention to shapes and colors. This is the principal lesson I learned from my master, the great chef Gualtiero Marchesi.

Roast Sambucana Lamb
with Goat Cheese, Chamomile,
and Pomegranate

Cook the lamb.
Cook the lamb rare in a saucepan with the butter, fennel, and the chamomile flowers. It should remain very pink. Keep warm.

Prepare the goat-cheese cream.
Bring the goat milk to a boil with the agar, remove from the heat, and leave to cool. Add the cheese and blend to obtain a cream.

Prepare the chamomile tea.
Heat the water to 195°F (90°C) in a saucepan, then remove from the heat. Add the chamomile and let infuse for 4 minutes. Strain and cool the tea.

Prepare the chamomile tea reduction.
Stir the tapioca flour into the cold chamomile tea and reduce to a smooth, honey-like consistency. Chill.

Prepare the pomegranate reduction.
Stir the tapioca flour into the pomegranate juice and reduce to a smooth, honey-like consistency. Chill.

Assemble the dish.
Slice the cleaned and trimmed artichokes very thinly and plunge them in a bowl of water with a little lemon juice. Drain them well, then season with a drizzle of olive oil and a little Maldon salt.
On four individual plates, gently place a spoonful of the goat-cheese cream and cover with the chamomile pollen. To the right of the cheese cream, sprinkle a few droplets of the chamomile and pomegranate reductions.
Lay the rack of lamb on the goat-cheese cream. Lay the artichoke slices on the lamb. Finish with the blanched hop or chrysanthemum shoots and a spoonful of the lamb juices.

Serves 4
Preparation time: 1 hour
Cooking time: 30 minutes

Ingredients
4 best ends of Sambucana lamb
2/3 tablespoon (10 g) butter
1 small branch dry, wild fennel
6 dried chamomile flowers
Salt, pepper

Goat-cheese cream
Scant ½ cup (100 ml) goat milk
1 pinch (1 g) of agar
3 ½ tablespoons (2 oz./50 g) fresh goat cheese

Chamomile tea
2 ⅓ cups (550 ml) water
2 tablespoons (10 g) chamomile (or other gently flavored herbal tea)

Chamomile tea reduction
4 tablespoons (1 ½ oz./40 g) tapioca flour

Pomegranate reduction
2 tablespoons (20 g) tapioca flour
6 pomegranates, blended to give 1 cup (250 ml) strained juice

Garnish
4 Ligurian artichokes, cleaned and trimmed
A little olive oil
Maldon salt
4 teaspoons chamomile pollen
½ cup (1 ½ oz./40 g) hop or chrysanthemum shoots

Ingredients

Sauce
4 cloves garlic
Milk for soaking
²/₃ cup (5 ½ oz./150 g) salted anchovies
¾ stick (3 oz./80 g) butter
1 cup (250 ml) olive oil

Accompaniment
Vegetables to cook: red beet, cardoon, potato, turnip, onion, Jerusalem artichokes, cabbage, pumpkin
Selection of raw vegetables: bell pepper, radishes, endive, fennel, celery, Treviso radicchio, leek, white onion, baby artichoke, cabbage, carrot, apple
Lemon juice

Optional
Polenta (see pp. 100-107)

Equipment
1 large terra-cotta casserole with a heat diffuser set over a flame
Traditional *fojots* or a tabletop hotplate

Techniques
Anchovies in Salt >> p. 26
Crudités >> p. 15
Polenta >> pp. 100–107

Anchovy Fondue ★★

Bagna cauda

This fondue is traditionally served in *fojots*: individual terra-cotta pots set over heat diffusers heated by candles.
Pieces of raw and cooked vegetables are dipped into the fondue. This is a very convivial winter dish for sharing, also served at wine harvest feasts.

Serves 4
Sauce preparation time: 30 minutes
Garlic soaking time: 1 hour
Vegetable preparation time: 20-30 minutes

Peel the garlic cloves. Soak 1 hour in milk so they become more digestible. Slice them finely then crush them.
Rinse the anchovies and remove their backbones.
Peel and cut the vegetables to be steamed into quarters or chunks. Steam them.
Peel and cut up the raw vegetables. Immerse those that tend to discolor (fennel, artichoke, cardoon, etc.) for a few minutes in water acidified with lemon juice, then dry them.
Display the assortment of vegetables on a platter.
Heat the butter and the olive oil in a terra-cotta casserole over low heat (so they do not burn) and very slowly soften the garlic for 15 minutes. When it becomes creamy, add the anchovies and stir with a spatula until they melt (5 minutes).
Serve this sauce in a fondue pot, either in individual *fojots* over candles, or in the casserole on a tabletop hotplate; then dip the vegetables into the hot sauce.

● Suggested food/wine match
Barbera, red wine from Alba or Asti DOC

● Chef's notes
If you are not partial to garlic, you can reduce its quantity or use whole cloves just to flavor the sauce, removing them before serving. You can also include white truffle to flavor this lighter version of the sauce: brush the truffle clean, wipe with a damp cloth, then cut into strips before adding. The current trend is to add a few tablespoons of whipping cream as well.
You can complement the vegetables with pieces of polenta (see pp. 100–107).

Veal *Tartare* with White Truffle ★

Carne all'albese

All'albese means typical of Alba, a town in Piedmont.
This is a recipe that shows off the famous white truffle to great advantage.
Veal is the ideal meat for this dish.

Serves 4
Preparation time: 20 minutes
Marinating time: 1 hour

Peel the garlic and chop. Squeeze the lemon juice.
Clean the truffle with a dry brush to remove the soil, using the tip of a knife to help if necessary. Wipe it with a damp cloth and pat it dry.
You can ask your butcher to chop the veal for the *tartare* by hand. Otherwise cut it up yourself into small pieces, then, with a very sharp large-bladed knife, chop it more and more finely.
Prepare a sauce with the garlic, olive oil, salt, and pepper. Mix well with the meat to season it. Marinate for about 1 hour. Only add the lemon juice just before serving, to prevent it from "cooking" the meat, which should remain pink.
Divide the *tartare* between the plates. Sprinkle with petals of white truffle finely shaved with a truffle mandolin.

● **Suggested food/wine match**
Barbaresco, DOCG red

● **Chef's notes**
In an ancient recipe, an anchovy, salted or in oil, is boned, crushed, and mixed into the sauce.
If you do not like garlic, simply spear a peeled clove on a fork and use it to mix the meat when you season it; it will enhance the flavor of the white truffle.
White truffles lose their aroma with time; they should be consumed within 5 days maximum. Wrap them in paper towel and place in a sealed glass jar in the vegetable compartment of the refrigerator.
White truffles cannot be cooked; they are too fragile.

Ingredients
12 oz. (350 g) loin of veal
2 cloves garlic
1 lemon
1 white truffle, preferably from Alba
2 tablespoons olive oil
Salt and freshly ground pepper

Equipment
1 truffle mandolin

Ingredients

1 lb. 5 oz. (600 g) veal roast (loin, rump, round)
1 carrot
1 stick celery
1 onion
¼ lemon
3 cloves
2 bay leaves
5 peppercorns
1 cup (250 ml) white wine
1 cup (7 oz./200 g) canned tuna in oil
4 anchovy fillets in oil
2 tablespoons capers
Salt

Mayonnaise
2 egg yolks
1 teaspoon mustard
1-1 ½ cups (250-350 ml) olive oil
2 tablespoons white wine
Salt

Veal with Tuna Sauce ★

Vitello tonnato (vitel tonné)

Serves 4
Preparation time: 20 minutes
Cooking time: 1 hour 30 minutes approximately

Peel and wash the vegetables. Cut the lemon in half. Place the carrot, celery, onion, lemon, cloves, bay leaves, peppercorns, and wine in 4 cups (1 liter) of salt water and bring to a boil.
Add the veal and cook for 1 hour 30 minutes approximately, then let cool down in its own stock.

Prepare the mayonnaise.
Beat the egg yolks in a bowl with a pinch of salt and the mustard.
Incorporate the olive oil gradually in a thin stream, whisking continuously until you have a thick consistency.
Thin the mixture with the white wine.

Flake the tuna. Chop the anchovy fillets and 1 tablespoon of the capers.
Gently mix with the mayonnaise.
Cut the veal into very thin slices, spread on a dish, then coat with the sauce and the rest of the capers. Cover with plastic wrap and place in the refrigerator until time to serve.

● Suggested food/wine match

Langhe, white DOCG

● Chef's notes

In the original recipe dating from the seventeenth century, the sauce is prepared with reduced veal stock mixed with hard-boiled egg yolk, capers, anchovies, and tuna passed through a chinois (fine mesh sieve).
You can serve this dish as an antipasto or as a main dish.

Piedmontese Ravioli with a Veal Stuffing ★ ★ ★

Agnolotti del Plin

Serves 4
Preparation time: 1 hour 30 minutes
Cooking time: 2 hours 10 minutes

A day ahead.
Prepare the vegetable stock (see p. 94).

Make 1 quantity of pasta dough using the recipe on p. 69, adding a tablespoon of olive oil. Leave to rest.

Prepare the ravioli stuffing.
Peel the garlic and crush the clove. Peel, wash, and dice the carrot, celery, and onion. Peel and wash the endives. Grate the Parmesan and nutmeg. Brown all the meat with 1 ¹/₃ tablespoons (20 g) butter and the oil in a pan, then add the vegetables and rosemary and cook for 5 minutes before adding the garlic. Season with salt and deglaze with the wine. Let it evaporate, then moisten with some of the vegetable stock. Cover and leave to simmer for 2 hours approximately, adding more stock if the meat looks at all dry.
Cook the endives in water, drain thoroughly (or dry them in a salad spinner). Sauté in the remaining butter, then chop them.
Once the meat is cooked, strain the juices and reserve for flavoring the *agnolotti*. Put the meat through the mincer at low speed to control the consistency of the stuffing. Add the endives, garlic, eggs, Parmesan, and nutmeg. Check the seasoning.

Assemble the ravioli.
Roll the pasta out into a single, thin sheet. Cut into strips, 2 ½ in. (5 cm) wide. Place little mounds of stuffing along the center of each strip at 1 in. (2 cm) intervals, then fold one side over the stuffing. Press well around each little mound to eliminate any air bubbles, then fold over the other side. Carefully pinch the dough between the mounds of stuffing so the ravioli are well sealed without trapping any air bubbles.
Once all the ingredients are used up, separate the ravioli by cutting along the sealed edges with a pasta cutter. You should have ravioli of approximately 1 ½ × ¾ in. (3 × 1.5 cm). Arrange them on a tray covered with a dry cloth, or on a drying rack.

Prepare the sauce.
Add the butter to the strained cooking juices and, if necessary, moisten with a little stock.

Cook the *agnolotti* in boiling water for 4 minutes. Remove them with a slotted spoon.
Pour over the sauce and serve with the Parmesan.

Ingredients

Pasta dough
1 quantity pasta dough (see p. 69)
1 tablespoon olive oil

Stuffing
10 oz. (300 g) loin or round of veal
7 oz. (200 g) boned rib or shoulder of pork
7 oz. (200 g) boned rabbit
1 clove garlic
1 carrot
1 stick celery
1 onion
10 oz. (300 g) endives
1 ¾ oz. (50 g) Parmesan
1 nutmeg
4 tablespoons (2 oz./50 g) butter
1 tablespoon olive oil
1 sprig of rosemary
½ cup (125 ml) red wine
4 cups (1 liter) vegetable stock (see p. 94)
2 eggs
Salt, pepper

Sauce
Cooking juices from the stuffing
2 tablespoons butter
Grated Parmesan to taste

● **Suggested food/wine match**
Dolcetto d' Alba, red DOC

● **Chef's notes**
In some restaurants these ravioli are served simply wrapped in a hot napkin after being cooked in boiling water so that the stuffing can be fully appreciated. The endives can be replaced by spinach or cabbage.

● **Did you know?**
Plin is the pinch between forefinger and thumb used to seal this shape of ravioli.

Ingredients

4 cups (1 liter) beef stock (or veal or poultry stock, but not using a stock cube; see p. 93)
1 white truffle, preferably from Alba
1 yellow onion
1 stick (4 oz./100 g) butter
2 cups (14 oz./400 g) risotto rice (*carnaroli, arborio, vialone nano*, etc.)
⅓ cup (80 ml) white wine
1 ½ oz. (40 g) Parmesan
Salt

Equipment

1 truffle mandolin

Technique

Risotto with Sparkling Wine >> p. 93

Risotto with White Truffles from Alba ★ ★

Risotto al tartufo

Serves 4
Preparation time: 20 minutes
Cooking time: 20 minutes

Prepare the beef stock (see p. 93).

Clean the truffle with a dry brush to remove the soil, using the tip of a knife to help if necessary. Wipe it with a damp cloth and pat it dry. Grate a quarter of the truffle and reserve the rest until the last minute. Grate the Parmesan. Peel and chop the onion.
Melt the butter in a heavy-bottom pan and soften the onion without coloring.
When translucent, add the rice. "Toast" the grains by rolling them vigorously around the base of the pan. Deglaze with the white wine. When the alcohol has evaporated, add the hot meat stock, ladle by ladle, without ever completely covering the rice, mixing well with each addition to distribute it evenly through the contents. Cook for 16 to 18 minutes. Taste and add salt if necessary.
Remove from the heat; add the Parmesan and the grated truffle. Mix well. Serve sprinkled with the remaining truffle, preferably shaved with a truffle mandolin in front of the diners.

● Suggested food/wine match
Langhe, white DOC

● Chef's note
You can replace the white truffle with black truffle.

Beef Braised in Barolo ★★

Brasato al barolo

Beef is part of the Piedmontese culinary tradition.
In the local dialect, *brasato* signifies that this dish was cooked in a pot on the
embers of the fire.

Serves 6
Preparation time: 1 hour
Marinating time: 6-24 hours
Cooking time: 3 hours

Peel the garlic and chop the cloves with the sage and rosemary. Wash
and peel the vegetables and cut into chunks.
Lard the meat with the bacon (insert the strips of bacon into the meat
using a larding needle), shape it, and tie it up with string. Marinate
for 6 to 24 hours in the wine with the vegetables, bay, nutmeg, and
cinnamon.
Remove the meat from the marinade, drain it, then roll it in the flour.
Brown the meat in a skillet with the butter and the olive oil. Add the
vegetables and let them color.
Moisten with the marinade; season with salt and pepper. Cover and cook
for 3 hours over very low heat.
At the end of the cooking process, when the sauce is well reduced,
remove the meat and cut into slices. Strain the sauce and pour it over the
meat.

● **Suggested food/wine match**
Barolo, red wine similar to Burgundy, DOCG

● **Chef's notes**
As an accompaniment, choose polenta (see pp. 100–107) or mashed potato.
Use the leftover cooking juices from the brasato *for flavoring fresh egg pasta
(tagliatelle, tagliolini, etc.).*
You can also cook the brasato *in the oven for 3 hours at 260°F (130°C), and
replace the Barolo with a wine of the same grape variety, Niebbolo.*

Ingredients
2 lb. (1 kg) rump or round of beef
2 cloves garlic
A few sprigs of sage
A few sprigs of rosemary
2 onions
1 carrot
1 stick celery
3 oz. (80 g) bacon, thinly sliced
3 cups (750 ml) Barolo wine
2 bay leaves
A pinch of nutmeg
1 cinnamon stick
2 tablespoons flour
1/3 stick (1 1/2 oz./40 g) butter
1 tablespoon olive oil

Marinated Eels ★★

Carpione d'anguille

This is an ancient marinade recipe that originated in the rice fields.
Its Italian name comes from a lake fish from the salmon family (*carpione*)
that was preserved in this way, allowing it to be eaten over several days.

Serves 4
Preparation time: 1 hour
Cooking time: 20 minutes
Marinating time: 1-2 days

Peel the garlic and chop the cloves. Peel the onions and cut into rounds.
Clean the eels and remove their skin if the fishmonger did not skin them.
Rinse well, cut into sections 3 to 5 in. (6 to 10 cm) long. Coat with the flour
and fry in cooking oil. Drain on a paper towel and sprinkle with salt.
Brown the sliced onion and chopped garlic in the olive oil in a skillet with
the bay leaves, sage, and peppercorns.
When the onions are cooked, add the vinegar and cook 10 minutes over
medium heat. Set aside. While the onions cool, arrange the pieces of fried
eel in a shallow dish. Spread the onions evenly over them and sprinkle
with oregano. Cover and leave to marinate for 1 to 2 days before serving
cold.

● Suggested food/wine match
Grignolino, red DOC

● Chef's notes
*Adapt this recipe to make marinated zucchini, veal escalopes, or lake or river
fish (carp, tench, trout, etc.).*
*This dish can be kept for several days in the refrigerator. It can be used in anti-
pasto or as a main course and would be a suitable choice for a picnic.*

Ingredients
1 lb. 12 oz. (800 g) eel (without skin)
2 cloves garlic
4 onions
1 ½ cups (5 ¼ oz./150 g) flour
Frying oil
2 tablespoons olive oil
2 bay leaves
2 sage leaves
10 peppercorns
2 cups (500 ml) good-quality red wine vinegar
1 tablespoon oregano
Salt

Ingredients

1 ⅓ lb. (600 g) fontina cheese (if unavailable,
   substitute Emmental, Gruyère, or Provalone)
1 ½ cups (350 ml) milk
Generous quantity of bread
⅔ stick (2 ¾ oz./80 g) butter
6 egg yolks
Salt and pepper

Optional
1 white truffle
Pickles for serving: gherkins, baby onions, etc.

Valdostana Fondue ★

Fonduta valdostana

This dish is the most typical of Val d'Aosta's hearty style of cooking,
made with fontina, a delicious, semi-soft PDO cow-milk cheese.

Serves 6
Preparation time for the cheese: 4 hours
Preparation time for the fondue: 30 minutes

Slice the fontina thinly and marinate in the milk for approximately
4 hours.
Slice the bread ready for toasting (after which it will be diced for dipping
in the fondue).
Melt the butter in a casserole (made of terra-cotta if possible); add
the cheese with half the milk from the marinade. Mix until the cheese
is completely melted.
Beat the egg yolks with the remaining milk, add to the melted cheese,
and stir until you have a smooth cream. Season with salt and pepper.
Serve in a fondue pot or in the casserole it was cooked in and place
on a hotplate in the center of the table.
Toast the bread on a griddle and cut it into cubes. Dip the pieces of bread
in the fondue with long-handled forks.

● Suggested food/wine match
Val d'Aosta, dry red DOC
Val d'Aosta, Pinot Grigio DOC

● Chef's notes
*To flavor the fondue, add a few thin slices of white truffle or mushroom (cleaned
with a dry brush to remove any soil, wiped with a damp cloth, and patted dry).
You can serve the fondue as antipasto or as a dish on its own.
Use any leftovers for polenta pasticciata, a gratin of polenta in slices (see p. 109).*

Bell Peppers with Anchovies and Garlic ★

Peperoni all'acciugata

Serves 4-6
Preparation time: 30 minutes
Cooking time: 30 minutes

Wash the peppers, cut them into quarters; remove the seeds
and white pith.
Rinse the salt from the anchovies, remove their backbone, then
chop them.
Peel and chop the garlic.
Put the butter and the olive oil in a skillet over low heat (they should
not color) and soften the garlic and anchovies. Stir in the milk. Add
the peppers, cook for 30 minutes.
Serve hot or cold. The mixture can also be served on slices of bread
toasted on a griddle.

● **Suggested food/wine match**
Grignolino d'Asti, red DOC

● **Chef's note**
*To make a lighter dish, peel the peppers with a serrated vegetable peeler
(for thin-skinned vegetables such as tomatoes), or roast them over a flame
and then let them cool down in an airtight container before removing the skins.*

● **Did you know?**
*Served at every table in Piedmont, this simple dish is usually considered an
antipasto but can also accompany meat or fish.*

Ingredients
4 yellow bell peppers
2/3 cup (5 ¼ oz./100 g) salted anchovies
2 cloves garlic
¼ stick (1 oz./30 g) butter
3 ½ tablespoons (50 ml) olive oil
3 tablespoons milk

Technique
Anchovies in Salt >> p. 26

Ingredients
4 sheets (8 g) gelatin
1 ²/₃ cup (400 ml) whipping cream
1 tablespoon milk
1 ¹/₃ cups (6 oz./175 g) confectioners' sugar
1 tablespoon rum

Caramel sauce
¾ cup (5 oz./150 g) granulated sugar
8 tablespoons (120 ml) water

Chocolate sauce
3 ½ oz. (100 g) dark chocolate
3 ¹/₃ cups (800 ml) hot milk

Fruit coulis
Red fruits, kiwi, mango, etc.
Confectioners' sugar to taste
Lemon juice to taste

Equipment
6 ramekins measuring 3-4 in. (6-8 cm) diameter
  (approximately 1 ½-3 in./3-6 cm deep)
1 sieve
1 stick blender

Panna Cotta ★★

Serves 6
Preparation time: 20 minutes
Chilling time: 8 hours

Prepare the panna cotta.
Wet the inside of the ramekins to enable the panna cotta to be turned out easily once they have chilled.
Soften the gelatin in a little cold water.
Heat the cream and milk in a saucepan with the confectioners' sugar, ensuring the mixture does not boil. Wring the water out of the gelatin and stir the gelatin into the mixture; leave on low heat a moment or two longer. Pass through a sieve, then stir in the rum. Pour the mixture into the ramekins and place in the refrigerator for 8 hours.
When ready to serve, turn out onto dessert plates, and pour over your chosen sauce.

Make the caramel sauce.
Make a dark caramel by heating the sugar in a saucepan with 3 tablespoons (50 ml) of the water to 350°F (180°C), shaking the pan gently and carefully monitoring the color, which will turn from pale to dark brown very quickly.
Chill immediately by standing the saucepan in cold water to stop the cooking process (be careful that the caramel does not splash you). Leave to cool, then add the remaining 5 tablespoons (70 ml) of water. Replace over the heat until the mixture is evenly melted and smooth. Remove the pan from the stove: the caramel is ready.

Make the chocolate sauce.
Break the dark chocolate into pieces and melt in a bain-marie. Once the chocolate has melted, gradually add the hot milk. Stir until the mixture is smooth.

Prepare the fruit coulis.
Wash the fruit and peel or trim as necessary. Choose from strawberries, raspberries, kiwi fruit, mangoes, etc. Mix with a stick blender, adding confectioners' sugar and a few drops of lemon juice to taste. Put the coulis through a sieve to remove raspberry seeds, if you wish.

● Suggested food/wine match
Borgo Maragliano, Loazzolo Vendemmia Tardiva DOC.
Cosseti, Brachetto d'Aqui DOCG

● Chef's note
Fifty years ago, panna cotta was only served in mountain hostels in the south of Piedmont, with caramel or chocolate sauce. Pairing it with fruit coulis is a recent innovation.

Lombardy

Nadia and Giovanni Santini

Our cuisine is a family affair. My husband Antonio's grandmother taught me the ritual of pasta making and their family technique for preparing risotto, as well as the importance of respecting and honoring local produce.

Today, I work together with my son Giovanni. Alberto, Giovanni's brother, assists Antonio in selecting wines and welcoming our guests. Our restaurant is small-scale, with no more than thirty covers per day. Each of our dishes is prepared from the heart.

We have been lucky enough to receive several awards in recent years, but we don't seek them out. We're happy doing what we do and will continue to work passionately for what inspires us the most: the quest for fine tastes and the desire to achieve perfection at every stage.

Risotto with Saffron Threads and Crispy Artichokes

Infuse the saffron threads for 1 hour in a small container filled with lukewarm water.

Prepare the artichokes.

Cut the stalks and remove the large leaves; cut the artichokes in two lengthwise. Remove the choke if necessary and slice them thinly. Put the tablespoon of butter and rosemary in a skillet, and add the slices of artichokes. Fry gently until crisp and golden.

Prepare the risotto.

Chop the onion finely. Put half of the butter in a saucepan and lightly brown the onion, then remove it from the pan and set aside. Add the rice all at once. Fry it gently, stirring with a wooden spoon.

Add the onion back to the pan. Moisten with a ladle of very hot stock and cook the rice over high heat, adding more stock as soon as it becomes absorbed. A few minutes before the rice is fully cooked, add the water infused with saffron. Finish cooking by adding the rest of the butter and Parmesan.

Stir the risotto, then put it in a dish with the crispy artichokes on top.

Serve immediately.

Preparation time: 30 minutes
Infusion time: 1 hour
Cooking time: 20 minutes

Ingredients
1 pinch (2 g) of saffron threads
2 purple artichokes
1 tablespoon (15 g) butter, for the artichokes
1 sprig of rosemary
1 small onion
¼ stick (1 oz./30 g) butter, for the risotto
Scant 1 ½ cups (8–10 oz./250–300 g) risotto rice
(e.g. *arborio*)
6 cups (1.5 liters) hot meat stock (see p. 93)
¼ cup (1 ½ oz./40 g) grated Parmesan
Salt

Risotto *alla Milanese* ★★

As for all the best-known Italian recipes, the recipe for risotto *alla Milanese* has been protected by a municipal designation (*Denominazioni Comunali: De.Co.*) of the city of Milan since 2007.

Serves 6
Preparation time: 30 minutes
Cooking time: 14-18 minutes

Peel and chop the onion finely. Chop the beef marrow.
Melt 3 ½ tablespoons (1 ¾ oz./50 g) of the butter and the beef marrow in a heavy-bottom pan. Add the onion and let it brown over low heat.
Add the rice and stir so that all the grains absorb the flavor of the other ingredients evenly, then leave to brown lightly over medium heat.
Increase the heat and mix in the stock (a ladle at a time) by stirring the rice with a wooden spoon, gently and frequently. As the liquid is absorbed, add more stock until the rice is cooked: 14 to 18 minutes, depending on the rice used. The cooking time is calculated from the moment the mixture returns to a boil after the first ladle of stock is added. The rice should be al dente.
If you are using powdered saffron, add it at the end of the cooking time to preserve its fragrance. If using saffron threads, mix them in a little stock and add two thirds of the way through the cooking process.
Once the cooking is complete, turn off the heat, add the rest of the butter, and stir with a wooden spoon until it has melted.
Add the Grana Padano and stir again gently to prevent the grains of rice breaking. Add salt if necessary.
The risotto should be slightly liquid, *all'onda* (i.e. wet), with the grains well separated but forming a creamy, homogenous whole. For best results, never cook more than 7 to 8 servings of risotto at a time.
Serve the risotto on warmed plates. Provide guests with spoons and extra grated Grana Padano.

● **Suggested food/wine match**
Ca'del Bosco, Curtefranca Rosso—Terre di Franciacorta DOC

● **Chef's note**
The risotto should be served as soon as it is ready. It should be the guests who wait for the risotto, never the other way round!

Ingredients
1 yellow onion
1 oz. (30 g) beef marrow
⅔ stick (2 ⅔ oz./75 g) butter
2 ⅔ cups (1 lb. 4 oz./550 g) risotto rice
(such as *arborio*)
10 cups (2.5 liters) hot beef stock (see p. 93)
1 pinch (2 g) saffron threads or powder
⅓ cup (2 oz./60 g) grated Grana Padano cheese
Salt

Technique
Risotto with Sparkling Wine >> p. 93

Ingredients

Dough for *pizzoccheri*
1 ¾ cups (10 oz./300 g) buckwheat flour
1 cup (3 ½ oz./100 g) bread flour
1 cup (250 ml) lukewarm water
2 eggs (optional)
1 tablespoon olive oil
Salt

Sauce
2 oz. (50 g) fontina or other quick-melting cheese
¾ oz. (20 g) Parmesan
1 onion
5 oz. (150 g) potatoes
6 oz. (200 g) chard (in summer) or cabbage
  (in winter) or spinach
A few sage leaves
1 clove garlic
¼ stick (1 oz./30 g) butter
Salt, pepper

Equipment
1 rolling pin
Pasta dryer (or dry dish towel)

● Chef's notes
To vary the flavor, add some black truffle paste to the sauce and decorate with shaved truffle.
To vary the cooking method, instead of heating the pizzoccheri with the sauce in the skillet, cook them in advance and bake them in the oven with thin slices of one of the cheeses on top. Sprinkle with Parmesan to serve.

Buckwheat Tagliatelle from Valtellina ★★

Pizzoccheri della Valtellina

Pizzoccheri are made with buckwheat flour, usually accompanied by a sauce made from local vegetables and cheeses.

Serves 4
Preparation time: 1 hour
Resting time for dough: 30 minutes
Cooking time: 25 minutes

Make the *pizzoccheri*.
Sift the flours together onto a smooth surface (preferably wooden) or into a large bowl. Make a well in the flour and pour in the lukewarm water and the eggs if using, oil, and the salt (in this order). Stir all this into the flour gradually, making sure that it does not overflow. When all the flour is incorporated, knead the dough as firmly as possible until it forms a smooth ball (approximately 10 minutes). Cover it completely with plastic wrap to protect it from the air.
Leave to rest for 30 minutes.
Once the dough has rested, roll it out on a flat surface (preferably wooden) from the center toward the outer edge, using a rolling pin. Give the dough a quarter turn (90 degrees) and turn it over. Do both frequently. Continue until you have a thin, uniformly rolled sheet (⅛ in./3 mm). Cut into small tagliatelle of approximately 2 ½ × ½ in. (6 × 1 cm).
If you do not have a pasta dryer, lightly flour a dry dish towel, lay it on a tray, and spread the tagliatelle out on it.

Prepare the sauce.
Dice the cheeses. Peel the onion and chop finely. Peel the potatoes and cut them into small cubes. Clean the chard (or cabbage or spinach) and cut it into ribbons.
Bring salted water to a boil. Cook the chard, cabbage, or spinach for 8 to 10 minutes. Add the potato and cook for 3 minutes longer. Add the *pizzoccheri* and let everything cook for an additional 4 minutes.
Soften the chopped onion, sage, and unpeeled garlic clove in the butter in a skillet.
Drain the pasta and vegetables (reserving some of the cooking water). Add to the skillet, adding the cheeses and a little of the cooking water. Serve very hot, seasoned with freshly ground black pepper.

● Suggested food/wine match
Rainoldi, Sassella Riserva—Valtellina superiore DOCG

Fricassee of Veal Sweetbreads ★ ★

Animelle in fricassea

The term *fricassea* traditionally describes a dish of white meat or veal sweetbreads with a sauce that uses a liaison of eggs and lemon juice at the end of the cooking time.

Serves 6
Soaking time for veal sweetbreads: minimum 4 hours
Preparation time: 30 minutes
Cooking time: 30 minutes

Soak the sweetbreads for a minimum of 4 hours in cold water. Change the water frequently.
Bring a pan of water to a boil to blanch the sweetbreads for 5 minutes. Remove their skin, rinse in cold water, and cut into pieces.
Peel and chop the onion. Brown it with the butter in a skillet and add the sweetbreads. Season with salt and pepper and let simmer for 15 minutes. Beat the eggs with the lemon juice and the stock in a bowl. Pour this over the sweetbreads and stir the mixture without letting it boil. As soon as the sauce thickens, serve very hot.

● **Suggested food/wine match**
Ca' del Bosco, Chardonnay—Curtefranca DOC

● **Chef's notes**
You can prepare this recipe with chicken, veal, or lamb, by adapting the cooking time.
You can also enhance it by adding previously blanched artichokes, cut into quarters. You can even prepare a vegetarian version using the artichokes without the sweetbreads, and substituting vegetable stock for the beef stock.

Ingredients
12 oz. (750 g) veal sweetbreads
1 onion
½ stick (2 oz./60 g) butter
2 eggs
Juice of 1 lemon
½ cup (125 ml) beef stock (see p. 93)
Salt, pepper

Ingredients

2 lb. (1 kg) tripe
½ cup (3 ½ oz./100 g) dried white beans
2 cups (10 oz./300 g) tomatoes, fresh or canned
1 stick celery
1 onion
1 carrot
3 ½ tablespoons (1 ¾ oz./50 g) butter
A few sage leaves
1 cup (250 ml) beef stock (see p. 93)
Grated Parmesan
Salt, pepper

Technique
Polenta >> pp. 100–107

Tripe *alla Milanese* ★

Trippa alla milanese

Serves 4
Soaking time for dried beans: 12 hours
Preparation time: 30 minutes
Cooking time: 4 hours

A day ahead.
Soak the dried beans in cold water for approximately 12 hours.

The next day, drain the beans and cook them in unsalted water (1 hour 30 minutes to 2 hours cooking time, or 40 to 50 minutes in a pressure cooker).
If necessary, peel the tomatoes (after immersing them for a few seconds in boiling water and then in cold water) and dice them.
Wash the celery, peel the onion and carrot, and chop them all finely.
Slice the tripe thinly.
Soften the vegetables in a saucepan with the butter and sage.
Add the slices of tripe. After 10 minutes, add the tomatoes and season with salt and pepper.
Cook for 2 hours over low heat. Moisten with stock as required to ensure that the tripe does not dry out.
Ten minutes before the end of the cooking time, add the cooked beans.
When fully cooked, the juices should be well reduced.
Serve sprinkled with grated Parmesan.

● Suggested food/wine match
Balgera, Grumello riserva—Valtellina superiore DOCG

● Chef's notes
To thicken the sauce, you can add a calf's foot, or 2 tablespoons of flour dissolved in a little cold stock.
Accompany the tripe with bread or grilled polenta (see p. 106).
You can also prepare the tripe without the beans.

Osso Buco ★ ★

Osso buco, which literally means "bone with holes," has been a traditional Milanese dish since the fifteenth century. It is traditionally served with a type of small skewer to help pry the marrow from the bone. This instrument is called *esattore* (meaning "tax collector") in Italian.

Serves 4
Preparation time: 30 minutes
Cooking time: 1 hour 30 minutes

Peel and chop the onion.

Prepare the *gremolata* condiment.
Remove the stalks from the parsley, peel the garlic and then chop the parsley and garlic clove finely with the lemon zest and anchovy.

Prepare the osso buco.
Make incisions with a knife around the edge of each piece of meat. Flour lightly and brown in a casserole with the butter. Deglaze with the wine and let it evaporate. Add the salt, pepper, and chopped onion. Cook a few minutes, add the peeled tomatoes, and moisten with the stock.
Let cook for 1 hour 30 minutes. At the end of the cooking time, the sauce should be fluid but not too thin and the meat should come away from the bone easily.
Add the *gremolata* to serve.

● Suggested food/wine match
Frecciarossa, Giorgio Odero—Oltrepò Pavese pinot nero DOC

● Chef's notes
The most classic accompaniment to osso buco is risotto alla Milanese (see p. 214). You can vary this by serving polenta, mashed potatoes, or peas, carrots, and green beans sautéed in butter.
If you use a pressure cooker, the cooking time will be reduced to about 45 minutes.

Ingredients
4 pieces of osso buco (veal shank or knuckle cut into thick slices of 1 ½-2 in./3-4 cm, weighing approximately 10 oz./300 g each)
1 onion
A few sprigs of parsley
1 small clove garlic
Zest of 1 lemon
1 anchovy in oil
2 tablespoons flour
2/3 stick (2 ½ oz./80 g) butter
250 ml (1 cup) white wine
1 cup (5 oz./150 g) peeled tomatoes
2 cups (500 ml) beef stock (see p. 93)
Salt, pepper

Equipment
Small skewers

Techniques
Polenta >> pp. 100–107
Peeled Tomatoes >> p. 42

Ingredients

1 guinea fowl, weighing approximately
  2 ½ lb. (1.2 kg), with its liver
2 dessert apples (approximately 8 oz./250 g)
3 ½ tablespoons (1 ¾ oz./50 g) butter
3 juniper berries
Cinnamon stick or powder
1 cup (250 ml) aromatic white wine
Juice of 1 lemon
1 cup (250 ml) beef stock (see p. 93)
4 oz. (120 g) fresh grapes
4 fresh figs
Salt, pepper

Guinea Fowl *alla Vignaiola* ★★

Faraona alla vignaiola

Serves 4
Preparation time: 20 minutes
Cooking time: 1 hour 15 minutes (30 minutes per lb./1 hour per kg)

Cut the liver into slices. Peel and core one of the apples.
Season the inside of the guinea fowl with salt and pepper and place
the apple in the cavity (to keep the meat moist during cooking).
Brown the guinea fowl in a casserole with half the butter and the juniper
berries. Add the slices of liver, season with salt and pepper, and add a
stick or a pinch of cinnamon and moisten with the wine. Let evaporate
and add the lemon juice.
Continue cooking (1 hour per 2 lb./1 kg), adding more stock if it begins
to look dry.
Meanwhile, halve the grapes and remove the seeds.
Peel the second apple and cut it into slices. Soften the grapes and
the apple slices in a saucepan with the rest of the butter.
Serve the guinea fowl with its cooking juices, the apples, and grapes.
Decorate each serving with a fresh fig.

● Suggested food/wine match
Rainoldi, Sfurzat di Valtellina DOCG

● Chef's notes
*You can vary the cooking method by following a very old recipe, typical of
Lombardy, for guinea fowl cooked in clay. Flavor the inside of the guinea fowl
with chopped bacon, rosemary, thyme, juniper, cinnamon, clove, nutmeg, and
bay; season with salt and pepper. Wrap it in slices of pancetta, then in a double
layer of dampened parchment paper. Lastly, cover it in a paste made of clay
mixed with water. Bake for 3 hours in a very hot oven (480°F/250°C). When the
guinea fowl is removed from the oven, break off the clay with a hammer and
serve.
If you do not have fresh figs, you can replace them with dried figs. Rehydrate
them and cook with the apple and grapes.*

Lombardy

Asparagus with Buttered Eggs and Parmesan ★

Asparagi al parmigiano

Ingredients
3 lb. (1.5 kg) green asparagus
4 eggs
½ stick (2 oz./60 g) butter
Grated Parmesan
Salt

Serves 4
Preparation time: 10 minutes
Cooking time: 15 minutes

Clean the asparagus. Stand them upright in a bunch in a saucepan with salted cold water reaching halfway up the stalks. Cook for 10 to 15 minutes.
During this time, cook the eggs in a skillet in butter.
When the asparagus is cooked, drain on paper towel or a clean cloth, then place in a dish.
Sprinkle the asparagus with grated Parmesan. Arrange the eggs on top (their heat will melt the cheese) and serve.

● Suggested food/wine match
Cavalleri, Rampaneto—Terre di Franciacorta DOC

● Chef's note
Once the asparagus is cooked, you can layer it with butter and Parmesan and bake in the oven.

Ingredients

1 ⅓ cups (7 oz./200 g) raisins
⅓ cup (80 ml) milk
2 sticks (8 oz./250 g) butter
1 orange
1 lemon
½ cup (2 ½ oz./70 g) chopped candied citrus peel
1 ¾ tablespoons (1 oz./25 g) fresh yeast
7 cups (1 lb. 8 oz./700 g) cake flour
2 whole eggs
5 egg yolks
1 ⅓ cups (8 oz./250 g) sugar
2 teaspoons (10 g) salt
1 vanilla bean or vanilla extract
2 tablespoons rum

Equipment

1 panettone mold, 12 in. (25 cm) in diameter

● Chef's notes

The Easter variation is made in almost the same way, but in the shape of a dove (colomba). It is also iced with egg white whisked with confectioners' sugar, ground almonds, and hazelnuts and, finally, decorated with blanched almonds.

For the dough to rise at 85°F (30°C), use the oven with just the light turned on.

If the dough becomes dry, replace the cloth with plastic wrap.

● Did you know?

It is unclear whether panettone emerged as the result of serious error or of grand passion, but it seems to have had its origins in fifteenth-century Milan. It is possible that someone by the name of Tonio invented it, hence "pane de Tonio," or possibly that it comes from the Milanese phrase, "pan del ton," which would translate as "cake of luxury."

Panettone ★ ★ ★

This sweet bread is traditionally eaten at Christmas and New Year and has become popular far beyond Italy. You can replace the raisins and candied peel with whole or chopped nuts (almonds, hazelnuts, pistachios, etc.), with chocolate chips (dark, white, or milk), or with other candied fruit (melon, raspberry, kiwi, etc.).

Serves 10
Preparation time: 1 hour
Soaking time: 15 minutes
Rising time for the dough: about 9 hours
Cooking time: 1 hour

Soak the raisins in water for 15 minutes. Take the milk from the fridge and let it come to room temperature. Soften the butter. Zest the orange and lemon. Dice the candied peel.

Dissolve the yeast in the milk and mix with 1 cup (3 ½ oz./100 g) of the flour to form a dough. Mark the surface with a cross, place in a floured bowl and cover with a cloth. Leave for 1 hour 30 minutes, sheltered from drafts at a temperature of approximately 85°F (30°C).

When the ball has doubled in volume, pour 3 cups (10 oz./300 g) of the flour onto the counter, form a well in the center, and place the risen dough in it. Add ¾ stick (3 ½ oz./100 g) of the butter, the eggs, and a scant ½ cup (100 ml) of water and knead well. Leave to rise again, covered with a cloth and sheltered from drafts at a temperature of approximately 85°F (30°C). Leave for 3 hours or until doubled in volume.

Make a well in the remaining 3 cups (10 oz./300 g) of flour and place the risen dough in the middle. Add the remaining stick (4 oz./125 g) of butter and knead. Drain the raisins.

Whisk the egg yolks with the sugar until thick and pale; add them to the dough with the salt and a scant ½ cup (100 ml) water. Knead the dough again for 10 minutes. Add the vanilla, rum, zest, raisins, and candied peel, and combine well.

Line a panettone mold with parchment paper. Butter and flour it before placing the dough in the mold, but do not fill more than two thirds full. Allow a final rise covered with a cloth, sheltered from drafts, at a temperature of approximately 85°F (30°C). Leave for 4 hours or until doubled in volume and slightly overlapping the rim of the mold. Remove the cloth and place in the refrigerator for 20 minutes. Mark the surface of the dough with a deep cross and place about 2 tablespoons butter in the middle.

Preheat the oven to 400°F (200°C). Bake for 10 minutes then lower the temperature to 350°F (180°C). Continue cooking for approximately 50 minutes.

Unmold and serve cold.

● Suggested food/wine match

Ceretto Moscato d'Asti DOCG (the traditional accompaniment)

Veneto
Trentino-Alto Adige
Friuli-Venezia Giulia

Massimiliano Alajmo

My *terroir* comprises the earth, the sea, and history. I like to highlight its specialty products in my cuisine–for example, salt cod, radicchio, free-range poultry, eels, rice, fish from the lagoon, and the famous Lamon beans, with their white pods veined with red.

The essence of a dish is revealed through its ingredients. Anyone wanting to discover my cooking must make a voyage to this hidden matrix that is a source of continual surprise. Then comes technique, but this is only a means, and in no way an end in itself.

The cuisine from Calandre is founded on three principles: lightness, depth, and evolution. We concentrate on sensory experiences. Among the five established senses, smell is the most powerful, the one that transports you instantly to taste. We are also searching for a sort of sixth sense that needs to be developed to fully appreciate the alchemy of cooking.

Duo of Asparagus with Eggs Mimosa

Prepare the white and green asparagus pulp.
Gently grate the two asparagus varieties into separate containers using a grater to obtain the pulp. Press the white asparagus pulp to extract the juice, filter, and set aside. Season the white and green pulp with the oil, salt, pepper, vinegar, and mustard.

Prepare the white asparagus juice and seasoned bread.
Mix the juice of the white asparagus in a bowl with the oil, vinegar, and salt.
Cut the bread into small dice and soak it in this juice. Strain and set aside.

Make the tarragon mayonnaise.
Boil the water with the vinegar and sprig of tarragon, then leave to infuse for 15 minutes. Mix the yolk with the soy sauce; add the tarragon-flavored water and vinegar mixture with a pinch of sugar. Add the grape seed oil in a thin stream, whisking continuously to form a mayonnaise. Season with salt and pepper. Pour the mayonnaise into a siphon fitted with a gas cartridge. Shake well and keep in the refrigerator for use later.

Prepare the deviled egg.
Boil the egg for 7 minutes, remove the shell, and crush it with a fork.
Season with the olive oil, salt, pepper, tarragon, mustard, and mayonnaise.
Mix gently to obtain a smooth cream.

Assemble the dish.
Arrange the following in a circle on each plate: a spoonful of white asparagus pulp, ½ spoonful of green asparagus pulp, 1 spoonful of egg mimosa, and 1 spoonful of bread flavored with asparagus juice.
Place a small mound of salad greens in the center, season with olive oil and tarragon vinegar, decorate with mayonnaise piped from the siphon, and top with the finely chopped tarragon and licorice. Sprinkle with olive oil and season with salt and pepper.

Serves 4
Preparation time: 30 minutes
Cooking time: 10 minutes

Ingredients
White and green asparagus pulp
10 oz. (300 g) white asparagus
8 oz. (250 g) green asparagus
½ tablespoon extra virgin olive oil
⅔ teaspoon (3 g) salt
2 drops red wine vinegar
1 dash Dijon mustard
Freshly ground black pepper

White asparagus juice and seasoned bread
⅓ cup (80 ml) white asparagus juice
3 oz. (80 g) plain sourdough bread
1 teaspoon extra virgin olive oil
2 drops red wine vinegar
1 pinch of salt

Tarragon mayonnaise
2 teaspoons water
1 teaspoon red wine vinegar
1 sprig of tarragon
1 (1 oz./22 g) egg yolk
2 drops soy sauce
1 pinch of sugar
½ cup (112 ml) grape seed oil
Salt, pepper

Deviled egg
1 egg
¼ tablespoon extra virgin olive oil
½ teaspoon salt
1 pinch of freshly chopped tarragon
1 dash Dijon mustard
1 teaspoon of mayonnaise from a siphon
Freshly ground black pepper

Garnish
Salad greens
Finely chopped tarragon
Licorice powder
Extra virgin olive oil
Freshly ground black pepper

Marinated Sardines ★

Sarde in saor

Marinated sardines is one of the oldest and most typical dishes of the Veneto region. A genuinely popular dish, this is simple and easy to prepare.

Serves 8
Preparation time: 40 minutes
Soaking time: 15 minutes
Resting time: 2 days

Soak the raisins in water for 15 minutes, then drain.
Peel and slice the onions.
Clean the sardines and remove the central bone, leaving the fillets whole.
Dip them in the flour then fry in the olive oil. When they are golden,
drain on paper towel and sprinkle with salt.
Fry the onions over medium heat in a skillet, season with salt and pepper
and add the sugar. When they are cooked, cool them by pouring over
the vinegar.
Arrange a layer of sardines on a platter or in a dish and cover them with
a layer of onions, a few pine nuts, a few bay leaves, peppercorns, juniper
berries, and raisins. Add another layer of sardines and then a layer
of onions and a few more spices.
Continue until all the ingredients are used up.
Marinate the sardines for 1 or 2 days in the refrigerator.
Serve as antipasto at room temperature.

● Suggested food/wine match
Maculan, Bidibi—Bregânze DOC

Ingredients
1 lb. (500 g) sardines (preferably small ones)
2 tablespoons raisins
4 onions
¼ cup (1 oz./30 g) flour
2 tablespoons olive oil
1 tablespoon sugar
½ cup (125 ml) good red wine vinegar
2 tablespoons pine nuts
A few bay leaves
A few peppercorns
A few juniper berries
Salt, freshly ground black pepper

Ingredients

8 fresh scallops (opened and prepared by
   the fishmonger, retaining the indented half
   of the shell)
1 clove garlic
1 bunch of parsley
1 ½ oz. (40 g) Parmesan
⅔ cup (1 ½ oz./40 g) fresh bread crumbs
2 tablespoons flour
⅓ stick (1 ½ oz./40 g) butter
¼ cup (60 ml) white wine
Salt, pepper

Gratin of Scallops ★

Capesante gratinate

Capesante can be served as an antipasto or as a main dish.

Serves 4
Preparation time: 20 minutes
Cooking time: 15 minutes

Peel the garlic and chop the clove. Wash and remove the stalks from the
parsley, then chop.
Grate the Parmesan and mix with the bread crumbs.
Rinse the scallops and dry them on paper towel.
Dip the scallops in flour and brown them for a few minutes in a skillet
with 2 teaspoons (10 g) of the butter. Set them aside.
Melt the rest of the butter in the skillet and quickly fry the parsley
and garlic before deglazing with the wine and removing from the heat.
Place each scallop in its shell, season with salt and pepper and
the prepared sauce, then sprinkle with the bread crumbs mixed with
Parmesan. Place under a broiler until the surface is golden brown
(8 to 10 minutes).

● **Suggested food/wine match**
Bastianich, Friulano—Colliorientalidel Friuli DOC

● **Chef's notes**
You can enrich the flavor of the sauce with chopped onions, or by adding some
béchamel sauce containing chopped hard-boiled egg and shrimp.
In the recipe for scallops alla veneziana *the scallops are simply cooked with*
olive oil, garlic, and parsley, then deglazed with a little lemon juice and served
in their shells.

● **Did you know?**
The Italian name for scallops, capesante, *dates back to the Middle Ages,*
when the empty shells were used for sprinkling holy water over a child being
baptized.

Veneto • Trentino-Alto Adige • Friuli-Venezia Giulia

Pasta with Cuttlefish Ink ★

Linguine al nero di seppia

Recipes including cuttlefish ink belong to the culinary tradition of Venice. Three very distinctive variations of these dishes follow.

Serves 4
Preparation time: 20 minutes
Pasta cooking time: follow packet instructions

Peel the garlic and chop the clove. Wash, remove the stalks of the parsley, and chop the leaves.
Peel and chop the onion.
Clean the cuttlefish and retain their ink sacs (see p. 125).
Slice the cuttlefish but keep their tentacles whole.
Fry the onion in a skillet with the olive oil.
When the onion becomes translucent, add the chopped garlic and cuttlefish, season with salt and pepper. Let the water that is released evaporate, then deglaze with the wine.
Add the ink sacs to the skillet. Use a spatula to pierce them, then leave the ink to melt.
Meanwhile, cook the pasta, drain it, and add to the sauce in the skillet. Sprinkle with a little chopped parsley and let the flavors mingle for 1 to 2 minutes. Serve immediately.

● **Suggested food/wine match**
Bertani, Sereole—Soave DOC

● **Chef's note**
If the sauce starts drying out, add a small ladle of the pasta cooking water to moisten it.

Ingredients
1 lb. (500 g) fresh cuttlefish
1 clove garlic
1 sprig of parsley
1 onion
2 tablespoons olive oil
½ cup (120 ml) white wine
1 lb. (500 g) linguine or spaghetti
Salt, pepper

Technique
Cleaning cuttlefish, extracting the ink ›› p. 125

Ingredients

1 lb. 3 oz. (600 g) cuttlefish
Fish stock (see shellfish stock, pp. 96-97)
1 onion
1 clove garlic
1 sprig of parsley
2 tablespoons olive oil
1 ⅓ cups (10 oz./280 g) risotto rice
Scant ½ cup (100 ml) white wine

Techniques

Risotto ›› pp. 90-91
Cleaning cuttlefish, extracting the ink ›› p. 125

Cuttlefish Ink Risotto ★★

Risotto al nero di seppia

Serves 4
Preparation time: 1 hour
Cooking time: 20 minutes
Preparation and cooking time for the stock: 30 minutes

Prepare the fish stock (see pp. 96-97), replacing the shrimp heads
and shells with fish heads and bones.
Peel and chop the onion. Peel the garlic; leave the clove whole. Wash the
parsley, remove the stalks, and chop the leaves.
Clean the cuttlefish, retaining their ink sacs (see p. 125). Cut the cuttlefish
into small squares.
Fry the onion with the olive oil in a saucepan. Add the garlic, parsley, and
cuttlefish. Mix thoroughly.
Add the rice and toast it over medium heat for several minutes.
Deglaze with the white wine and add the ink sacs.
Cook the risotto, adding a little fish stock whenever the rice begins
to dry out (see pp. 90-91).
Remove from the heat and serve immediately, sprinkled with freshly
chopped parsley.

● Suggested food/wine match

Bertani, Sereole—Soave DOC

Ingredients

1 lb. 3 oz. (600 g) small cuttlefish
1 clove garlic
1 onion
2 tablespoons olive oil
Scant ½ cup (100 ml) white wine
2 tablespoons tomato sauce
Parsley, chopped

Technique

Cleaning cuttlefish, extracting the ink ›› p. 125

Cuttlefish in Their Ink ★

Seppie al nero

Serves 4
Preparation time: 20 minutes
Cooking time: 20 minutes

Follow the method for the pasta with cuttlefish ink recipe (facing page),
but do not cut the small cuttlefish up–keep them whole. Add the tomato
sauce after the wine, before adding the ink sacs. No need to add rice or
pasta; sprinkle with a little chopped parsley and serve immediately.

● Suggested food/wine match

Bertani, Sereole—Soave DOC

Ingredients

Bigoli pasta
3 cups (10 oz./300 g) all-purpose flour
3 cups (10 oz./300 g) durum wheat
   semolina flour
3 medium eggs
¾ cup (160 ml) water
Salt

Sauce
1 duck, with its liver and preferably other giblets
2 onions
2 carrots
2 sticks celery
3 cloves
½ stick (2 oz./60 g) butter
2 tablespoons olive oil
1 sprig of rosemary
2 sage leaves
3 juniper berries
1 cup (250 ml) white wine
Grated Parmesan
Salt, pepper

Equipment

1 *bigolaro* pasta extruder or meat grinder

 **Chef's notes**

You can add pomegranate juice to the sauce.
Variation: Bigoli in salsa *is another well-known recipe, prepared with onions softened in olive oil, with anchovies then added to them before mixing with the* bigoli *and chopped parsley.*

Bigoli with Duck Sauce ★★

Bigoli in salsa d'anatra

The recipe for *bigoli* with duck sauce originated between Thiene and Zane (Vicenza). Today, it is widely known throughout the Veneto region. The original version of the sauce for *bigoli* was prepared with the giblets (liver, stomach, heart, etc.) of a duck to be poached and then served as a main dish. The *bigoli* were cooked in the fatty duck stock. Food habits have changed since then; it is also more difficult to buy a whole duck with its giblets nowadays. The recipe is therefore often simplified and prepared with the flesh of the duck.

Serves 8
Preparation time: 30 minutes
Resting time: 1 hour
Cooking time: 1 hour 35 minutes

Prepare the *bigoli*.
Mix the flours together, make a well in the center, and stir in the eggs, water, and salt.
Knead well until you have a firm, smooth dough. Cover with plastic wrap and let rest for 1 hour (at room temperature).

Make the sauce.
Meanwhile, wash and peel all the vegetables. Chop one of each.
Bone the duck and chop the flesh finely (or put it through a meat grinder); set aside. Put the carcass and liver (and any more duck giblets you may have) into a saucepan, and cover with water. Pierce the whole onion with the cloves and add to the saucepan with the whole carrot and celery stick. Season with salt and prepare a stock by simmering everything together for 1 hour 30 minutes over low heat. Remove the liver and giblets, let cool, and chop finely. Set aside.
Remove the chopping blade from the meat grinder, if using, and replace it with a mincing disc with ⅛ in. (4 mm) diameter holes.
When the *bigoli* dough has rested, divide the ball equally into three and put each one through the grinder or *bigolaro* pasta extruder.
Be sure to separate the *bigoli* as they pass through the holes to prevent them from sticking to each other. Flour well and lay them on a dry cloth.
Color the chopped or ground duck in the butter and olive oil in a saucepan over medium heat. Add the chopped vegetables, rosemary, sage, and juniper berries. When the vegetables become translucent, add the chopped liver and any other giblets, and deglaze with the white wine. When the wine has evaporated, moisten with a little stock and cook for 1 hour to 1 hour 30 minutes.
Strain the remaining stock into another saucepan (add a little water if it has reduced significantly) and cook the *bigoli* in it for 5 minutes. Strain, then pour the duck sauce over the pasta and serve with the grated Parmesan.

● **Suggested food/wine match**
Maculan, Pinot Nero Breganze DOC

Cipriani's Carpaccio ★

Carpaccio di Cipriani

This dish is often served as an appetizer. You can dress the carpaccio with just olive oil, salt, pepper, and lemon juice, then sprinkle over a few shavings of Parmesan and/or thinly sliced mushrooms. If you have a meat slicer, you can slice a piece of raw beef extremely thinly if you freeze it first.

Serves 4
Preparation time: 30 minutes

Prepare the sauce.
Make a mayonnaise: beat the egg yolk with a pinch each of salt and pepper, the vinegar, and mustard. Add the olive oil in a thin stream, whisking continuously until you have a thick emulsion.
Thin the mayonnaise with the lemon juice, Worcestershire sauce, and milk, to give it a pouring consistency.

Arrange the slices of beef on individual plates, dress with 2 tablespoons of sauce, and place a few arugula leaves on top.
Serve at room temperature.

● Suggested food/wine match
Conte Brandolini, Vistorta—Friuli Grave DOC

● Did you know?
This dish was created in 1950 by Giuseppe Cipriani in his restaurant, Harry's Bar, in Venice. Wanting to prepare an original dish for one of his clients who could not eat cooked meat, he created a recipe for raw meat of the finest quality, sliced very thinly. It was dressed with his "universal" sauce and decorated with arugula. He named the dish after the great Venetian painter Vittore Carpaccio (c. 1465–1525/1526), in recognition of the artist's prominent use of red.

Ingredients
14 oz. (400 g) very thinly sliced beef (rump, fillet, etc.), lean or marbled with fat, according to your taste
1 ½ oz. (40 g) arugula

Sauce
1 egg yolk, at room temperature
1 tablespoon white wine vinegar
2 tablespoons mustard
Scant 1 cup (200 ml) olive oil
1 tablespoon lemon juice
1 teaspoon Worcestershire sauce
2 tablespoons milk
Salt, pepper

Technique
Octopus Carpaccio >> p. 131

Ingredients

4 slices of calf's liver (1 lb./500 g)
2 lb. 10 oz. (1.2 kg) onions (preferably
  white onions from Chioggia)
2 tablespoons olive oil
¼ stick (1 oz./30 g) butter
A few sage leaves
½ cup (120 ml) white wine or stock
  (chicken or vegetable, see pp. 93 or 94)
Salt, pepper

Technique
Polenta >> pp. 100–107

Calf's Liver *alla Veneziana* ★★

Fegato alla veneziana

By replacing the figs with onions in a recipe dating back to the Romans, Venetians have created one of the signature dishes of Venetian cuisine: *fegato alla veneziana*.

Serves 4
Preparation time: 30 minutes
Cooking time: 20 minutes

Prepare the stock, if using (see pp. 93 or 94).
Peel the onions and chop them. Cut the liver into strips.
Cook the onions over low heat in a skillet with the olive oil, butter, and ¾ cup (150 ml) water. At the end of 20 minutes they should be cooked and the water completely evaporated. Increase the temperature and, when the onions are sizzling, add the sage and liver. Moisten with the white wine or stock. Season with salt and pepper, mix well, then leave to cook for 5 minutes.
The calf's liver should not be overcooked or underdone. You can accompany it with polenta or mashed potato.

● Suggested food/wine match
Speri, Sant'Urbano Valpolicella Classico Superiore—Veneto DOC

● Chef's notes
Traditionally, a liver pâté is made with the leftovers of calf's liver alla vene-ziana, and then served sliced or as a spread. Chop the leftovers very finely in a food processor and mix with an equal quantity of butter. Place in a bowl and chill in the refrigerator.
Fegato alla veneziana is a recipe that you can vary in simple ways: replace the sage with parsley, the wine with vinegar or lemon juice, the calf's liver with pig's liver, etc.

Baked Knuckle of Pork ★ ★ ★

Stinco al forno

This is a filling dish served with polenta or baked potatoes, to enjoy in the mountain chalets of Trentino-Alto Adige and Friuli.

Serves 4
Preparation time: 30 minutes
Cooking time: 2-3 hours

Prepare the stock (see pp. 93 or 94). Preheat the oven to 350°F (180°C). Avoid using forks to handle the knuckles. It is very important not to puncture the meat in order to keep the juices inside, so the meat remains succulent.
Brown the meat all over with the olive oil and butter in a roasting dish set on the stove top.
Add the rosemary, thyme, sage, and unpeeled garlic, then deglaze with the white wine.
Season with salt and pepper and bake in the oven for about 2 hours. During the cooking, moisten the meat with stock if it appears dry. The base of the dish should never dry out, but nor should the meat be surrounded by liquid.
Once the meat is cooked, return the dish to the stove top and finish glazing it on all sides, keeping it well moistened with the sauce.

● Suggested food/wine match

Cantina Cortaccia, Lagrein—Trentino-Alto Adige DOC

● Chef's notes

This dish can be accompanied by polenta, or by potatoes that you can cook in the oven at the same time as the pork (add midway through the cooking time, cut into cubes).
The white wine can be replaced by beer.
In some areas, this dish is prepared with shin of veal, requiring a slightly longer cooking time.

Ingredients

2-4 pork knuckles (depending on the weight: 3-4 lb./1.5-2 kg)
2 tablespoons olive oil
2 tablespoons butter
A few sprigs of rosemary
A few sprigs of thyme
A few cloves garlic
1 cup (250 ml) white wine
A few sage leaves
4 cups (1 liter) stock (poultry or vegetable, see p. 93 or p. 94)
Salt, pepper

Technique
Polenta >> pp. 100–107

Ingredients

2 lb. (1 kg) stockfish
1 lb. (500 g) onions
1 bunch of parsley
2 oz. (50 g) Parmesan
2 cups (500 ml) olive oil
3 salted anchovies
3-4 tablespoons (¾-1 oz./20-30 g) flour
Scant ¼ cup (50 ml) milk
Salt, pepper

Equipment

1 casserole, terra-cotta or stainless steel

Techniques

Anchovies in Salt >> p. 26
Polenta >> pp. 100–107

Stockfish *alla Vicentina* ★ ★ ★

Stoccafisso alla vicentina

Stockfish was introduced to Venetian cuisine in the fifteenth century, as an alternative to fresh fish.

Serves 8

Soaking time: 3-4 days
Preparation time: 30 minutes
Cooking time: 4 hours 30 minutes

A few days ahead.
Soak the stockfish for 3 to 4 days (depending on the thickness) in cold water. Change the water every 4 hours.

On the same day (or, even better, the day before).
Remove the skin and bones from the fish and then cut it into pieces.
Peel and chop the onions. Wash, remove the stalks from the parsley, and chop enough to give you 2 tablespoonfuls. Grate the Parmesan.
Brown the onions in a skillet with half the olive oil.
Add the anchovies; let them melt. Remove from the heat and add the parsley.
Divide the mixture in two. Place the first half on the bottom of a terra-cotta or stainless steel casserole. Lightly flour the pieces of fish, arrange them in a layer on top of the onions, then cover with the rest of the mixture.
Add the milk, Parmesan, salt, pepper, and the rest of the olive oil; the pieces of fish should be completely covered.
Leave to simmer for 4 hours 30 minutes, rotating the saucepan on the heat from time to time without stirring the contents.
Serve with a creamy polenta (see pp. 100-107).

● Suggested food/wine match

Bertani, Le Lave—Veneto IGT

● Chef's notes

When you buy the stockfish, ask if it requires beating with a wooden mallet to tenderize its fibers.
If you cannot get hold of stockfish, prepare the recipe with salt cod. This first requires soaking for 48 hours in cold water, which should be changed as often as possible.
The flavor of this dish develops if it is served the day after it is made.
You can reduce the cooking time to 1 hour 30 minutes using a pressure cooker over low heat.

● Did you know?

In 1890 the owner of a restaurant called Polenta e Baccalà in Vicenza created this dish, which very quickly became popular. The Venerable Brotherhood of Baccalà alla Vicentino was later created to protect the original recipe.

Baked Radicchio *alla Trevisana* ★

Radicchio alla trevisana

There are several varieties of salad from the Veneto that are cultivated around the towns for which they are named.
There are two varieties of Treviso radicchio: the early (short), and the late (long), which is only harvested from November onward.

Serves 6
Preparation time: 10 minutes
Cooking time: 10-15 minutes

Preheat the oven to 350°F (180°C).
Clean and wash the radicchio, shake them well, and divide each into two halves.
Place them on a baking sheet, drizzle with olive oil, sprinkle with salt, and bake for 10 to 15 minutes.

⬤ **Suggested food/wine match**
Conte Brandolini, Pinot Grigio—Friuli Grave DOC

⬤ **Chef's notes**
You can also grill the radicchio (see p. 16), or deep-fry them after flouring or dipping them in a very light fritter batter.
Alternatively you can serve radicchio as a salad with pancetta, browned first in a skillet for a few minutes.

Ingredients
2 lb. (1 kg) radicchio (preferably from Treviso)
Olive oil
Salt

Technique
Grilled Vegetables >> p. 16

Ingredients

4 eggs
Scant ½ cup (100 ml) strong espresso coffee
²/₃ cup plus 2 tablespoons (5 oz./150 g) sugar
2 tablespoons rum or brandy (optional)
1 ²/₃ cups (14 oz./400 g) mascarpone cheese
8 oz. (250 g) ladyfinger cookies
Cocoa powder

Equipment

One 8 × 15 in. (20 × 30 cm) dish

Tiramisu ★

Tiramisù

This classic layered cream dessert can be varied in many ways. Add fresh fruit (pineapple, raspberries, strawberries, etc.); vary the alcohol for flavoring the mascarpone; or replace the ladyfingers with leftover panettone, amaretti, pavesini, speculoos or other cookies.

Serves 12

Preparation time: 20 minutes
Chilling time: 12 hours
Resting time: 1 day

A day ahead.
Separate the eggs. Whisk the whites until stiff.
Prepare four very strong espresso coffees (scant ½ cup/100 ml).
Whisk the egg yolks with ²/₃ cup (4 oz./125 g) of sugar until thick and pale. Add the rum or brandy, if using, and whisk again. Gently stir in the mascarpone until the mixture is smooth.
Fold the egg whites into the mixture using a spatula.
Make a syrup by boiling a scant ½ cup (100 ml) of water and the remaining 2 tablespoons of sugar.
Remove from the heat, mix with the coffee, and leave to cool.
Dip the cookies quickly into this mixture, crust side up. Arrange them in a single layer in a dish or individual ramekins.
Cover with the mascarpone mixture and cover with plastic wrap.
Refrigerate for at least 12 hours.
Depending on the size of your dish or ramekins, you can alternate several layers of cookies and mascarpone.

Before serving, sprinkle the entire surface of the tiramisu with cocoa.

Variation: lemon tiramisu
Replace the coffee for soaking the cookies with lemon juice.
Add limoncello and/or the zest of an unwaxed lemon to the mascarpone cream instead of the rum or brandy.

● Suggested food/wine match

An espresso coffee for the classic tiramisu
A glass of limoncello for the lemon tiramisu

● Chef's note

The ideal cookies for tiramisu are ladyfingers (savoiardi). By dipping them crust side up, you prevent the cream from softening them too much.

● Did you know?

Tiramisu only made its first appearance in the twentieth century, probably during the early 1970s at the Beccherie restaurant in Treviso. It was claimed to be the creation of the pastry chef there, Roberto Linguanotto, who combined mascarpone, ladyfinger cookies (sponge fingers), and coffee with a traditional recipe called sbatudin, *consisting of egg yolks and sugar, which used to be given to children, convalescents, and the elderly as a "pick-me-up"—*tiramisù *in Italian.*

Liguria

Flavio Costa

We are fortunate to live in a region that is particularly fertile, in terms of fish, meat, and produce from the soil. Vegetables mostly come to us from the Albenga plain: purple artichokes, beef tomatoes, violet asparagus, all kinds of green vegetables and aromatic herbs, beans from Pigna (classified by Presidio Slow Food), and basil from Prà.

The sea–unpolluted and very cold–is teeming with oily fish (tuna and swordfish), white fish (bass, sea bream, and red porgy), crustaceans (San Remo or Santa Margherita lobsters), and shellfish. Meat such as rabbit, lamb, kid, and game also feature in our culinary tradition.

As my cooking is intuitive, I like to do the shopping myself, every morning. This is the best way to keep a check on the quality of raw ingredients. I love to accompany the fishermen at night and I always come away with ideas. I work a lot by eye, even when measuring out ingredients, and I rarely combine more than three main ingredients in the same dish. I do not use much cream or butter, and not many spices either, to allow the natural flavors to come out fully.

My sense of taste was developed during my childhood with the help of my mother, who is herself an excellent cook and now helps me in the restaurant. If I had not chosen to be a chef, I would have undoubtedly become a farmer or a vine grower.

Cream of Trombetta Zucchini with Cuttlefish Ink and Candied Lemon Zest

Serves 4
Preparation time: 40 minutes
Cooking time: 30 minutes

Ingredients

2 lb. (1 kg) zucchini, preferably trombetta
14 oz. (400 g) cuttlefish
2 shallots
1 leek
2 1/3 cups (550 ml) extra virgin olive oil
A ladle of fish stock
1 unwaxed lemon
Scant 1 cup (200 ml) water
½ cup (3 ½ oz./100 g) sugar
1 sprig of fresh dill
A few rosemary flowers
Salt

Peel and chop the shallots. Clean and dice the zucchini. Boil them in salted water with the shallots until cooked.

Clean and dice the cuttlefish. Remove the ink sacs and set aside.

Chop the leek finely and soften in a skillet with a tablespoon of the olive oil. Add the cuttlefish; cook for a few minutes then add the ink mixed with the fish stock. Season with salt and let cook for 15 to 20 minutes.

To prepare the candied lemon zest, cut the peel into julienne and add to a small saucepan of boiling water for 3 minutes (it should remain slightly bitter), then drain. Prepare a syrup by boiling the water with the sugar, add the drained zest and cook until translucent (about 5 minutes).

Finish preparing the cream by mixing the drained zucchini and shallots with some of the cooking liquid using a stick blender, and drizzle in the remaining olive oil.

Serve the cream of zucchini in soup plates. Add a spoonful of cuttlefish, a sprig of dill, some candied zest, and rosemary flowers.

Chickpea Galette ★★

Farinata

Almost everywhere, *farinata* is a dish served on its own, although it can accompany aperitifs or be eaten at teatime—or anytime, for the sheer pleasure of it.

Serves 8
Preparation time: 5 minutes
Resting time: 4 hours minimum
Cooking time: 30 minutes

About 5 hours before the meal, mix the flour with 6 cups (1.5 liters) of water in a bowl, using a whisk, until smooth and free of lumps. Leave it to rest for at least 4 hours.
Skim off the foam that forms on the surface and season with salt. Preheat the oven to 400°F (200°C).
If you do not have a copper *farinata* tray, line a baking sheet with parchment paper, oil it lightly, and place in the oven for 5 minutes to heat up.
Pour the olive oil into the mixture and whisk thoroughly. Spread it over the hot baking sheet to a thickness of approximately ½ in. (1 cm) and bake for 30 minutes until it forms a golden crust.
Serve immediately, and pass round a pepper mill so your guests can season to taste.

● Suggested food/wine match
The most classic match is Spuma (a popular soda made of sugar, water, and caramel), or Durin Ormeasco Di Pornassio—Liguria DOC

● Chef's notes
Before cooking, you can embellish the farinata by sprinkling its surface with very finely sliced scallions (such as oneglia), rosemary (traditional in Savona), or with thin slices of purple artichoke.
The result can be good when cooked in an oven, but the best farinata is cooked over a wood fire. The most important thing is to serve it very hot, as soon as it comes out of the oven.

● Did you know?
Farinata is a humble dish that goes back to the ancient Greeks and Romans. Made from chickpeas, it provided an alternative to wheat flour, which was very expensive.

Ingredients
4 cups (1 lb./500 g) chickpea flour
Scant ½ cup (100 ml) olive oil
Salt, pepper

Equipment
1 copper *farinata* tray, or baking sheet
and parchment paper

Ingredients

5 cups (1 lb./500 g) + 1 tablespoon all-purpose
   flour
1 cup plus 2 tablespoons (280 ml) water
½ cup (120 ml) olive oil
3 bunches young chard
½ cup (3 ½ oz./100 g) grated Parmesan
A few sprigs of marjoram
2 cups (1 lb./500 g) ricotta
8 eggs
2 tablespoons butter
Salt, pepper

Equipment

1 deep tart mold
1 pastry brush

● **Chef's note**

*You can replace the chard with purple artichokes
and a little onion.*

● **Did you know?**

The traditional recipe uses quagliata *or* presciseua
*cheeses, but their limited production means that
they are replaced by ricotta these days.*

Easter Pie ★ ★

Torta pasqualina

This pie is a traditional dish—known as "lean"—that has been made at Easter
in Genoa since the Middle Ages.

Serves 8
Preparation time: 40 minutes
Resting time: 1 hour
Cooking time: 50 minutes

Mix the 5 cups (1 lb./500 g) flour, water, salt, and half the oil together
to make a firm, smooth dough. Divide it into six balls, cover with a dish
towel, and let rest for 1 hour at room temperature.
Bring a pan of salted water to a boil. Trim and wash the chard,
then blanch it. Drain and slice it, then mix with the tablespoon of flour,
half the Parmesan, and the marjoram.
Mix the ricotta with rest of the olive oil, two eggs, a pinch of salt,
and the remaining Parmesan.
Roll out the balls of dough into very thin sheets (traditionally there
would have been thirty-three sheets to symbolize Christ's age,
but today to allow for the frenetic pace of modern life, the number
has been reduced to six or eight).
Lightly oil a deep tart mold. Line it with the first sheet of pastry, which
should overlap the edge by approximately ½ in. (1 cm). Brush it all over
with olive oil and lay the second sheet on top. Repeat twice more, taking
care that the layers of dough stick to each other as little as possible.
Spread the chard mixture evenly over the base of the pastry and then
carefully spread the ricotta mixture on top. Make six indentations with
the back of a tablespoon and break an egg into each one, adding a pinch
of salt and the 2 tablespoons butter.
Roll out the remaining balls of dough and cover the pie in the same way
as you did for the base. Once all the layers are in place, roll the edges
of the pie to make a pretty border around it.
Prick the surface with a fork (being careful not to pierce the egg yolks),
sprinkle with olive oil, and bake in the oven at 400°F (200°C) for
50 minutes.
The pie can be served as soon as it comes out of the oven but its flavor
will develop as it cools down.

● **Suggested food/wine match**

Bio Vio, Aimone Vermentino—Riviera Ligure Di Ponente DOC

Fresh Pasta with Pesto ★★

Trofie al pesto

Trofie are pasta in the shape of a corkscrew, typical of the Recco region near Genoa.

Serves 4
Preparation time: 1 hour
Resting time: 1 hour
Pasta cooking time: 3-5 minutes

Prepare the *trofie*.
Mix the flour, water, and a pinch of salt into quite a firm, smooth dough.
Divide it into pieces about the size of a small bean.
Press down gently while rolling each piece diagonally by hand on the counter, to give it the shape of a corkscrew measuring 1 ½ in. (4 cm) long.
Let them rest for 1 hour.

Make the pesto.
Meanwhile, peel the garlic. Wash and carefully dry the basil, removing the leaves by hand from any stalks that seem fibrous. Pound the kosher salt and garlic in a mortar, then add the basil leaves, continuing to press down with the pestle in a circular movement. Incorporate the pine nuts and both cheeses. Add the olive oil in a thin stream, whisking continuously to obtain a smooth, creamy emulsion.

Just before the meal, cook the *trofie* in a large saucepan of boiling salted water. When they are cooked (3 to 5 minutes), drain them, retaining 2 tablespoons of the cooking liquid to thin down the pesto.
Mix the *trofie* with the pesto sauce and serve immediately.

● **Suggested food/wine match**
Lunae Bosoni, Vermentino Lunae—Colli di Luni DOC

● **Chef's notes**
For authentic pasta with pesto, enrich the pasta cooking water with green beans and potatoes cut into small pieces.
To keep your pesto for several days in the refrigerator, transfer to a small glass jar and cover with olive oil before sealing.
Ideally, do not add the cheeses until just before serving.
Basil has a fragile aroma and oxidizes very quickly when it comes in contact with metal. Prepare the pesto in a mortar made of stone with a wooden pestle, if possible; you can use a knife or blender but the aroma will be lost. Also, avoid using Thai basil, as its minty quality is not suitable for this recipe.

Ingredients
Trofie
4 cups (12 oz./400 g) bread flour
2/3-1 cup (220 to 240 ml) water
Salt

Pesto
1 clove garlic
2 bunches European basil
1 teaspoon kosher salt
1 tablespoon pine nuts
1/3 cup (2 oz./50 g) grated Parmesan
1/3 cup (2 oz./50 g) grated pecorino, preferably Sardinian
2/3 cup (150 ml) olive oil

Equipment
1 stone mortar with wooden pestle

Technique
Pasta Dough >> p. 69

Ingredients

¼ cup (²/₃ oz./20 g) dried porcini
7 oz. (200 g) white haricot beans (in the pod)
5 oz. (150 g) peas (in the pod)
5 oz. (150 g) fava beans (in the pod)
1 clove garlic
1 potato
1 onion
2 zucchini
6 cabbage leaves
7 oz. (200 g) green beans
6 chard, endive, or borage leaves
1 carrot
2 tomatoes
3 tablespoons olive oil
Grated Parmesan
Grated pecorino
Pesto (see p. 262)
Salt

Equipment

1 vegetable mill or stick blender (optional)

Minestrone Soup ★

Minestrone

This popular recipe highlights the flavors of spring vegetables, which complement the taste of the pesto.

Serves 4
Preparation time: 20 minutes
Cooking time: 2 hours

Soak the dried porcini in lukewarm water for 10 minutes, then drain and chop them.
Wash and shell the fresh haricot beans, peas, and fava beans (if these are large, peel them as well).
Peel the garlic and chop the clove finely. Peel and wash all the other vegetables and cut them into small pieces. Bring 8 cups (2 liters) of water to a boil in a stockpot, and add the tomatoes for a few seconds so that they will peel easily. Remove with a slotted spoon and take off the skins. Salt the water, then return the peeled tomatoes to the pan, together with the porcini and the rest of the vegetables.
Add the olive oil and cook for 2 hours over low heat.
Serve with Parmesan, pecorino, and pesto.

● **Suggested food/wine match**
Fontanacota, Sciac-trà—Ormeasco di Pornassio DOC

● **Chef's notes**
Once the minestrone soup is ready, you can add pasta or rice and cook according to the packet instructions.
You can also pass the soup through a vegetable mill, or use a stick blender, to give it a smoother texture.

Rabbit with Olives ★★

Coniglio alla sanremese

Traditional Ligurian cuisine features mostly white meat, such as rabbit and poultry, but also, to a lesser extent, veal, lamb, kid, and pork.

Serves 8
Preparation time: 20 minutes
Marinating time: 30 minutes
Cooking time: 1 hour 30 minutes approximately

Ask your butcher to joint and bone the rabbit when you buy it, retaining the head and offal.
Marinate the rabbit pieces in 1 cup (250 ml) of vinegar mixed with 3 cups (750 ml) water for 30 minutes.
Meanwhile, simmer the rabbit's head and offal in 1 ⅔ cups (400 ml) salted water for 15 minutes minimum, over medium heat.
Peel the onions and chop. Finely chop the walnuts.
Pat the marinated rabbit pieces dry and heat in a pan, without fat, so that water still contained in the meat evaporates.
Transfer the pieces of rabbit to a large stockpot with the olive oil and brown them.
Add the chopped onions, unpeeled garlic, walnuts, and herbs; season with salt. When the onions are well colored, deglaze with the wine, then let everything simmer for approximately 1 hour.
Once the offal is cooked, remove it from its stock, and chop it up. Remove the head and discard. Add the chopped offal back to the stock and use this stock to moisten the rabbit while it is cooking.
Add the olives 5 minutes before the end of the cooking time.

● Suggested food/wine match

Maccario Dringenberg, Rossese di Dolceacqua Posaù superiore—Rosse DOC

● Chef's note

Serve a vegetable puree with the rabbit, or roasted potatoes. You can use the cooking juice, without the olives, for flavoring pasta.

Ingredients

1 jointed and boned rabbit with its liver, and preferably other offal
1 cup (250 ml) wine vinegar
2 onions
2 tablespoons walnut kernels
3-4 tablespoons olive oil
8 cloves garlic
1 sprig of thyme
1-2 bay leaves
1 sprig of rosemary
4 cups (1 liter) red wine
20 *riviera* (or Provençal) olives
Salt

Ingredients

1 lb. 5 oz. (600 g) red mullet

4 tablespoons tomato coulis, either store-bought
   or homemade (see p. 44)

½ oz. (15 g) dried porcini

2 tablespoons capers in salt

2 anchovies in salt or olive oil

1 small carrot

1 stick celery

1 onion

Olive oil

1 clove garlic

A few sprigs of parsley

2 tablespoons pine nuts

¼ cup (120 ml) white wine

A handful of fresh bread crumbs

Salt, pepper

Techniques
Anchovies in Salt >> p. 26

Tomato Coulis >> p. 44

Red Mullet *alla Genovese* ★★

Triglie alla genovese

Serves 4

Preparation time: 40 minutes

Cooking time: 20-30 minutes

Prepare in advance.

Make the tomato coulis, if using homemade (see p. 44).

Soak the dried porcini in lukewarm water for 10 minutes.

If very salty, rinse the capers and anchovy fillets under running water.

Peel the carrot, celery, and onion, and chop them. Soften them in a skillet with a little olive oil and add the anchovies.

Peel the garlic, then chop the clove. Wash the parsley and chop.

Finely chop the capers and the pine nuts.

When the vegetables become translucent, add the drained porcini, capers, garlic, parsley, and pine nuts. Deglaze with the wine. Add the tomato coulis and season with salt.

Preheat the oven to 400°F (200°C).

Wash and clean the mullet. Lay them on a baking sheet and cover with the sauce. Sprinkle with bread crumbs and bake. Allow 20 to 30 minutes cooking time approximately (depending on the size). The fish will be cooked once the eyes have turned completely white.

● Suggested food/wine match

Ottaviano Lambruschi, Costa Marina—Colli di Luni Vermentino DOC

● Chef's notes

Choose red mullet rather than sand mullet as they have a better flavor and finer texture. They are recognizable by their dorsal fin, which is colored rather than transparent, their brighter color, and rounder head.

This alla Genovese recipe can also be prepared with other fish such as monkfish, swordfish, red snapper, hake, mackerel, etc.

Octopus *all'Inferno* ★★

Polpo all'inferno

Polpo all'inferno—meaning "octopus in hell"—is the Ligurian name for octopus cooked in boiling water with potatoes.

Serves 4
Preparation time: 20 minutes
Cooking time: 1 hour 30 minutes

Clean and thoroughly rinse the octopus under fresh water.
Peel the garlic and the onion. Peel and wash the carrot and the potatoes. Wash the tomatoes.
Place a large saucepan of water over the heat and add the carrot, onion, garlic, tomatoes, herbs, and the chili, if using. You can also add a cork, as this is thought to help the octopus become tender.
When the water comes to a boil, slowly and gradually add the octopus, and let cook for 1 hour.
Add the potatoes for approximately 20 minutes, or until cooked.
Remove the octopus and potatoes from the saucepan (discard everything else). Serve dressed with a good olive oil and season with salt and freshly ground black pepper.

● **Suggested food/wine match**
Poggio dei Gorleri, Pigato Albium—Riviera Ligure di Ponente DOC

● **Chef's notes**
Choose octopus caught on the rocks. They can be recognized by the double row of suction cups on their tentacles; these should be longer than their heads. Frozen octopus can also be used for this recipe.

Ingredients
2 or 3 octopus, weighing 2 ½-3 lb.
(1.2-1.5 kg) in total
5 cloves garlic
1 onion
1 carrot
2 lb. (1 kg) potatoes
4 tomatoes
1 sprig of rosemary
1 bay leaf
1 chili (optional)
Olive oil to taste
Salt, pepper

Equipment
1 cork (optional)

Technique
Cleaning octopus >> p. 126

Ingredients

4 purple artichokes with their stalks
Vegetable stock (see p. 94)
⅓ oz. (10 g) dried porcini
½ cup (1 oz./30 g) + 1 tablespoon bread crumbs
½ cup (125 ml) milk
2 cloves garlic
A few sprigs of parsley
A few sprigs of marjoram
2-3 tablespoons (1 oz./30 g) grated Parmesan
2 tablespoons olive oil
½ cup (120 ml) white wine
Salt, pepper

Stuffed Artichokes ★

Carciofi ripieni

Stuffed vegetables are very common in Liguria. Zucchini and their flowers, onions, eggplants, mushrooms, and artichokes can all be stuffed for serving with aperitifs or as antipasti.

Serves 4
Preparation time: 10 minutes
Cooking time: 30 minutes

A day ahead.
Prepare the vegetable stock (see p. 94).

On the same day, prepare the vegetables.
Soak the dried porcini in water and the ½ cup of bread crumbs in the milk. Peel the garlic. Wash the parsley and remove the thickest stalks.
Thoroughly clean the artichokes. Remove the tough, outer leaves and cut off a third of the remaining tip. Roll the artichokes on the kitchen counter, pressing down on them to make them easier to open out.

Prepare the stuffing.
Cut the stalks from the artichokes, dry the drained porcini with a cloth or paper towel, squeeze the moisture from the bread crumbs, and chop all three with the parsley and garlic.
Add the marjoram, Parmesan, salt, and pepper.
Fill the artichokes with this stuffing, sprinkle them with the tablespoon of bread crumbs, and place in a saucepan. Sprinkle with 2 tablespoons of olive oil.
Heat to a simmer and then add the white wine, let it evaporate then add a ladle of vegetable stock. Cover and simmer for 30 minutes over a low heat.

● **Suggested food/wine match**
Terre Bianche—Arcana Bianco RLP Pigato DOC

● **Chef's notes**
Artichokes from Liguria are so tender that they can be eaten raw, in salad. Thoroughly clean the artichokes, slice very finely, and season with olive oil, lemon juice, salt, and pepper.
You can also cook the stuffed artichokes in the oven for 30 minutes at 350°F (180°C).

Jelly Tart ★★

Crostata

This is a simple, homely recipe using homemade jelly that is very quick to prepare.

Serves 8
Preparation time: 20 minutes
Resting time: 30 minutes
Cooking time: 30 minutes

Prepare the *pasta frolla* (sweet pastry dough).
Cut the butter into small pieces, soften to room temperature, and mix them with the flour. Add the sugar, the orange flower water or the Marsala, the whole egg and egg yolk, and a pinch of salt.
Mix everything together very quickly so the heat from your hands does not melt the butter too much. When you have a smooth ball of dough, wrap it in plastic wrap and place it in the refrigerator for 30 minutes.

Butter and flour a fluted tart mold. Divide the dough into two balls, one smaller than the other (roughly two thirds to one third). Roll out the largest ball to a thickness of ¼ in. (5 mm). Line the mold with the pastry, trim the edges, and prick the base with a fork.
Spread the jelly evenly over the base of the pastry.
Preheat the oven to 400°F (200°C).
Roll out the smaller ball of pastry to the size of the tart.
Cut into strips ¾ in. (2 cm) wide with a serrated dough cutter. Make a lattice of the strips on the surface of the tart, attaching them firmly to the rim.
Bake for 30 minutes, until the dough is golden brown.

● **Suggested food/wine match**
Bisson, Sciacchetrà Passito—Cinque Terre DOC

● **Chef's notes**
Sprinkle the surface of the tart with slivered almonds.
You can replace the jelly with pastry cream or chocolate cream (see Italian trifle p. 295); with ricotta mixed with sugar, or mascarpone mixed with sugar and eggs, or with rice cooked in milk mixed with eggs and the zest of a lemon.

Ingredients
1 stick (4 oz./100 g) butter
2 cups (7 oz./200 g) all-purpose flour
½ cup (3 ⅓ oz./100 g) sugar
1 tablespoon orange flower water or Marsala
2 eggs (1 whole plus 1 yolk)
Salt
Butter and flour for preparing the tart mold
10 oz. (300 g) jelly (jam), preferably homemade

Equipment
1 fluted tart mold, 12 in. (28 cm) diameter
1 serrated dough cutter (see p. 168)

Emilia-Romagna Marche

Massimo Bottura

It was under the kitchen table, where I used to hide when I was small, that I first discovered I wanted to become a chef. When my mother, my aunt, and my grandmother were kneading the dough for tortellini on the same table, I would feel a sense of profound well-being. Several years later, in response to a strong imperative closely linked to this childhood memory, I abandoned my law studies to devote myself to cuisine.

There is no contradiction between modernity and *terroir*. Modern cooking is the refined expression of a territory. It is often forgotten that tradition is not static, but the result of an evolution.

At Osteria Francescana, we still look at the world from under the table. We are trying to project the best of the past toward the future through a filter of critical thinking, free from any nostalgia. The modern chef puts aside his ego and tries to sublimate the raw ingredients by lovingly handling and examining them, and through study and interpretation. This allows one to realize the essential role that is played by the fisherman, the farmer, or the cheese maker, well before the chef plays his role.

Tortellini with a Creamy Parmigiano Reggiano Sauce

Serves 4

Preparation time: 45 minutes
Resting time: 30 minutes
Cooking time: 35 minutes

Ingredients
4 cups (1 liter) capon stock (see p. 93)

Pasta dough
5 cups (1 lb./500 g) bread flour
5 eggs

Stuffing
7 oz. (200 g) pork
7 oz. (200 g) veal
1 ½ oz. (50 g) sausage meat
1 ½ oz. (50 g) Modena ham aged 24 months
1 ½ oz. (50 g) beef marrow
1 ½ cups (10 oz./300 g) grated Parmigiano Reggiano
2 tablespoons extra virgin olive oil

Creamy sauce
3 tablespoons (50 ml) mineral water
1 cup (7 oz./200 g) grated Parmigiano Reggiano

Prepare the dough.
Sift the flour onto the kitchen counter and make a hole in the middle; add the eggs and mix thoroughly. Knead the dough vigorously for 15 minutes until you have a smooth ball.
Cover it with a dish towel and leave it to rest for 30 minutes. Roll it out as evenly and as thinly as you possibly can.

Make the stuffing.
Chop the pork and veal and brown in a saucepan with the extra virgin olive oil.
Brown the sausage meat separately and add to the pork and veal; finish cooking. Remove from the heat and leave to cool. Add the diced ham.
Mix well and add the beef marrow. Put the mixture through the meat grinder twice and add the Parmesan. Mix well again and set aside.

Assemble the tortellini.
Cut the rolled-out pasta into 1 ½ in. (3.5 cm) squares and place a small spoonful of stuffing in the middle of each one. Dip your finger in a bowl of water and run it along two edges of the square. Fold the dough over to form a triangle and press the edges down gently to close the tortellini. Draw the two bottom corners of the triangle together to form a handkerchief shape. Press tightly to seal.
Cook the tortellini in the stock.

Make the creamy sauce.
In a Thermomix, heat the water to 175°F (80°C) and add the Parmesan little by little. Increase the speed and the temperature to boiling point, then lower the temperature to 140°F (60°C), continuing to mix. Alternatively, heat the water to 175°F (80°C) in a saucepan, then pour it over the Parmesan little by little, constantly whisking energetically.

Pour this creamy sauce into the bottom of a deep plate and place the cooked tortellini on top.

Galette ★

Piadina romagnola

The *piadina* is a very simple way of using wheat flour to make a quick and nutritious snack.

Serves 8-10
Preparation time: 5 minutes
Resting time: 1 hour
Cooking time: 4-6 minutes

Mix all the ingredients together to obtain a fairly firm dough.
Cover with a dish towel and let rest for 1 hour.
Divide the dough into eight to ten balls. Roll them out into 10 to 12 in. (25 to 30 cm) rounds, $1/10$ to ¼ in. (2 to 6 mm) thick, according to your taste (bear in mind that they will become thicker as they cook).
Piadini should be cooked quickly: 2 to 3 minutes on each side over high heat in a cast-iron skillet (a pancake skillet, for example). Turn them over several times.
Bubbles will form on the surface that are characteristic of *piadini*; prick them with a fork so the galettes can cook evenly.

● Suggested food/wine match

Rinaldini, Vecchio Moro—Lambrusco dell'Emilia IGT

● Chef's notes

Piadini can be stuffed with ham, sausage, fresh or melted cheese, or vegetables sautéed with garlic (chard, spinach, mushrooms, eggplant, etc.). They need to be eaten while they are still very hot.
You can add 1 teaspoon ($1/8$ oz./4 g) of yeast or baking soda to the dough to make the piadini *rise a little.*

Ingredients
9 cups (2 lb./1 kg) all-purpose flour
$2/3$ cup (5 oz./150 g) lard or olive oil
1 cup (250 ml) milk
$2/3$-1 scant cup (150-200 ml) water
Salt

Equipment
1 cast-iron (pancake) skillet

Ingredients

1 lb. (500 g) green Ascolane olives
  (or other large green olives)
3 ½ oz. (100 g) lean pork
8 oz. (220 g) veal
1 oz. (30 g) chicken breast
1 onion
1 carrot
1 celery stick
Nutmeg
Olive oil
1 sprig of rosemary
½ cup (120 ml) white wine
2 eggs
¾ cup (4 oz./120 g) grated Parmesan
Sufficient quantity of oil for deep frying
Flour for coating
Bread crumbs for coating
Salt, pepper

Equipment

1 cherry pitter
1 food processor

Stuffed Green Olives ★★★

Olive ascolane

These can be served as an aperitif or as part of *Fritto all'ascolana*, a selection of fried food typical of the region.

Serves 8
Preparation time: 1 hour
Resting time: 30 minutes
Cooking time: 25 minutes

Prepare the olives.
Wash the olives. Remove the pits with a cherry pitter, or by forming a spiral around the pit with a knife. Immerse them in salted water to prevent them discoloring.

Make the stuffing.
Dice all the meat. Peel the onion and the carrot, wash and peel the celery, then chop all three. Grate a little nutmeg.
Brown the meat in a skillet with a little olive oil. Add the rosemary and the chopped vegetables. When they become translucent, deglaze with the wine, and let evaporate. Season with salt and cook for 10 minutes, adding a little water if the mixture seems dry.
Chop the stuffing in a food processor. Stir in one egg yolk, the grated nutmeg, and Parmesan, then season with pepper. Leave to rest in the refrigerator for 30 minutes.

Stuff the olives with small balls of the stuffing or reshape those that were cut into spirals around the stuffing. Beat the remaining egg (the second yolk and the two whites). Heat the frying oil in a deep pan. Prepare three plates: one with flour, the other with the beaten egg, and the third with the bread crumbs. Roll the stuffed olives in each of these in turn, in the same order.
The olives are now ready to be fried in the oil until golden.
Place on paper towel to remove excess oil.

● **Suggested food/wine match**
Umani Ronchi, Vellodoro—Terre di Chieti pecorino IGT

● **Chef's note**
It is becoming more and more fashionable to replace the meat with fish.

Baked Lasagna ★★

Lasagne e vincisgrassi

A variation of baked lasagna typical of the Marche region, *vincisgrassi* is a dish in which rectangles of pasta are baked with a meat and tomato sauce, with added béchamel sauce and Parmesan. The recipe sometimes includes chicken giblets, sweetbreads, or truffles.

Serves 6
Preparation time: 1 hour 15 minutes
Cooking time: 1 hour

Prepare the fresh pasta dough in advance.
Follow the recipe on p. 69. Roll out the dough thinly and cut into rectangles approximately 5 × 7 in. (12.5 × 17.5 cm).

Prepare the Bolognese sauce.
Proceed as described on p.52.

Make the béchamel sauce.
Melt the butter in a saucepan over low heat, sprinkle with the flour and mix to obtain a white roux. Off the heat, pour in a little milk and mix well. Whisk in the rest of the milk until you have a smooth sauce without any lumps. Replace over the heat and bring to a boil, stirring continuously. Let the sauce cook for a few minutes. It should remain fairly liquid, as it will thicken while baking in the oven. Season with salt and a little freshly grated nutmeg.

Cook the pasta.
If the fresh pasta is homemade, precook the sheets before arranging them in the baking dish. Dampen a dish towel and place it on the counter. Prepare a bowl of iced water with a teaspoon of salt and 1 teaspoon of oil for each 4 cups (1 liter) of water; also prepare a saucepan of water with the same proportions of salt and oil and bring it to a boil. Cook three to five rectangles of pasta at a time for 3 seconds, then remove with a skimmer and immerse immediately in the bowl of iced water before they begin to dry. Drain them and lay them side by side on the damp cloth.

Assemble the lasagna.
Preheat the oven to 350°F (180°C). Generously butter an ovenproof dish. Pour in a thin layer of béchamel, then lightly layer the ingredients in the following order (this is the detail that will give the lasagna its texture): a layer of pasta, slightly overlapping, followed by béchamel, then Bolognese sauce, then grated Parmesan, and so on until all the ingredients are used up. Ensure there is enough béchamel sauce in the corners of the dish to prevent them drying out. If need be, add a little water. Bake for approximately 1 hour.

● **Suggested food/wine match**
Umani Ronchi Cumaro—Rosso Conero Coast DOCG

Ingredients
Pasta dough
14 oz. (400 g) fresh egg pasta dough (see p. 69)

Sauce
1 lb. 12 oz. (800 g) Bolognese sauce (see p. 52)

Béchamel sauce
1 stick (4 oz./100 g) butter
1 cup (3 ½ oz./100 g) flour
4 cups (1 liter) milk
Nutmeg
Salt, pepper
½ cup (3 ½ oz./100 g) grated Parmesan

Techniques
Pasta Dough ›› p. 69
Bolognese Sauce ›› p. 52

● **Chef's notes**
If you want to give the sauce extra flavor, add some presoaked dried porcini.
If you want to lighten the dish, replace the béchamel with a velouté sauce (made with stock instead of milk). If you want to use green lasagna, add spinach to the fresh pasta dough (see table, p.79). The rectangles of lasagna can be prepared in advance: they keep very well, raw or cooked, in the refrigerator or freezer.

Ingredients

Chicken stock
1 chicken carcass
1 onion
1 carrot
1 stick celery
Salt

Galantine
1 boneless chicken, 2 ½–3 lb. (1.2-1.5 kg),
  with its liver
Butter
1 tablespoon brandy
2 eggs (optional)
1 calf's foot
½ cup (3 ½ oz./100 g) pistachio nuts
Salt, pepper

Stuffing
3 ½ oz. (100 g) Parma ham
3 ½ oz. (100 g) mortadella
3 ½ oz. (100 g) sausage meat
7 oz. (200 g) ground veal
1 egg
⅓ cup (1 ¾ oz./50 g) grated Parmesan
Nutmeg
2 tablespoons sweet wine (Passito, Marsala,
  vin santo, etc.)

Equipment
1 piece muslin (or a fine mesh dishcloth)
Kitchen twine
1 oval dish

● Chef's notes
*If you want a more sophisticated galantine, clean
a truffle (see veal tartare with white truffle, p. 192),
and dice it finely with the liver.*
*For an even grander version, replace the chicken
liver with foie gras.*

● Did you know?
*This recipe from Bologna dates from the Renais-
sance and is one of the traditional family dishes
served on festive occasions.*

Galantine of Chicken with Pistachios ★ ★ ★

Galantina di pollo con pistacchi

It is well worth the effort to present this eye-catching dish at a summer party.

Serves 8
Preparation time: 45 minutes
Cooking time: 2 hours
Cooling time: 6 hours minimum

Prepare the stock in advance.
Put the chicken carcass into a large pan of salted water with the onion, carrot, and celery. Bring to a boil then simmer for 1 hour 30 minutes. Strain it and put back over very low heat.

Prepare the galantine.
Soften the chicken liver in a saucepan with a little butter. Season with salt and pepper, then moisten with the brandy. Cut it into small dice. If using, prepare the two hard-boiled eggs (cook for 10 minutes in boiling water, cool down in cold water, then shell them).

Make the stuffing.
Cut the ham and the mortadella in small strips. Mix with the sausage meat and ground veal. Add the egg, Parmesan, pinch of nutmeg, and the sweet wine. Season with salt and pepper. Mix well.

Make up the galantine.
Lay the boned-out chicken on its back on the kitchen counter and spread the stuffing over it evenly. Sprinkle over the diced liver and pistachios. Place the hard-boiled eggs in the center.
Roll up the chicken and sew it together tightly. Wrap it in muslin and tie up the ends firmly with kitchen twine. Place it in the pan of stock with a calf's foot and cook for approximately 2 hours.
When you remove the chicken from the stock, put it in an oval dish to cool for 6 hours at least. Once cooled, you can remove the muslin. Meanwhile strain the stock, pour it into a bowl, and cover with plastic wrap. Place in the refrigerator until it has set to a jelly.
Before serving, dice the jelly.
To serve, slice the galantine, sprinkle with a little of the diced jelly and accompany with a salad.

● Suggested food/wine match
Enrico Vallania, Malago' colli—Bolognesi DOC

Cotechino Sausage "In Jail" ★★★

Cotechino in galera

Cotechino sausage has its origins in the Po plain.

Serves 6
Preparation time: 30 minutes
Cooking time: 25 minutes approximately

Prepare in advance.
Make the meat stock (see p. 93), and choose your *cotechino* sausage.

On the same day.
Cook the *cotechino* as recommended by the artisan who made it,
or according to the packet instructions.
Remove the stalks from the spinach and wash it. Peel the onion,
peel and wash the carrot and celery, then chop them.
Soften the spinach with about 2 tablespoons butter and the peeled
garlic clove in a skillet. Let cool, then remove the garlic.
Lay the slice of beef on the kitchen counter and flatten it with a meat
tenderizer. Lay the ham and spinach over it, then place the cooked
cotechino in the center.
Roll up the beef and tie firmly with kitchen twine. Brown in a saucepan
in the remaining butter. Add the vegetables, bay leaves, wine, and stock.
Season with salt, and cook for 20 minutes over medium heat.
When the cooking time is completed, remove the twine, and cut the roll
into slices. Strain the cooking juice to serve with the meat.

● **Suggested food/wine match**
Moro di Rinaldini, Vigna del Picchio Rosso—Emilia-Romagna IGT

● **Chef's note**
*As a variation, you can replace the beef with veal or make it without the
spinach.*

● **Did you know?**
*Legend has it that in 1511, during the siege of Mirandola, a town near Modena,
the inhabitants were forced to use every part of the pig. They therefore created
a sausage made from the feet, flavored with spice.*

Ingredients
⅔ cup (150 ml) stock (see p. 93)
1 *cotechino* sausage, weighing 1 lb. (500 g)
1 piece of beef, approximately 14 oz. (400 g);
ideally a piece of rump steak cut by a butcher
2 ½ oz. (80 g) Parma ham, sliced
2 lb. (1 kg) spinach
1 onion
1 carrot
1 stick celery
1 clove garlic
⅓ stick (1 ½ oz./40 g) butter
2 bay leaves
⅔ cup (150 ml) Lambrusco wine
Salt

Equipment
1 meat tenderizer
Kitchen twine

Ingredients

4 trout (river or salmon)
¼ cup (⅔ oz./20 g) dried porcini
1 shallot
2 lemons
Scant 1 cup (200 ml) olive oil
½ cup (2 oz./50 g) slivered almonds
Scant ½ cup (100 ml) dry white wine
4 sprigs of rosemary
1 tablespoon plus 4 teaspoons butter
Salt, pepper

Baked Trout with Porcini ★

Trota alla montanara

Serves 4
Marinating time: 1-2 hours
Preparation time: 20 minutes
Cooking time: 25-30 minutes

Prepare in advance.
Soak the porcini in a little water for 10 minutes, then chop.
Peel and chop the shallot. Squeeze the juice of the lemons. Clean the trout and marinate them in the olive oil, salt, and lemon juice for 1 to 2 hours in the refrigerator.

Soften the chopped shallot in a skillet with the tablespoon of butter, and add the porcini and almonds. Deglaze with the white wine and let evaporate.
Preheat the oven to 350°F (180°C).
Lay four sheets of parchment paper on the kitchen counter and butter them. Place a trout in the center of each one. Put a teaspoon of butter in each of the belly cavities and place a quarter of the shallot mixture on each trout, finishing with a sprig of rosemary. Season with salt and pepper and close up the parchment paper to completely envelop the trout.
Bake for 25 to 30 minutes, then serve immediately.

● **Suggested food/wine match**
Tre Monti, Vigna Rocca—Albana di Romagna DOCG

● **Chef's note**
Brown river trout found locally are traditionally used for this dish. They are recognizable by the black, red, and violet markings on their skin. Salmon trout (of American origin and much easier to raise) would make a perfectly acceptable alternative for this recipe, which is typical of the Parma hills.

Bolognese Fava Beans ★

Fave alla bolognese

Serves 4
Soaking and precooking time (if dried beans): follow packet instuctions
Preparation time: 20 minutes
Cooking time: 20 minutes

Prepare in advance.
If you have chosen dried beans, soak then cook them according to the
packet instructions.
Prepare the meat stock (see p. 93).

On the same day.
If using fresh beans, shell them. Blanch them in a saucepan of boiling
water for 3 to 5 minutes (depending on their size), and then drain.
If they are very big, remove their outer skin as well.
Peel the onions and chop them. Chop the ham and finely dice the
mortadella. Soften the onion in the olive oil in a saucepan with the ham.
Add the beans and mortadella, season with salt, pepper, and freshly
grated nutmeg. Mix together, add a ladle of stock, cover and cook for
20 minutes over low heat.

● Suggested food/wine match

Francesconi Paolo, Limbecca sangiovese—Romagna superiore DOC

● Chef's notes

*Choose small beans as they will be the sweetest and most tender. The bigger
they are, the tougher they will be. In contrast, the pods of very young fava
beans are good to eat.*
*You can replace the ham and mortadella with precooked pork rind, as is
often the case in Emilia-Romagna. Equally, flavored lard can be substituted,
or* guanciale, *a type of unsmoked charcuterie made from ox cheek.*

Ingredients
2 ½ lb. (1.2 kg) fresh fava beans or
10 oz. (250 g) dried beans
2 white onions
1 ½ oz. (40 g) cooked ham
1 ½ oz. (40 g) mortadella
1 tablespoon olive oil
Nutmeg
1 ladleful of meat stock (see p. 93)
Salt, pepper

Ingredients
7 oz. (200 g) ladyfingers or other soft cookie
Some candied fruit to decorate

Pastry cream
4 egg yolks
1 cup (4 ½ oz./130 g) sugar
²/₃ cup (2 oz./60 g) flour
2 cups (500 ml) milk
1 vanilla bean
A little butter

Chantilly cream
1 cup (250 ml) whipping cream
1 tablespoon confectioners' sugar

Syrup for dipping
Scant 1 cup (200 ml) water
1 cup (3 ⅓ oz./100 g) sugar
1 cup (250 ml) *rosolio* (rose liqueur)
1 ²/₃ cups (400 ml) *alkermès* (very sweet liqueur
  of medieval origin made from spices)

Equipment
1 deep cake mold

Italian Trifle ★★

Zuppa inglese

This is a rich layered dessert whose Italian name translates as "English soup."

Serves 6
Preparation time: 1 hour
Cooking time: 10 minutes
Cooling time: 1 hour 30 minutes

Make the pastry cream.
Beat the egg yolks with the sugar until thick and pale; add the flour.
Stir in the milk little by little and place over low heat, stirring continuously.
Do not allow the cream to come to a boil–it can separate. As soon as it
begins to simmer, remove from the heat and pour onto a baking sheet or
into a bowl. Melt a little butter and spread it over the surface of the cream
to prevent it forming a skin. Cover with plastic wrap and leave to chill in
the refrigerator for approximately 1 hour.

Prepare the Chantilly cream.
Whip the cream (straight from the refrigerator so that it is really cold)
with the confectioners' sugar until stiff. Cover with plastic wrap and put
back in the refrigerator.

Prepare the syrup.
Dissolve the sugar in the water over low heat. When it is completely
melted, divide the syrup between two small bowls. Add the rose liqueur
to one and the *alkermès* to the other.

Brush a mold with a little of the pastry cream.
Dip the ladyfingers alternately in the two syrups and line the bottom
of the mold. Cover them with a layer of pastry cream and continue to
alternate the dipped ladyfingers and pastry cream. Finish with a layer
of ladyfingers. To finish, cover with the Chantilly cream.
Decorate with slices of candied fruit.
Keep cool and serve at room temperature.

⬤ **Suggested food/wine match**
La Stoppa, Vigna del Volta—Emilia malvasia passito IGT

⬤ **Chef's notes**
You can replace the ladyfingers with different soft cookies.
*For a two-color Italian trifle, flavor half of the pastry cream with grated dark
chocolate or cocoa powder.*
If you do not have rose liqueur or alkermès, *replace them with rum, kirsch, or
a liqueur made from fruit or a different flower.*

⬤ **Did you know?**
*This dessert would have been prepared for
the first time by cooks at the court of the
d'Estes—the dukes of Ferrara—in the sixteenth
century. It was probably adapted from a recipe
for English trifle that reached them via commer-
cial exchanges with England.*

Tuscany
Umbria

Valeria Piccini

The Maremma is untamed land compared
to the rest of Tuscany. Its unspoiled nature has
allowed farming and cattle rearing to develop
to a sustainable level that remains respectful
of the environment. So, why look elsewhere?
The ingredients for my dishes grow all around
me, particularly in the vegetable gardens of Caino,
enabling us to be self-sufficient. Among our best
indigenous products, I have a particular fondness
for the Chianina and Maremmana breeds of cattle,
and for pork from Cinta Senese. Game, particularly
wild boar, is also very much part of the local
gastronomic tradition.

I was not formally trained but am self-taught and
have always been passionate about cooking; I have
learned everything from my mother-in-law.
My training as a chemist has made me pay
particular attention to discipline and accuracy,
and has allowed me to understand the importance
of attention to detail and nuances.

My cuisine is modern, but deeply rooted in
tradition. I search for lightness in my cooking,
while retaining the flavors of the past.

Lamb in Sauce

Cut up the shoulder of lamb into pieces without removing the bones. Trim the cutlets (to be cooked later for adding to the finished dish).

Brown the pieces of lamb in the extra virgin olive oil with one clove of garlic and the rosemary. Deglaze with the wine and let evaporate.

Add the tomato paste diluted in water, season with salt, and cook for at least 1 hour over low heat.

Meanwhile, prepare the *crostini* by browning the dry bread in the oven at 350°F (180°C) for 10 minutes. Lightly rub them with the second clove of garlic.

Brown the cutlets in a skillet.

Place some crostini on the base of each plate. Lay some pieces of lamb shoulder on top with a generous spoonful of the sauce and decorate with the cutlets.

Serves 4
Preparation time: 40 minutes
Cooking time: 1 hour 45 minutes

Ingredients
1 shoulder of lamb, on the bone
4 lamb cutlets
Extra virgin olive oil
2 cloves garlic
1 sprig of rosemary
1 cup (250 ml) white wine
2 tablespoons tomato paste
1 cup (250 ml) water
Slices of dry bread
Salt

Tuscany • Umbria

Bruschette and *Crostini* ★

These are Tuscany's most traditional antipasti, found on every table in every season, often accompanied by charcuterie.

Serves 8
Preparation time: 45 minutes
Cooking time: 30 minutes

Prepare the *fettunta* (*fetta unta* means, literally, "oily slice").
Sprinkle the slices of grilled bread with a top-quality olive oil (extra virgin, from the first cold pressing), preferably the new season's oil.

Prepare the *bruschette*.
Peel the garlic and crush half the clove. Wash the basil and thyme, remove their leaves, and chop them.
Peel the tomatoes with a serrated vegetable peeler, or after immersing them in boiling water for a few seconds and then in cold water. Cut the flesh into small cubes and mix well with the crushed garlic, basil, thyme, and olive oil. Season with salt. Rub the slices of grilled bread with the remaining half of the garlic clove. Spread them generously with the tomato mixture.

Make the mushroom *crostini*.
Clean the mushrooms and dice them. Wash the parsley, remove the stalks, and chop. Peel the garlic and chop. Dilute the tomato paste in a small ladle of stock. Brown the mushrooms in a skillet with a little olive oil, the parsley, and garlic. Once the water from the mushrooms has evaporated, deglaze with the wine. Let evaporate. Add the diluted tomato paste; season with salt and pepper and cook for 10 minutes.
Generously spread the slices of grilled bread with the mixture.

Prepare the chicken liver *crostini*.
Peel and chop the half-onion, the capers, chicken livers, and anchovies. Fry the onion in a skillet with a little olive oil; add the capers, livers, and anchovies and continue cooking for 3 minutes.
Deglaze with the wine. Dissolve the flour in a little warm water and stir it into the mixture in the skillet; season with salt and pepper and leave to cook for an additional 5 minutes.
Generously spread the slices of grilled bread with the mixture.

Make the anchovy *crostini*.
Thoroughly drain the oil from the anchovies. Butter the slices of grilled bread and lay one anchovy on each slice.

● **Suggested food/wine match**
La Mozza I Perazzi Morellino di Scansano DOC

Ingredients

Fettunta
8 slices of grilled country bread
(if possible, use bread without salt)
Top-quality olive oil

Bruschette
8 slices of grilled country bread
1 clove garlic
A few basil leaves
A few sprigs of thyme
2 ripe tomatoes
Olive oil
Salt

Mushroom *crostini*
4 slices grilled country bread, cut in half
14 oz. (400 g) mushrooms (button mushrooms, porcini, or other)
A few sprigs of parsley
1 clove garlic
1 tablespoon tomato paste
Scant ½ cup (100 ml) white wine
1 stock cube (or meat stock, see p. 93)
Olive oil
Salt, pepper

Chicken liver *crostini*
4 slices of grilled country bread, cut in half
½ onion
1 tablespoon capers
5 oz. (150 g) chicken livers
2 anchovy fillets in oil
Olive oil
Scant ½ cup (100 ml) Tuscan vin santo
(sweet wine); otherwise brandy, Marsala, white wine, etc.
1 teaspoon flour
Salt, pepper

Anchovy *crostini*
4 slices of grilled country bread, cut in half
8 anchovy fillets in oil
Butter

Ingredients

14 oz. (400 g) stale bread
1 lb. 8 oz. (700 g) ripe tomatoes or
  14 oz. (400 g) canned, peeled tomatoes
1 onion
4 cloves garlic
A few sprigs of basil
2 sage leaves
2 tablespoons olive oil plus extra for serving
4-8 cups (1-2 liters) water or meat stock
  (see p. 93)
Grated Parmesan
Salt, pepper

Tomato and Bread Soup ★

Pappa al pomodoro

This soup is a rustic Tuscan recipe that transforms stale bread into a flavorsome gourmet dish for all the family.

Serves 4
Preparation time: 15 minutes
Soaking time: 4-5 hours
Cooking time: 30 minutes

Soak the stale bread in a bowl of cold water for 4 to 5 hours.
If necessary, peel the tomatoes (after immersing in boiling water for a few seconds and then in cold water). Remove the seeds and cut them in quarters.
Peel and chop the onion; peel the garlic and cut the cloves into thin rounds. Wash the basil.
Squeeze the bread to remove the water. Heat the olive oil in a saucepan and add the onion; when it begins to soften, add the garlic and bread, and let turn golden brown. Add the tomatoes, basil, and sage, and a minute later enough stock or water to cover.
Cook for 30 minutes: the soup should become thick and creamy.
Serve with a drizzle of olive oil and pass the Parmesan and a pepper mill around the table.

● Suggested food/wine match
San Fabiano in Calcinaia, Famalgallo—Chianti Classico DOCG

● Chef's notes
Pancotto is a similar recipe for bread soup, but without the tomato, and with a bay leaf instead of the basil. The soup has a beaten egg and grated pecorino stirred in it to serve.
There is also a recipe for a cold version called panzanella. This is a sort of tabbouleh, prepared with stale bread dipped in water that is squeezed and then crumbled before having cucumber, tomato, red onions, basil, olive oil, and wine vinegar added to it.
The quality of the bread and the tomatoes obviously determine the flavor of this very simple dish.

Pappardelle with Hare Sauce ★★

Pappardelle al sugo di lepre

Tuscany and Umbria have a strong tradition of hunting. During the season, there are numerous village fairs devoted to cuisine that uses game.

Serves 4
Marinating time: 6 hours
Preparation time: 45 minutes
Cooking time: 45-50 minutes

Prepare in advance.
Peel the carrots and onion, wash and peel the celery, and cut them all into large pieces.
Marinate the hare for 6 hours in 4 cups (1 liter) of the red wine, the carrots, onion, celery, herbs, and spice.

Make the pasta.
Roll out the fresh pasta dough and roll it up lengthwise (see p. 69). Cut the roll into slices 1 to 1 ¼ in. (2.5 to 3 cm.) wide. Take one end of each slice and uncoil it. Lay the *pappardelle* on a pasta dryer or on a dry dish towel.

Assemble the dish.
Drain the meat and put it through a grinder. Discard the liquid from the marinade, reserving the vegetables, herbs, and spice.
Chop the vegetables finely and brown them in a saucepan with the olive oil, herbs, and spice. Add the meat and color it well.
Add the tomato paste, let the mixture cook for 5 minutes, then cover with the second liter of red wine. Leave to cook for an additional 40 minutes until the sauce is well reduced. Season with salt and pepper.
Bring a large pan of salted water to a boil and cook the pappardelle for 2 to 3 minutes.
Drain and mix in the hare sauce before serving.

● **Suggested food/wine match**
Col d'Orcia, Brunello di Montalcino DOCG

● **Chef's note**
You can of course replace the hare with any other game: wild boar, venison, etc.

Ingredients
1 lb. (500 g) boneless hare (or rabbit)
2 carrots
1 onion
2 sticks celery
8 cups (2 liters) red wine
2 bay leaves
2 sprigs of rosemary
5 cloves
10 oz. (300 g) fresh pasta dough (see p. 69)
Scant ½ cup (100 ml) olive oil
⅓ cup (2 oz./60 g) tomato paste
Salt, pepper

Equipment
1 meat grinder
1 fresh pasta dryer or clean dish towel

Technique
Pasta Dough >> p. 69

Ingredients

4 oz. (120 g) black truffle
1 clove garlic
A few sprigs of parsley
12-14 oz. (400-500 g) spaghetti
4 anchovy fillets in oil
Scant ½ cup (100 ml) olive oil
Salt

Spaghetti with Truffle and Anchovy ★★

Spaghetti alla norcina

Serves 4
Preparation time: 10 minutes
Pasta cooking time: follow packet instructions

Clean the truffle. Peel the garlic and chop the clove with the truffle. Wash the parsley, remove the stalks, and chop enough for 2 tablespoonfuls. Cook the spaghetti.
Melt the anchovies in the olive oil in a saucepan, using a fork to crush them. Add the garlic and truffle, leave to cook for 3 minutes, keeping the heat low as they burn very easily. Season with salt if needed.
Drain the spaghetti and mix it into the sauce over the heat.

● **Suggested food/wine match**
Rocca di Fabbri, Trebbiano—Umbria IGT

● **Chef's notes**
You can add 5 oz. (150 g) of sausage meat: brown it over low heat in the pan with the other ingredients.
To clean the black truffle, brush it with a small brush, rinse quickly under warm water, and wipe it carefully with paper towel.

● **Did you know?**
Norcia, or Nursia as it is sometimes known, lies in the southeast of Umbria, and is famed for its hunting, for its hams, salamis, and sausages made from the local wild boar, and for its black truffles. Castelluccio di Norcia IGT lentils also come from this region. The title of this recipe derives from the area; pork butcher's shops throughout Italy are now known as norcineria.

Fish Stew *alla Livornese* ★ ★

Cacciucco alla livornese

This fisherman's dish was originally created to make use of less well-known fish that were therefore more difficult to sell. Now all the coastal towns in Tuscany have developed their own version.

Serves 8
Preparation time: 20 minutes
Cooking time: 1 hour 10 minutes

Peel the onion and chop finely. Peel the garlic cloves and crush one clove (keeping the other for rubbing the toast); wash the parsley, remove the stalks, and chop enough for 2 tablespoonfuls; deseed the chili and chop finely. If necessary, peel the tomatoes (after immersing for a few seconds in boiling water, then in cold water). Cut the peeled tomatoes into quarters.
Clean the octopus and cuttlefish thoroughly (see pp. 125-26); cut them into pieces. Clean all the fish (leaving them whole). If necessary, cut the dogfish into pieces. Wash the crustaceans.
Brown the onion in a saucepan with the crushed garlic, chopped parsley, and sage in a little olive oil. Add the peeled tomatoes, the tomato paste, and the chili, leave to cook for 20 minutes. Add the octopus and cuttlefish, cook for 10 minutes.
Add the fish, beginning with the largest and finishing with the smallest to ensure the cooking is even.
Leave to cook for about 20 minutes (depending on the size of the fish), stirring very gently so they do not break up.
Five minutes before the end of the cooking process, add the spiny lobsters.
Toast the slices of bread on a griddle, rub with the remaining garlic clove, drizzle with olive oil, and place the fish on top, taking care not to break up the more fragile fish.

● Suggested food/wine match

Fertuna, Plato Rosso—Maremma Toscana IGT
San Fabiano, Cerviolo chardonnay bianco di Toscana IGT

● Chef's notes

You can add a handful of cleaned mussels 10 minutes before the end of the cooking time.
For a more refined version, remove the fillets from the fish and set them aside. Cook the bones and heads with the tomato and the vegetables then pass everything through a vegetable mill. Cook the octopus, cuttlefish, and fish fillets in the resulting sauce.

Ingredients

1 lb. (500 g) octopus and/or cuttlefish
and/or calamari
2 lb. (1 kg) fish (mackerel, red mullet, redfish,
grenadier, red snapper,
large moray eels, conger eel, bar, or
any rock fish for soup)
10 oz. (300 g) dogfish
16 spiny lobsters and/or king-size shrimp
1 onion
2 cloves garlic
A few sprigs of parsley
1 Thai/bird (bird's eye) chili, or to taste
1 lb. (500 g) fresh, ripe tomatoes or
10 oz. (300 g) canned, peeled tomatoes
2 sage leaves
2 tablespoons olive oil
1 teaspoon tomato paste
8 slices of bread
Salt

Techniques
Cleaning cuttlefish, extracting the ink ›› p. 125
Cleaning octopus ›› p. 126

Ingredients

1 fish weighing 3 lb. (1.2 kg) approximately
  (bass, sea bream, rascasse, turbot, etc.)
2 cloves garlic
A few sprigs of parsley
4 potatoes
4 purple artichokes
4 tomatoes
Oregano
2 tablespoons black olives
1 tablespoon butter
1 teaspoon olive oil
2 tablespoons white wine
1 lemon
Salt, pepper

Whole Baked Fish *all'Isolana* ★★

Pesce all'isolana

Serves 4
Preparation time: 15 minutes
Cooking time: 40 minutes

Peel the garlic cloves and crush. Wash the parsley and remove the stalks.
Peel and wash the potatoes, then slice very thinly.
Wash the artichokes, remove the tough, outer leaves, cut off the tips,
and slice finely. Wash the tomatoes and cut into slices.
Season the sliced vegetables with the garlic, oregano, olives, salt,
and pepper.
Preheat the oven to 350°F (180°C).
Rinse the fish and make two incisions diagonally on each side. Place
the tablespoon of butter and the parsley in the belly cavity.
Lightly oil a baking sheet with the olive oil and place the fish in the
middle. Distribute the diced vegetables around it. Place in the oven.
After 10 minutes cooking time, sprinkle with the white wine. Cook for an
additional 40 minutes (or until the eyes of the fish are completely white),
basting from time to time with the lemon juice.
Serve the fish with the vegetables.

⬤ Suggested food/wine match
Fertuna, Droppello—Adremma Toscana IGT

⬤ Chef's note
You can replace the artichokes with capers, eggplant, or porcini.

Wild Boar Stew ★★

Cinghiale in umido

This recipe is a great classic of Umbrian and Tuscan cuisine, especially in the Maremma area, in southern Tuscany, north of Lazio.

Serves 6
Marinating time: 10 hours minimum
Preparation time: 30 minutes
Cooking time: 2 hours 30 minutes approximately

A day ahead, prepare the marinade.
Peel the 2 cloves of garlic, then chop the cloves. Wash and peel
the marinade vegetables, then cut into large pieces.
Put the meat in a large bowl with the wine and vegetables, chopped
garlic, juniper berries, rosemary, and bay leaf. Leave to marinate for
at least 10 hours.

On the same day.
Remove the meat from the marinade and strain it. Chop the rosemary.
If necessary, peel the tomatoes (after immersing in boiling water for
a few seconds, then in cold water). Peel and chop a third clove of garlic.
Cut the meat into pieces and dip in the flour. Brown in a saucepan with
the olive oil. When the meat is well colored, add the rosemary and garlic,
cook for a few minutes, then deglaze with a glass of wine from the
marinade. When the wine has evaporated, add the peeled tomatoes
and season with salt and pepper.
Cook for 20 minutes then moisten with the stock. Leave to cook
for 2 to 2 ½ hours, until the sauce has thickened.

● **Suggested food/wine match**
Badia a Coltibuono Chianti Classico Riserva DOCG

● **Chef's notes**
This dish can be served with potatoes or polenta.
You can use the rest of the sauce to flavor pasta.

Ingredients
2 lb. 10 oz. (1.2 kg) wild boar (ideally loin)
1 sprig of rosemary
4 fresh ripe tomatoes or
8 oz. (250 g) canned, peeled tomatoes
1 clove garlic
3-4 tablespoons flour
2 tablespoons olive oil
1 $2/3$ cups (400 ml) stock
(meat or vegetable, see pp. 93 and 94)
Salt, pepper

Marinade
2 cloves garlic
1 carrot
1 stick celery
1 onion
3 cups (750 ml) red wine
5 juniper berries
1 sprig of rosemary
1 bay leaf

Techniques
Pasta Dough >> p. 69
Polenta >> pp. 100–107

Ingredients

1 pork loin, weighing 3 ½ lb. (1.5 kg)
2 cloves garlic
A few sprigs of rosemary
5 cloves
1-2 teaspoons olive oil
Salt, pepper

Spiced Roast Pork with Rosemary and Garlic ★

Arista

This is a tasty staple of Tuscan cooking. The ideal way to roast the pork would be on a spit, but it is also delicious when roasted in an oven. Whichever method you use, serve it with potatoes or green vegetables such as Catalan chicory, *cime de rapa* (turnip leaves), Tuscan black cabbage, spinach, or chard, moistened with some of the roasting juices.

Serves 6-8
Preparation time: 10 minutes
Cooking time: 1 hour approximately

Preheat the oven to 400°F (200°C). Lightly oil a roasting pan or ovenproof dish with the olive oil.
Peel the garlic cloves and chop with half of the rosemary. Season with salt and pepper. Spread some of this mixture over the meat.
With the tip of a knife, pierce small holes in the meat; insert the rest of the mixture and the 5 cloves.
Use kitchen twine to tie up the meat, securing the remaining sprigs of rosemary around it (see facing page).
Place the meat in the roasting pan or dish and roast for about 1 hour, basting it with its cooking juices from time to time and turning it over so that it browns evenly on all sides.
Serve either warm or cold, but most importantly it should be sliced very thinly.

● **Suggested food/wine match**
Tenuta San Guido, Le Difese—Toscana IGT

● **Chef's note**
You can replace the rosemary with wild fennel seeds and sprigs of fennel that you can wrap around the roast.

● **Did you know?**
Arista is a recipe for pork roasted with aromatic flavorings dating back to the fourteenth century. The word comes from the Greek aristos meaning "the best."

Florentine Bean Stew ★

Fagioli all'uccelletto

Serves 4
Soaking time: 10 hours
Preparation time: 5 minutes
Cooking time: 2 hours-3 hours 30 minutes

A day ahead.
Soak the beans in cold water for at least 10 hours.

On the same day.
Cook the beans in salted water with a bay leaf and a pinch of baking
soda over low heat (faster cooking can result in them breaking up)
for 2 to 3 hours.
During this time, peel the garlic. If necessary, peel the tomatoes
(after immersing for a few seconds in boiling water, then in cold water),
then chop.
Drain the beans. Fry the garlic with the olive oil in a saucepan. Add
the sage leaves and the beans, cook for 10 minutes.
Add the chopped tomatoes, season with salt, and cook for another
20 minutes.
Serve with a drizzle of olive oil and freshly ground black pepper.

● **Suggested food/wine match**
Col d'Orcia, Sant'Antimo Pinot Grigio DOC

● **Chef's note**
If you use fresh beans from the pod, the cooking time will only be 15 minutes.

Ingredients
1 ½ lb. (700 g) white beans (*cannellini*)
1 bay leaf
1 pinch of baking soda
2 cloves garlic
14 oz. (400 g) ripe tomatoes or 10 oz. (250 g)
canned, peeled tomatoes
2 tablespoons olive oil
2 sage leaves
Salt, freshly ground black pepper

Ingredients

Whole spices for the panforte
½ oz. (15 g) piece cinnamon bark
Small piece of mace
½ teaspoon cubeb (tailed) peppercorns
½ teaspoon coriander seeds
½ teaspoon cloves
½ teaspoon nutmeg, grated separately

Panforte
5 oz. (150 g) candied orange
5 oz. (150 g) candied melon
7 oz. (200 g) blanched almonds
¼ cup (1 oz./30 g) cocoa powder
⅓ cup (4 ½ oz./125 g) honey
⅔ cup (4 ½ oz./125 g) granulated sugar

Polverino
1 teaspoon cocoa powder
1 teaspoon ground cinnamon
1 teaspoon ground coriander

Confectioners' sugar, for dusting

Equipment

1 mortar or coffee grinder
1 sheet rice paper 9 in. (22 cm) wide
One 8 in. (20 cm) diameter tart ring
1 spatula

Panforte ★★★

This is an ancient recipe for a cake from Siena, traditionally prepared for Christmas as an offering to seigneurs and to clergy.

Serves 6
Preparation time: 40 minutes
Cooking time: 30 minutes
Cooling time: at least 2 hours

Reduce the whole spices for the *panforte* to a powder in a mortar or coffee grinder. Add the grated nutmeg.
Cut the candied fruit into small pieces and mix them with the almonds, cocoa, and ground spices.
Mix the *polverino* ingredients together.
Preheat the oven to 300°F (150°C).
Place the tart ring on a sheet of rice paper.
Melt the honey in a saucepan with the sugar and heat to fondant (soft ball) stage. Place a sugar thermometer in the pan and measure 239°F–242°F (115°C–117°C). Once the desired temperature is reached, stand the pan in cold water to stop the cooking process.
You can recognize the fondant (soft ball) stage by dropping a small spoonful of the syrup into a bowl of very cold water and trying to shape it into a small ball with your fingers in the water; the syrup should easily form a soft ball while in the water but will flatten out once removed.
Stir the fondant into the almond mixture and spread it over the rice paper inside the tart ring. Smooth the surface with a spatula, sprinkle with the *polverino*, and bake for 30 minutes.
Leave to cool. Give the *panforte* a shake to remove any excess *polverino*, then sprinkle with plenty of confectioners' sugar.

● Suggested food/wine match
Col d'Orcia, Pascena—Moscadello di Montalcino DOC

● Did you know?
Panforte literally means "strong bread" in Italian, reflecting its spicy and peppery flavors.

Almond *Cantuccini* Cookies ★ ★

Cantuccini

Few meals in Tuscany end without a couple of *cantuccini* to dip into homemade or locally produced *vin santo*, sweet Tuscan wine.

Serves 8-10
Preparation time: 5 minutes
Cooking time: 40 minutes

Ingredients
9 oz. (250 g) almonds
4 eggs, separated
1 vanilla bean or vanilla extract
2 ½ cups (1 lb. 2 oz./500 g) granulated sugar
5 cups (1 lb. 2 oz./500 g) all-purpose flour
1 teaspoon baking soda
Zest of 1 orange
1 tablespoon aniseed (optional)
Salt

Preheat the oven to 300°F (150°C). Toast the almonds for 10 minutes, then chop them.
Whisk the egg whites until stiff. Slit the vanilla bean in two lengthwise and scrape out the seeds.
Beat the egg yolks with the sugar until pale and light. Add the flour, baking soda, vanilla seeds, a pinch of salt, and the orange zest. Mix everything together, stir in the almonds and gently fold in the egg whites.
Increase the oven temperature to 375°F (190°C).
Place a sheet of parchment paper on a baking sheet.
Divide the mixture into two balls and form two sausage shapes 2 in. (5 cm) in diameter.
Place them on the baking sheet and cook for 20 minutes in the oven. As soon as they begin to color, remove them. Cut each "sausage" into slices approximately 1 in. (2 cm) thick.
Turn down the oven to 340°F (170°C) and place the slices on the baking sheet. Cook them for 5 minutes then turn them over and cook for an additional 5 minutes, by which time the *cantuccini* should be nicely crunchy.
Leave to cool.

● **Suggested food/wine match**
Badia Coltibuono, VinSanto—Chianti Classico DOC

● **Chef's notes**
For a chocolate version, replace 2 tablespoons of the flour with 2 tablespoons of cocoa powder.
Store the cantuccini *in a tin to keep them crunchy.*

● **Did you know?**
These crunchy twice-baked cookies traditionally come from the city of Prato, near Florence, and date back to at least the sixteenth century.

Lazio
Abruzzo
Molise

Niko Romito

My region, Abruzzo, has a heritage that's just waiting to be discovered. It has everything: sea, hills, and mountains. There is no doubt that its value is expressed through its products. Identity, research, creativity, food, and *terroir* all come together here. My region has had a profound influence over me—and not only on my cuisine.

My love of intellectual effort and uncompromising research led me to become a chef, and also gave me a mix of uncertainty and pride. But it is above all the desire to create a challenge for myself that drives me. My cuisine is sincere, expressing a strong and clear identity. My inspiration is derived from the agricultural and pastoral traditions and from an extensive knowledge of the produce of the woods, fields, and hills of this marvelous region.

The dishes I cook are also creative and innovative, and I believe that there should be the same link between modernity and tradition in cuisine as there is between the past and the present in all other fields.

Lamb Served Four Ways

Prepare the lamb and artichokes.

Remove the bone from the best end of lamb with a boning knife. Season with salt and pepper and brown in a nonstick skillet in a little olive oil and the thyme for 2 to 3 minutes. Remove from heat, let cool, then cut the meat into medallions 1 in. (2 cm) thick. Clean the artichokes, cut into quarters, and cook them until completely tender in a cast-iron casserole with 2 tablespoons of oil, the rosemary, chopped garlic, and mint leaves. Mix in a food processor, then sieve the mixture to obtain a smooth puree. Using a pastry bag, pipe a generous layer of it onto the medallions of meat. Place in the freezer. When the medallions are frozen hard, dip them in flour, then in the beaten egg, and finally in bread crumbs. Let them thaw in the refrigerator for about 2 hours.

Meanwhile blend the *mostaccioli* with the grape must to obtain a mealy consistency. If necessary, add 1 tablespoon of water. Deep-fry the medallions of lamb in a pan filled with peanut oil.

Make the lamb *tartare*.

Select the leanest pieces of the leg of lamb and chop them finely with a knife. Season them with the lemon juice, chopped thyme, olive oil, salt, and pepper.

Prepare the rack of lamb.

Thoroughly clean the cutlets by removing the thin layer of skin on the bones. Divide the rack into four pairs of cutlets. Sprinkle with salt, and brown in a little oil until they develop a nice surface crust. Chop the almonds and the herbs mix them together. Season with salt and pepper. Coat the lamb with this mixture and finish cooking in the oven at 350°F (180°C) for 8 minutes.

Make the lamb sandwich.

Mix the flour, sugar, eggs, yeast, water, and a pinch of salt in a large bowl; gradually add the softened butter to the mixture. When you have a smooth dough, transfer it to a loaf pan and bake at 350°F (180°C) for 20 minutes. Remove from the oven, leave to cool, and then cut the bread into slices ½ in. (1 cm) thick. Cut these into rounds 2 in. (5 cm) in diameter with a cookie cutter. Dip them in the beaten egg yolks, sprinkle them with sesame seeds, and fry them in a preheated nonstick skillet with about 2 teaspoons butter. Season the ground meat with salt, pepper, and thyme. Form sandwiches by dividing the meat mixture between half the bread rounds; place the remaining halves on top. Place the sandwiches in the oven at 340°F (170°C) for 6 minutes.

Assemble the dish.

Place a hot lamb medallion on each plate; arrange a drop of *mostaccioli* sauce next to each one.

Shape rounds of the *tartare* using a cookie cutter and place them next to the medallions. Finely chop the black olives and sprinkle a few over the *tartare*.

Complete each arrangement with a rack of lamb and a sandwich.

Decorate with a small mint leaf.

Serves 4
Preparation time: 5 hours
Cooking time: 35 minutes
Freezing time: 4 hours

Ingredients

Lamb and artichokes
10 oz. (300 g) best end of lamb
Extra virgin olive oil
1 sprig of fresh thyme
2 lb. (1 kg) purple artichokes
2 sprigs of rosemary
2 cloves garlic, chopped
A few small mint leaves
Flour (for coating)
1 egg (for coating)
Bread crumbs (for coating)
5 oz. (150 g) *mostaccioli* (soft almond and honey cookies from Abruzzo)
1 oz. (30 g) grape must (available from specialty stores or online)
2 ¼ cups (550 ml) peanut oil (for frying)
Salt, pepper

Tartare
7 oz. (200 g) boned leg of baby lamb
Juice of ¼ lemon
2 sprigs of fresh thyme, chopped
Drizzle of extra virgin olive oil
¼ cup (50 g) black olives, pitted, to finish

Rack of lamb
2 racks of lamb, each weighing 14 oz. (400 g)
Extra virgin olive oil
2 oz. (60 g) peeled almonds
2 sprigs of fresh thyme
2 sprigs of rosemary
A few mint leaves
A few marjoram leaves

Lamb sandwich
5 cups (17 ½ oz./500 g) bread flour
2 tablespoons (¾ oz./25 g) sugar
3 eggs
¾ cake (½ oz./15 g) fresh compressed yeast
Scant ½ cup (100 ml) water
1 ¼ sticks (5 oz./140 g) butter, softened
½ cup (5 ¼ oz./150 g) egg yolks, beaten
1/3 cup (1 ¾ oz./50 g) sesame seeds
2 teaspoons (10 g) butter (for frying)
3 ½ oz. (100 g) ground shoulder of lamb
1 sprig of fresh thyme, chopped

Spaghetti *alla Chitarra,*
Lamb and Bell Pepper Sauce ★ ★

Spaghetti alla chitarra, ragu di agnello e peperoni

Serves 4
Preparation time: 30 minutes
Resting time: 30 minutes minimum
Cooking time: 1 hour 10 minutes

Prepare in advance.
Make the stock (from a cube or see pp. 93-94).

Prepare the spaghetti.
Mix the flour, eggs, and salt together until you have a firm, smooth dough.
Cover with plastic wrap and leave to rest for at least 30 minutes.
Divide the dough into eight balls and roll out each one to a thickness of ¼ in. (5 mm). The sheets should be narrower than your pasta "guitar."
Using the rolling pin, press each sheet of dough on the guitar until they separate into spaghetti. Flour them and leave them to dry on a pasta dryer or dish towel.

Make the lamb and bell pepper sauce.
Dice the meat and slice the bell peppers thinly. Finely chop the tomatoes.
Heat the olive oil in a saucepan with the unpeeled garlic cloves and bay leaves.
Add the meat and brown it for 15 minutes, and then deglaze with the wine.
Add the bell peppers and the tomatoes, season with salt and pepper.
Cover and cook over moderate heat for approximately 1 hour. If the sauce seems dry during the cooking time, add one or two ladles of stock.

Cook the spaghetti in a saucepan of boiling water for 10 minutes (or according to the packet instructions, if using dried spaghetti).
Drain and add the sauce and pecorino.

● Suggested food/wine match
La Valentina, Spelt-Montepulciano d' Abruzzo DOC

Ingredients
Spaghetti
4 cups (14 oz./400 g) durum wheat semolina flour
2 teaspoons (10 g) salt
2 eggs, at room temperature
(Alternatively, you can use dried spaghetti: follow packet instructions)

Lamb and bell pepper sauce
10 oz. (300 g) lamb
2 bell peppers
2 ripe tomatoes or 7 oz. (200 g) canned, peeled tomatoes
2 tablespoons extra virgin olive oil
2 garlic cloves
2 bay leaves
Scant ½ cup (100 ml) white wine
A few ladles of stock (from a cube or see pp. 93 and 94)
Grated pecorino
Salt, pepper

Equipment
1 pasta "guitar" (see illustration p. 168)
1 pasta dryer or dish towel

Technique
Peeled Tomatoes >> p. 42

Ingredients

7 oz. (200 g) *guanciale* (cured pork cheek flavored
   with herbs) or pancetta (unsmoked bacon)
4 eggs
½ cup (3 ½ oz./100 g) grated pecorino
   or Parmesan
Pepper
14-16 oz. (400-500 g) spaghetti

Spaghetti Carbonara ★

Spaghetti alla carbonara

The origins of the recipe for carbonara sauce are undetermined, but almost
certainly recent, dating from the end of World War II.

Serves 4
Preparation time: 15 minutes
Pasta cooking time: follow packet instructions

Cut the *guanciale* into matchsticks and fry them in a skillet. Remove
from the heat.
Using a fork or whisk, mix the eggs with the cheese in a large bowl
until smooth and creamy. Season with freshly ground black pepper.
Cook the spaghetti and drain it, but not too thoroughly.
Reheat the cooked pasta in the skillet with the *guanciale*. Combine it
with the sauce in the bowl and mix together rapidly.

● Suggested food/wine match
Sergio Mottura, Civitella Rosso—Civitella of Agliano IGT

● Chef's notes
*This is the most streamlined version of the recipe. A fundamental issue is
whether or not to add an unpeeled garlic clove to the* guanciale *in the skillet and then remove it before serving. There is also debate about whether to
include onions, parsley, egg white, etc.*
*You can replace the pecorino with Parmesan cheese, the egg white with liquid
cream, or the spaghetti with* bucatini *or* rigatoni.
*It is common to find carbonara sauce served with tagliatelle all over the world,
but nothing could be more wrong: tagliatelle is an egg pasta from Emilia that
does not go well with a sauce that is also made from eggs.*

● Did you know?
*This dish might have been named in honor of the Carbonari ("charcoal burn-
ers"), members of a liberal and patriotic secret society of the early nineteenth
century, or simply because charcoal workers popularized it. A further theory
is that it was so named because the large quantity of ground pepper that is
added made the dish appear black as coal.*

Lazio • Abruzzo • Molise

Bucatini all'Amatriciana ★

The name of this dish derives from the town of Amatrice, Lazio, northeast of Rome and near the border with the Abruzzo region.

Serves 4
Preparation time: 15 minutes
Cooking time: 30 minutes

Peel the onion and chop. Grate the pecorino.
Wash the tomatoes; if necessary, peel them with a serrated vegetable peeler (or after immersing them in boiling water for a few seconds, then in cold water). Remove the stalk, core, and also the seeds if you wish, then chop them.
Dice the *guanciale* and brown it in the olive oil in a skillet. When it is nicely crisp, add the chopped onion. As soon as the onion becomes translucent, add the chili pepper and the tomatoes. Season with salt and cook for 10 minutes.
Bring a large pan of salted water to a boil and cook the *bucatini* pasta (according to the packet instructions). Drain and add them to the sauce in the skillet and sprinkle over the pecorino.
Serve immediately.

● Suggested food/wine match
Poggio le Volpi, Baccarossa Lazio IGT

● Chef's note
You can replace all or part of the pecorino with Parmesan, and the bucatini *with spaghetti or rigatoni.*

Ingredients
1 onion
3 ½ oz. (100 g) pecorino
1 lb. 12 oz. (800 g) ripe tomatoes or 14 oz. (300 g) canned, peeled tomatoes
4 oz. (120 g) *guanciale* (pork cheek aged with herbs) or pancetta (unsmoked bacon)
2 tablespoons olive oil
1 Thai/bird (bird's eye) chili, or to taste
14-16 oz. (400-500 g) *bucatini*
Salt

Equipment
1 serrated vegetable peeler

Ingredients

3 ½ oz. (100 g) *guanciale* (cured pork cheek flavored with herbs) or pancetta (unsmoked bacon)
4 lb. (1.8 kg) oxtail and ox cheek (e.g. 1 tail and 2 cheeks)
1 clove garlic
1 carrot
1 onion
A few sprigs of parsley
8 sticks celery
2 tablespoons raisins
2 tablespoons olive oil
3 cloves
1 cup (250 ml) red wine
1 lb. (500 g) peeled tomatoes
1 tablespoon pine nuts
1 teaspoon unsweetened cocoa
Salt, pepper

Equipment

1 degreasing ladle

Technique
Peeled Tomatoes >> p. 42

Braised Oxtail ★ ★

Coda alla vaccinara

This dish originated on the streets of Regola, the neighborhood where most of the *vaccinari*—workers from the Roman slaughterhouses—lived.

Serves 4
Preparation time: 1 hour
Cooking time: 4 hours

Peel the garlic, carrot, and onion and chop them all. Wash the parsley, remove the stalks, and chop finely. Wash the celery and cut the sticks into sections. Soak the raisins in water.
Chop the *guanciale*.
Rinse the ox meat several times thoroughly under running water and cut into pieces. Bring a saucepan of water to a boil. Add the meat and cook for 30 minutes. Drain the meat. Degrease the stock with a degreasing ladle and set aside.
Color the pieces of meat in a large casserole (preferably made of terracotta), with the olive oil and *guanciale*. Add the carrots, onions, garlic, parsley, and the cloves.
When the vegetables become translucent, deglaze with the red wine. Add the peeled tomatoes and 1 glass of water; season with salt and pepper, cover, and cook for 3 hours over low heat. Stir from time to time, adding a little stock if necessary to prevent the mixture drying out. Add the celery and cook 20 minutes more, then add the pine nuts, soaked raisins, and cocoa. Continue cooking for a few minutes.
At the end of the cooking time, the sauce should be quite thick and the meat should come away from the bone easily.
Serve hot, with good-quality bread.

● Suggested food/wine match
Castel de Paolis, Campo Vecchio Rosso—Lazio IGT

● Chef's notes
You can reduce the cooking time for the meat to 1 hour by using a pressure cooker.
The original traditional recipe recommends cooking both oxtail and cheeks together. You can nevertheless prepare this dish without the ox cheeks, or without the cocoa.

Baked Shoulder of Lamb ★★

Abbacchio

Abbacchio is a milk-fed lamb weighing less than 17 lb. (8 kg). This recipe is a typical Roman festive dish, enjoyed at Easter in particular.

Serves 4
Preparation time: 40 minutes
Cooking time: 2 hours

Peel the garlic; chop the garlic clove with the rosemary and sage, reserving a few sprigs and leaves. Peel and chop the potatoes. Preheat the oven to 400°F (200°C).
Lard the meat and add the reserved sprigs of rosemary and sage leaves; place in a roasting pan. Season with the chopped garlic, rosemary, and sage, and salt and pepper. Add the potatoes. Sprinkle everything with olive oil.
Place in the oven. After 15 minutes cooking time, sprinkle with wine, and lower the oven temperature to 350°F (180°C). Leave to cook for 1 to 1 ½ hours, turning the meat and potatoes round from time to time to ensure they cook evenly.

● **Suggested food/wine match**
Falesco, Montiano Rosso—Lazio IGP

● **Chef's notes**
You can add a few onions with the potatoes.
An ancient version of this recipe calls for a sauce made from vinegar, anchovies, garlic, and rosemary, pounded together in a mortar, to be added to the lamb 15 minutes before the end of the cooking time.

Ingredients
1 leg or 1 shoulder of milk-fed lamb, approximately 2 lb. (1 kg)
1 clove garlic
A few sprigs of rosemary
A few sage leaves
4 potatoes
1 slice fat bacon
Olive oil
2/3 cup (150 ml) white wine
Salt, pepper

Ingredients

2 pigeons
1 clove garlic
1 onion
1 carrot
1 stick celery
2 cups (500 ml) red wine
1 sprig of parsley
1 sprig of rosemary
A few sage leaves
A few bay leaves
1 sprig of thyme
Olive oil
1 tablespoon flour
3 tablespoons wine vinegar
3 anchovies in oil, drained
Salt

Techniques
Broiled or grilled polenta >> p. 106
Fried polenta >> p. 106

Salmi of Pigeon ★★

Piccioni in salmi

This recipe is very widespread in central Italy and is an ideal way to soften the strong flavor of game.

Serves 4
Marinating time: 12 hours minimum
Preparation time: 1 hour 30 minutes
Cooking time: 1 hour 20 minutes

Cut up the pigeons. Peel the garlic, onion, and carrot. Wash and clean the celery.
Marinate the pigeon with the wine, herbs, and vegetables for at least 12 hours. Strain the marinade and chop the vegetables and herbs, setting them and the marinade aside.
Brown the pigeon in olive oil in a saucepan. Add the chopped vegetables and herbs from the marinade. Leave to simmer for 10 minutes, stirring frequently.
Mix in the flour and salt then deglaze with the vinegar and some of the wine from the marinade. Leave to cook for approximately 1 hour, basting when necessary with the rest of the marinade.
At the end of the cooking time, remove the pieces of pigeon and place them in a serving dish.
Melt the fillets of anchovy in the sauce, strain it, then pour over the pigeons.

● **Suggested food/wine match**
Di Majo Norante, Don Luigi—Molise DOC

● **Chef's note**
Serve the salmi with slices of bread toasted on a griddle, or grilled or fried polenta (see p. 106).

Scampi au Gratin ★

Scampi gratinati

This is an original recipe by the Roman Ada Boni. Her cookbook *Il Talismano della Felicità* (The Talisman of Happiness) was published for the first time in 1929 and is still considered a definitive reference on classic Italian cuisine.

Serves 6
Preparation time: 10 minutes
Marinating time: 1 hour
Cooking time: 8-10 minutes

Clean the langoustines, then split the shell along the underside and open them up, taking care that they remain in one piece. Marinate in the cognac for 1 hour. Drain them and place on a baking sheet.
Preheat the oven to 400°F (200°C).
Season the langoustines with olive oil, salt, and pepper, then sprinkle with bread crumbs.
Cook for about 8 to 10 minutes, just long enough for them to brown nicely.
Serve them hot, with lemon wedges.

● Suggested food/wine match
Sergio Mottura, Latour a Civitella—Grechetto di Civitella of Agliano IGT

Ingredients
6 ½ lb. (3 kg) medium-sized langoustines
1 cup (250 ml) cognac
Olive oil
1 ²/₃ cups (3 ½ oz./100 g) bread crumbs
1 lemon
Salt, pepper

Ingredients

4 *mammole* or purple artichokes
Juice of 1 lemon
Sufficient quantity of oil for deep frying
Salt, pepper

Deep-Fried Artichokes ★ ★

Carciofi alla giudia

This recipe uses the Roman artichokes known as *mammole*, which are small and purple.

Serves 4
Preparation time: 20 minutes
Cooking time: 20 minutes approximately

Wash and clean the artichokes. Using a small knife, remove the tough outer leaves and cut off the tip, then go round the artichoke cutting off all the dark-colored parts. Next, remove the most fibrous outer layer of the stalk, taking care not to separate it from the artichoke. They will now be ball-shaped, with their stalks firmly attached.
Fill a bowl with cold water and add the lemon juice. Immerse the artichokes in the acidulated water and leave for 10 minutes (to avoid discoloration). Drain them and gently shake them to remove excess water. Roll them one by one between your hands, rubbing them gently to open up the leaves. Season the inside with salt and pepper.
Heat the frying oil to 280°F/140°C and deep-fry the artichokes for 7 to 8 minutes, stalk pointing downward. Increase the temperature of the oil to 320°F/160°C and cook for an additional 7 to 8 minutes.
To make the artichokes crispier, spray a little cold water on the oil's surface; fry for 2 more minutes, then drain on paper towel.
Serve immediately.

● **Suggested food/wine match**
Poggio le Volpi, EPOS—Frascati DOC

● **Did you know?**
This very ancient recipe originated in the Jewish quarter of Rome, hence its name in Italian, "Jewish-style artichokes." Grown in abundance in the vicinity of the city, artichokes were affordable for everyone, even the poorest.

Sweet Buns ★ ★ ★

Maritozzi

These sweet buns are a specialty of this part of Italy, especially during fasting periods such as Lent, when religious prohibitions were strict. The original recipe used olive oil instead of butter.

Makes 12 buns
Preparation time: 4 hours
Rising time: 1-2 hours
Cooking time: 10 minutes

Remove the egg and butter from the refrigerator in advance so they come to room temperature.
Crumble the yeast and dilute it in a tablespoon of warm water.
Mix it with ½ cup (1 ¾ oz./50 g) of the flour and the honey in a bowl. Cover with a dish towel and let stand until the dough has doubled in volume (between 15 minutes and 1 hour).
Mix the dough with the rest of the flour, the egg, butter, salt, and sugar. Add a little water if necessary.
Knead until you have a smooth, supple ball of dough. Let rise in a large bowl covered with a cloth until it has doubled in volume again (between 1 and 2 hours).
Meanwhile soak the raisins in lukewarm water, dry them with a dish towel, and dust with a little bit of flour. Cut the candied orange peel into small pieces. Butter a baking sheet.
When the dough has risen, add the raisins, pine nuts, and candied orange peel.
Knead thoroughly, then divide the dough into twelve pieces. Shape each one into a small oval bun and place on the baking sheet. Cover with a dish towel and leave them to double in volume (between 1 and 2 hours).
Meanwhile, prepare the Chantilly cream (see p. 295), and a syrup, with 2 tablespoons of sugar and 1 tablespoon of water. Preheat the oven to 400°F (200°C).
Bake the buns for 6 to 8 minutes: they should be a nice golden color. Lightly brush with the syrup and put them back in the oven for 1 to 2 minutes so the coating can dry.
Just before serving, split them lengthwise without separating the two halves (see photo), and fill them with the whipped Chantilly cream, then sprinkle with confectioners' sugar.

● Suggested food/wine match
Castel de Paolis, Bianco Cannellino—Frascati DOC

Ingredients
1 ¼ cakes (1 oz./25 g) fresh yeast
2 ½ cups (9 oz./250 g) + 1 tablespoon cake flour
1 teaspoon honey
1 egg
3 ½ tablespoons (1 ¾ oz./50 g) butter, plus extra for the baking sheet
Salt
2 ½ tablespoons (1 oz./30 g) sugar
3 tablespoons (1 oz./30 g) raisins
2/3 oz. (20 g) candied orange peel
¼ cup (2/3 oz./20 g) pine nuts
Chantilly cream, made with 1 cup (250 ml) cream and 1 tablespoon confectioners' sugar (see Italian trifle, p. 295)
2 tablespoons superfine (castor) sugar for the glaze
Confectioners' sugar for dusting

● Chef's notes
You can vary the recipe in other ways by replacing the raisins, pine nuts, and candied orange peel with caraway seeds, and/or the water with milk. Maritozzi can also be served without the Chantilly cream.

● Did you know?
These buns were often exchanged between engaged couples on Saint Valentine's Day, giving them the name maritozzo, *derived from the Italian* marito *(husband).*

Campania

Alfonso Iaccarino

It would not be wrong to say that I was hotel-born, as I am descended from four generations of hoteliers. It was my grandfather Alfonso, a wonderful person, who taught me everything. He loved cooking with the local produce, and when I was small he would take me to visit the farmers to source different products. Pasta, mozzarella, and especially our tomatoes, that grow so well in the Mediterranean climate and the volcanic earth, all symbolize Naples and its surrounding area. Then there is the sea, always present and very important to me because it provides me with great energy.

Terroir is at the heart of my understanding of gastronomy. My cuisine may be modern, but it respects local tradition. This respect also needs to be demonstrated through a change in production methods. For example, on my twenty acres (eight hectares) of land, I have always used organic and biodynamic methods. Mother Nature teaches you to respect the seasons, and above all to be patient. I have learned to listen to her.

Rigatoni Timbale *alla Vesuviana*

(dedicated to Maria Orsini Natale)

Serves 4
Preparation time: 1 hour
Cooking time: 45 minutes

Ingredients
1 oz. (30 g) bread
¼ cup (60 ml) milk
2 oz. (60 g) ground pork
2 eggs
2–3 (10 g) cloves garlic, peeled and chopped
Scant ¼ cup (50 ml) extra virgin olive oil,
plus extra for frying
50 basil leaves
9 oz. (250 g) mozzarella, finely chopped
½ oz. (15 g) onion, peeled and chopped
1/3 cup (2 oz./50 g) peas
9 oz. (260 g) rigatoni
7 oz. (200 g) meat and tomato sauce
Salt, pepper

Prepare the meatballs.
Soak the bread in 1 ½ tablespoons (20 ml) of the milk; squeeze gently. Make small meatballs with the ground pork, the milk-soaked bread, one egg, and the chopped garlic. Season with salt and pepper and fry in a little olive oil.

Prepare the basil sauce.
Blanch 30 of the basil leaves and blend them with the olive oil to make a basil sauce. Strain and set aside but keep warm.

Prepare the mozzarella sauce.
Warm the remaining 3 tablespoons (40 ml) milk and add ½ cup (2 ½ oz./70 g) of the chopped mozzarella. Cook together in a bain-marie, then mix well and strain. Set aside but keep warm.

Brown the chopped onion in a skillet in a little olive oil, then add the peas and sauté. Hard-boil the second egg for 7 minutes in boiling water. Cool and chop finely.
Set aside a few basil leaves for decoration, and then chop the remaining leaves. Preheat the oven to 340°F (160°C).
Cook the rigatoni for 3 minutes. Heat the meat and tomato sauce. Mix the rigatoni with half of the meat and tomato sauce and half of the basil sauce.

Assemble the timbales.
In four individual aluminum molds approximately 3 ¼ in. in diameter and 1 ½ in. high (8 cm × 4 cm), lined with plastic wrap, assemble the timbales: first place half of the remaining chopped mozzarella on the base, then line the sides with the rigatoni and fill with the peas, chopped egg, meatballs, and chopped basil. Top with the last of the chopped mozzarella.
Bake for 14 minutes. Turn out onto a plate and pour over the three sauces: the remaining meat and tomato sauce, the mozzarella sauce, and the remaining basil sauce. Decorate with the remaining basil leaves and a drizzle of olive oil.

Tomato and Mozzarella Salad ★

Caprese

Caprese—tomato and mozzarella salad—is the emblem of Italian cuisine the world over, with the red tomatoes, white mozzarella, and green basil representing the colors of the national flag.

Serves 4
Preparation time: 5 minutes

Wash the basil and remove the leaves from the stalks. Wash the tomatoes.
Cut the tomatoes and mozzarella into slices that are 1/8 in. (3 mm) thick.
Lay alternate slices of tomato and mozzarella on a plate.
Alternatively, cut each tomato into sixths, without slicing all the way through, and place a slice of mozzarella between each segment of tomato.
Season with the olive oil and salt. Sprinkle over a few basil leaves and serve.

● **Suggested food/wine match**
Grotta del Sole, Asprinio D'Aversa—San Cipriano D'Aversa DOC

Ingredients
4 ripe tomatoes
1 lb. 5 oz. (600 g) buffalo mozzarella,
from Campania if possible (2 balls or 1 braid:
see illustration p. 159)
4 tablespoons extra virgin olive oil,
from the first cold pressing
A few fresh basil leaves
Salt

Ingredients

4 ½ lb. (2 kg) mussels
1 clove garlic
A few sprigs of parsley
1 lemon
Scant ½ cup (100 ml) white wine
A few slices of bread
Olive oil for brushing the toasted bread
Freshly ground black pepper

Mussels with Black Pepper ★

Impepata di cozze

This recipe appeared for the first time in *Il Cuoco Galante* (The Gallant Cook) by Vincenzo Corrado, the first compendium of southern Italian cooking, published in 1773.

Serves 4
Preparation time: 30 minutes
Cooking time: 20 minutes

Discard any mussels that have broken shells or that do not close when tapped.
Clean them by scraping any barnacles from the shells, remove the beards, and rinse thoroughly.
Peel the garlic. Wash and remove the stalks from the parsley and chop. Wash the lemon and cut into quarters.
Place the mussels with the peeled garlic in a saucepan over the heat. Once the shells have all opened, sprinkle them with the white wine and plenty of pepper.
Stir, then remove from the heat. Strain off the juice. Discard any mussels that have not opened.
Toast the slices of bread on a griddle and brush with a little olive oil. Serve the mussels in shallow plates or in a large bowl with their juice, the chopped parsley, and the lemon wedges. Pass the grilled bread around the table.

● Suggested food/wine match
Grotta del Sole, Falanghina dei Campi Flegrei, Coste di Cuma DOC

● Chef's notes
Mussels are best during the summer months (when there is no "r" in the month). They should preferably be eaten within 3 days of being harvested.

Spaghetti with Clams ★

Vermicelli alle vongole

Spaghetti alle vongole is one of the best-known Neapolitan dishes in the world. In Naples, *vermicelli* is the name for slightly thicker spaghetti, whereas in the United States and elsewhere it denotes a slightly thinner strand.

Serves 4
Preparation time: 15 minutes
Soaking time for clams: 1 hour
Pasta cooking time: follow the packet instructions

Soak the clams in cold salted water for 1 hour to remove any sand.
Wash the parsley, remove the stalks, and chop 2 tablespoonfuls. Peel the garlic and chop the cloves.
Rinse the clams under running water until no sand remains, then let drain.
Cook the clams in a large skillet with 1 tablespoon of the parsley, the garlic, and olive oil. When the clams are all open, sprinkle with a tablespoon of flour. Stir, season with pepper, and deglaze with the wine.
Cook the pasta in a large pan of salted water, then drain.
Reheat the pasta with the clams and the second tablespoon of parsley.
Serve the pasta with the clams in their shells.

● Suggested food/wine match
Mastroberardino, Nova Serra—Greco di Tufo DOCG

● Chef's notes
It is very important not to overcook clams to prevent them becoming rubbery. You can replace the clams with cockles, razor clams, or other shellfish.

Ingredients
2 lb. 4 oz. (1 kg) clams
1 sprig of parsley
2 cloves garlic
4 tablespoons olive oil
1 tablespoon flour
Scant ¼ cup (50 ml) white wine
14-16 oz. (400-500 g) *vermicelli*
(large Neapolitan spaghetti)
Salt, pepper

Ingredients

¼ cup (1 ½ oz./40 g) capers in salt
1 sprig of parsley
2 cloves garlic
½ cup (3 ½ oz./100 g) black olives
Chili (to taste)
14 oz. (400 g) canned, peeled tomatoes or
  1 lb. 8 oz. (700 g) fresh, ripe tomatoes
2 tablespoons olive oil
8 fillets anchovies in oil
14-16 oz. (400-500 g) penne
Salt, pepper

Technique
Peeled Tomatoes >> p. 42

Penne *alla Puttanesca* ★

Puttana being the Italian word for a "lady of the night," *alla puttanesca* literally means "in the style of a prostitute." This dish does not seem to have existed before 1950. For some, it originated in what were known as the "Spanish" neighborhoods of Naples, where prostitutes were numerous; for others it was created in Ischia, the whim of a restaurateur in search of a quick meal for clients in a hurry; for yet others, it was a Provençale with loose morals working in Naples who made the dish, inspired by ingredients native to her country of origin.

Serves 4
Preparation time: 30 minutes
Cooking time: 25 minutes

Rinse the salt-preserved capers thoroughly in lukewarm water and drain.
Wash the parsley, remove the stalks, and chop 1 tablespoonful.
Peel the garlic and crush. Remove the pits from the olives. Finely chop the chili.
If necessary, peel the tomatoes (after immersing for a few seconds in boiling water, then in cold water).
Fry the garlic in the olive oil in a skillet. Add the chili, anchovies, olives, and capers.
Add the tomatoes and half of the parsley; cook for 15 minutes.
Meanwhile, cook the pasta (according to the packet instructions).
Check the seasoning and mix the cooked pasta with the sauce and the rest of the chopped parsley.

● **Suggested food/wine match**
Tenuta Vicario—Fiano di Avellino DOCG

● **Chef's notes**
A very similar recipe, pasta alla Vesuviana *is prepared in almost the same way, except the parsley is replaced with oregano, the olives are green, there are no anchovies, and there is much more chili!*
You can use capers in vinegar, but the sauce will naturally be more acidic.

● **Did you know?**
Generally, grated Parmesan cheese is not served with this dish.

Neapolitan Beef Roulade ★ ★

Polpettone alla napoletana

This is a traditional gourmet way of making good use of leftover meats and other foods.

Serves 8
Preparation time: 40 minutes
Cooking time: 1 hour 15 minutes

Make the roulade.
Hard-boil two of the eggs, immerse in cold water for a few minutes, then shell them, leaving them whole.
Soak the bread in the milk, then squeeze it.
Peel the garlic and chop the cloves. Wash the parsley and remove the stalks; chop 1 tablespoonful. Wash the basil and remove the stalks.
Slice the provolone cheese very thinly.
Mix the ground meat with the stale bread, Parmesan, pecorino, remaining two raw eggs, parsley, and garlic. Season with salt and pepper.
Preheat the oven to 400°F (200°C). Lightly oil a baking sheet.
Spread the mixture on a sheet of a parchment paper. Arrange the slices of ham over it followed by a few basil leaves, the slices of provolone cheese, and the hard-boiled eggs.
Holding the ends of the parchment paper tightly, and starting at the long edge, roll the mixture away from you into a sausage shape, as you would a jelly (Swiss) roll. Remove the paper and place the "sausage" on the baking sheet.
Bake for approximately 15 minutes, turning the roulade round regularly to ensure it cooks evenly. Then reduce the oven temperature to 350°F (180°C) and cook for an additional 30 minutes.

Prepare the tomato sauce.
Puree the tomatoes in a food processor. Peel and crush the garlic, and soften in a saucepan with the olive oil. Add the pureed tomatoes to obtain a tomato coulis, then add the tomato paste. Season with salt and pepper, and let simmer for 15 minutes. Add the basil and remove from the heat.

Remove the roulade from the oven when cooked. Slice, and serve with the tomato sauce.

● **Suggested food/wine match**
Mastroberardino, Radici—Taurasi DOCG

● **Chef's note**
You can cook the roulade for 10 minutes in the tomato sauce before serving.

Ingredients
Roulade
14 oz. (400 g) ground beef
3 ½ oz. (100 g) thinly sliced cooked ham
4 eggs
7 oz. (200 g) stale bread
1 ⅔ cups (400 ml) milk
2 cloves garlic
1 sprig of parsley
A few fresh basil leaves
3 ½ oz. (100 g) mature provolone cheese
⅓ cup (1 ¾ oz./50 g) grated Parmesan
⅓ cup (1 ¾ oz./50 g) grated pecorino

Olive oil
Salt, pepper

Tomato sauce
14 oz. (400 g) peeled tomatoes
1 clove garlic
2 tablespoons olive oil
1 tablespoon tomato paste
A few basil leaves
Salt, pepper

Technique
Peeled Tomatoes >> p. 42

Ingredients

1 rabbit, weighing 3-4 lb. (1.2-1.5 kg),
  jointed (your butcher can do this)
1 cup (250 ml) vinegar
2 tablespoons olive oil
1 bulb garlic
1 cup (250 ml) white wine
A few sprigs of parsley
A few sprigs of marjoram
A few sprigs of thyme
14 oz. (400 g) peeled tomatoes or
  1 lb. 8 oz. (700 g) fresh, ripe tomatoes
1 Thai/bird (bird's eye) chili, or to taste
1 cup (250 ml) stock (see p. 93)
Salt

Technique
Peeled tomatoes >> p. 42

Braised Rabbit with Tomatoes and Herbs ★★

Coniglio all'ischitana

Serves 4
Preparation time: 20 minutes
Maceration time: 30 minutes
Cooking time: 1 hour 15 minutes

Add the vinegar to 8 cups (2 liters) of water and macerate the rabbit pieces in this for approximately 30 minutes, then drain and pat them dry. Brown the pieces of rabbit in the olive oil in a saucepan with the whole bulb of garlic.
Deglaze with the wine and leave to cook for 15 minutes.
Meanwhile wash the parsley, remove the stalks, and chop. Chop the other herbs. If necessary, skin the tomatoes (after immersing for a few seconds in boiling water, then in cold water).
Add the peeled tomatoes, the chopped herbs, and the chili to the rabbit and season with salt.
Cook for a further 45 minutes, basting with the stock if needed.
Serve the rabbit with the sauce and with the garlic cloves, which will be meltingly soft by now.

● Suggested food/wine match
Tenuta Vicario, Aglianico—Campania IGT

● Chef's notes
Do not try to brown more than two or three pieces of rabbit at a time, to allow them to color evenly on all sides.
Serve the rabbit with homemade fries, as is the tradition in Ischia.
Use any leftover sauce for flavoring pasta: bucatini or penne liscie, for example.

Octopus *alla Luciana* ★★

Polpi alla luciana

The Luciani are the inhabitants of Santa Lucia—a district of Naples—who were once renowned for fishing octopus.

Serves 4
Preparation time: 30 minutes
Cooking time: 1 hour 30 minutes

Peel the garlic and chop. Wash the parsley, remove the stalks, and chop 1 tablespoonful.
Thoroughly clean the octopus (see p. 126). Put the octopus in a saucepan with the olive oil, chili, oregano, garlic, and the chopped parsley.
Lay a piece of parchment paper on top, then place a lid on the pan.
Cook for 30 minutes without lifting the lid.
Meanwhile, peel the tomatoes if necessary (after immersing for a few seconds in boiling water, then in cold water).
Add them to the saucepan with the capers and olives, and leave to cook for 1 hour longer.

● Suggested food/wine match

Mastroberardino, Riadici—Fiano di Avellino DOCG

● Chef's notes

Serve this dish with bread, either fresh or grilled.
You can also use the recipe as a sauce for linguine.

Ingredients
2 lb. 8 oz. (1.2 kg) baby octopus
2 cloves garlic
1 sprig of parsley
Olive oil
1 Thai/bird (bird's eye) chili, or to taste
½ teaspoon oregano
14 oz. (400 g) peeled tomatoes or
1 lb. 8 oz. (700 g) fresh ripe tomatoes
1 oz. (30 g) small capers
(the best are from Pantelleria)
1 ¾ oz. (50 g) black olives
(the best are from Gaeta)
Salt

Techniques
Cleaning octopus ›› p. 126
Peeled Tomatoes ›› p. 42

Ingredients

12 shrimp
1 carrot
1 onion
A few sprigs of parsley
2 tablespoons olive oil
Thai/bird (bird's eye) chili (to taste) or pepper
1 cup (250 ml) white wine
Salt

Technique
Candied Tomatoes >> p. 46

Shrimp *alla Vesuviana* ★

Gamberi alla vesuviana

Serves 4
Preparation time: 15 minutes
Cooking time: 20 minutes

Rinse the shrimp in cold water and wipe dry with paper towel.
Wash and peel the carrot and onion, and chop. Wash the parsley, remove the stalks, and chop.
Soften the carrot and onion in a skillet with the olive oil and chili (or pepper).
Add the shrimp and let them color.
Add the parsley, season with salt, and deglaze with the wine.
Cook for an additional 5 to 8 minutes (depending on the size of the shrimp) and serve.

● **Suggested food/wine match**
Grotta del Sole, Lacryma Christi bianco del Vesuvio DOC

● **Chef's notes**
Add a few candied tomatoes (see p. 46) at the same time as the chopped parsley. You can also use this recipe as a sauce for linguine.

Eggplant *Parmigiana* ★

Parmigiana di melanzane

Serves 6
Preparation time: 1 hour
Resting time: 1 hour
Cooking time: 45 minutes

Cut the eggplant into slices approximately ¼ in. (5 mm) thick, put them in a colander, and sprinkle with kosher salt. Let drain for approximately 1 hour. (This is not necessary if the eggplants are very fresh.) Rinse them and then dry thoroughly.
Fry them in oil in a skillet and then place on paper towel.
Peel the tomatoes if necessary (after immersing for a few seconds in boiling water, then in cold water). Prepare a Neapolitan tomato sauce using the tomatoes, onion, basil (reserving a little for layering later on), and parsley (see p. 51).
Preheat the oven to 350°F (180°C). Lightly oil a baking sheet.
Cut the mozzarella into thin slices.
Spread 1 tablespoon of tomato sauce on the base of the serving dish, place a layer of eggplant slices on top, then a few slices of mozzarella. Sprinkle with Parmesan and a few chopped basil leaves. Continue layering the ingredients in this order until they are all used up.
Finish with a layer of tomato sauce sprinkled with Parmesan.
Place in the oven for approximately 45 minutes. Serve hot or cold.

● **Suggested food/wine match**

Mastroberardino, Lacrimarosa—Campania IGT

● **Chef's notes**

You can prepare a lighter version of eggplant parmigiana *by roasting the eggplant, or a richer version with deep-fried eggplant coated in egg and bread crumbs (as in the original recipe).*
You can also replace the eggplants with zucchini.
This recipe should not be confused with eggplants alla parmigiana, *a completely different recipe that is typical of Emilia-Romagna.*

Ingredients
3 lb. 5 oz. (1.5 kg) eggplants
Frying oil
1 lb. 12 oz. (800 g) peeled tomatoes or
3 lb. 5 oz. (1.5 kg) fresh ripe tomatoes
1 onion
A few basil leaves (for the
Neapolitan sauce and for layering)
A few parsley leaves
3 balls mozzarella, weighing
approximately 4 oz. (125 g) each
Scant cup (5 ¼ oz./150 g) grated Parmesan
Kosher salt
Salt

Techniques
Neapolitan Tomato Sauce >> p. 51
Peeled Tomatoes >> pp. 42

Ingredients

Pasta frolla dough
1 ¼ sticks (5 ¼ oz./150 g) butter
3 cups (10 oz./300 g) cake flour
¾ cup (5 oz./150 g) sugar
1 whole egg plus 2 egg yolks
Salt

Filling
10 oz. (300 g) soft wheat
Scant 1 cup (200 ml) milk
⅓ stick (1 ½ oz./40 g) butter
1 cup (7 oz./200 g) sugar
1 pinch of cinnamon powder
1 vanilla bean
1 lemon
3 ½ oz. (100 g) mixed candied peel
5 eggs
1 ¾ cups (14 oz./400 g) ricotta
  (preferably sheep milk)
1 tablespoon orange flower water
1 tablespoon confectioners' sugar

Equipment

1 tart mold 10 in. (24 cm) in diameter
1 serrated dough cutter (see p. 168)

● Chef's notes

It is increasingly common to find canned pre-cooked wheat for sale in Italian grocers, made specifically for this recipe (there is even often a photo of the tart on the can).
This dish can also be made with cooked rice (as in Benevento), with barley, or with other cereals.

● Did you know?

Pasta frolla forms the basic tart shell in Italy. It is the equivalent of shortcrust pastry; here a sweetened version is used.
In the version of this tart to be found on the Sorrento coast, pastry cream is added to the filling.

Easter Tart ★ ★ ★

Pastiera pasquale

This cake is associated with Easter, and its recipe varies according to family traditions and where it is made.

Serves 8
Preparation time: 1 hour
Soaking time: 10-12 hours
Resting time: 20 minutes
Cooking time: 1 hour 30 minutes

A day ahead.
Soak the wheat for 10 to 12 hours in water.
Drain, then cook in fresh water for 45 minutes over low heat. Drain again.

Make the *pasta frolla* dough.
Remove the butter from the refrigerator in advance so that it is at room temperature, then dice it. Rub the butter into the flour with a little salt until the mixture resembles fine bread crumbs. Sprinkle in the sugar and combine. Add the whole egg and the two yolks; work together quickly and lightly until the dough is evenly mixed and forms a ball. Cover with plastic wrap and let rest for 20 minutes in the refrigerator.

Prepare the filling.
Meanwhile, place the cooked wheat in a saucepan with the milk, butter, sugar, cinnamon, and the vanilla bean split in two lengthwise, its seeds scraped out and also added.
Cook for 10 minutes, and let the mixture cool.
Wash the lemon, peel it, and chop the peel finely. Dice the candied peel.
Separate the eggs and whisk the whites until stiff.
Mix the ricotta with the egg yolks, lemon peel, orange flower water, and candied peel; fold in the egg whites and lastly the cooked wheat.
Preheat the oven to 350°F (180°C).
Butter a 10 in. (24 cm) tart mold, and line the base with parchment paper. Using your fingers, spread three quarters of the *pasta frolla* dough over the base and sides of the mold. Fill the dough case with the wheat mixture and smooth over the surface.
Spread out the remainder of the dough on the kitchen counter and cut strips ½ in. (1 cm) in width with a serrated dough cutter. Form a lattice over the tart.
Bake for approximately 1 hour until the tart is a nice amber color, then let cool (1 day would be ideal) before sprinkling with confectioners' sugar to serve.

● Suggested food/wine match

Villa Matilde, Eleusi Passito IGT

Rum Baba ★ ★ ★

Babà

The rum baba is originally from Lorraine in France and dates from the eighteenth century. It was brought to Naples by French chefs and became a popular Neapolitan specialty. It was named in honor of Ali Baba from the tale *One Thousand and One Nights*.

Makes 12 babas
Preparation time: 30 minutes
Rising time: 2 hours 30 minutes
Cooking time: 30 minutes

Prepare the baba dough.
Remove the butter from the refrigerator so that it is at room temperature, then work it with a spatula until it is soft.
Dissolve the yeast in the milk in a bowl and stir in ½ cup (1 ¾ oz./50 g) of the flour.
Cover with a dish towel and let the dough rise for 1 hour. Beat the eggs with the sugar and mix into the softened butter, along with the zest of 1 lemon and a pinch of salt.
Put the rest of the flour in a large bowl, make a well in the center, and mix in the risen dough and egg mixture. Knead thoroughly until you have a smooth, elastic dough.
Butter and flour twelve dariole molds (truncated, cone-shape molds). Half fill them with the dough, and leave to rise until the dough has doubled in volume (1 hour 30 minutes approximately).
Toward the end of this time, preheat the oven to 350°F (180°C).
When the dough has risen again, bake the babas for approximately 20 minutes; test the cooking by inserting a wooden toothpick, which should emerge dry.
Unmold them and cover with a dish towel.

Make the syrup.
Boil the water with the sugar and the zest of the orange and lemon. Strain and add the rum. Immediately immerse the babas in the rum syrup, remove, and let cool on a rack.

Make an apricot glaze.
Melt the jelly in 3 tablespoons of hot water. Brush the babas generously with this glaze. Serve with Chantilly cream and pass round the bottle of rum for diners to add for themselves.

● Chef's notes
If you have prepared the babas in advance, keep them in the fridge. Do not add the Chantilly cream until they are to be served.
You can replace the rum in the recipe with limoncello, a lemon liqueur that is typical of the region.

Ingredients
Babas
3 ½ tablespoons (1 ¾ oz./50 g) butter
1 ⅔ tablespoons (1 oz./25 g) fresh yeast
2 tablespoons milk
3 cups (10 oz./300 g) cake flour
5 eggs
2 tablespoons (1 oz./25 g) sugar
Zest of 1 lemon
Salt

Syrup
Scant ¼ cup (50 ml) water
1 cup (7 oz./200 g) sugar
Zest of 1 orange
Zest of 1 lemon
Scant ¼ cup (50 ml) rum

Apricot glaze
5 tablespoons apricot jelly
3 tablespoons hot water

Butter and flour for preparing the dariole molds
Generous quantity of Chantilly cream for serving
Generous quantity of rum for serving

Equipment
Twelve 2 in. (5 cm) diameter dariole
(truncated cone) molds
1 cooling rack
1 pastry brush

● Did you know?
This dessert is now so anchored in Neapolitan tradition that the word "baba" is used as a synonym for "beautiful."

Calabria

Gaetano Alia

Calabria yields an abundance of natural produce that forms part of a well-defined local culture: beans and lentils from Mormanno; bottarga (pressed tuna roe) and tuna from Pizzo Calabro; bergamot, cultivated between Villa San Giovanni and Gioiosa Ionica; cedars in the Cosenza region; red onions from Tropea, etc. All of this exceptional produce, when handled with skill, allows marvelously colorful, aromatic dishes to be created.

Of course, all good cooking must respect the seasons. My culinary creations are anchored in the local *terroir* and linked to tradition. I have tried to lighten these dishes by adopting a quicker method of cooking.

A cuisine comprises a range of experiments perfected over the course of several millennia. In Calabria, the Greeks, the Arabs, the Albanians, as well as others, have all left their mark on the local gastronomy. We should make use of our historical memory to create modern versions of traditional dishes. The exchange with other culinary traditions is of prime importance to me.

Tripoline Pasta with Salt Cod and Crushed Green Olives

Make the sauce.
Finely chop the onions and bell peppers. Heat the olive oil in a skillet large enough to eventually take the cooked pasta, and soften the chopped onions and bell peppers. Add the salt cod and cook for a few minutes.

Add the cherry tomatoes and cook for another 10 minutes. When the sauce is almost cooked, add the olives and chili, if using. Continue cooking the sauce, and then flavor with the basil and mint.

Prepare the flavored bread crumbs.
Mix the bread crumbs with your choice of finely chopped fresh herbs. Lightly toast the breadcrumb mixture in a small skillet for a few minutes, making sure it does not burn.

Prepare the pasta and assemble the dish.
Cook the pasta al dente in plenty of salted water. Drain and add to the sauce in the skillet. Heat through, then sprinkle with the herb and breadcrumb mixture. Serve immediately.

373

Serves 4

Preparation time: 20 minutes
Cooking time: 20 minutes

Ingredients
14 oz. (400 g) salt cod, presoaked in water and cut into small pieces
14 oz. (400 g) *tripoline* pasta
1 onion (preferably a white onion from Castrovillari or a red onion from Tropea)
1 small green bell pepper
1 small red bell pepper
1/3 cup (75 ml) extra virgin olive oil
14 oz. (400 g) cherry tomatoes, peeled and chopped
1/3 cup (2 ½ oz./70 g) crushed green olives or pitted black olives in salt
1 chili (optional)
A few small basil and mint leaves
1 cup (2 oz./50 g) fresh bread crumbs
A selection of fresh herbs (e.g. parsley, basil, mint, fresh oregano, thyme, wild fennel, chives, lemon verbena), finely chopped
Salt

Ingredients

1 cup (250 ml) olive oil
Hot dried chilies (to taste)

● **Chef's note**
Chop the chilies if you want the oil to turn spicy more quickly.

● **Did you know?**
Chili oil is known as "holy oil" (olio santo) in the southern part of the country, where the process of macerating the chilies in oil is called "sanctification"!

Chili Oil ★

Olio santo

Use this spicy oil to enhance the flavor of a variety of breads, pasta, pizza, and sauces.

Makes 1 cup (250 ml) oil
Preparation time: 5 minutes
Maceration time: 3 weeks minimum

Remove the stalks from the chilies; put them in a glass container, preserving jar, or bottle.
Cover with the olive oil and leave to macerate for a minimum of 3 weeks, in a cool, dry place away from the light.

Ingredients

1 eggplant
Fresh, strong chilies (to taste)
1 yellow and 1 red bell pepper
2 green tomatoes
2 oz. (50 g) button mushrooms
1 clove garlic
1 stick celery
1 cup (250 ml) olive oil
1 tablespoon kosher salt
Salt

Chili Relish ★★

Piccantino

Piccantino is a very spicy chili spread found in Calabrian grocery stores, called *bomba* (bomb).

Makes one 8 oz. (250 g) jar
Preparation time: 5 minutes
Resting time: 1 hour
Maceration time: 4 weeks

Wash, then cut the eggplant into ¼ in. (5 mm) slices. Place in a colander, cover them with the kosher salt, and leave for at least 1 hour. Rinse and dry on paper towel.
Chop the chilies.
Wash and peel the vegetables. Dice them finely (¼ in./5 mm cubes).
Mix and season them with plenty of salt and chopped chili.
Pour the mixture into a glass jar. Cover with a weight and leave for 3 weeks in a cool, dry place away from the light.
Look at them every week and remove any water that has appeared by tipping the jar but without removing the weight.
At the end of the three weeks, remove the weight, carefully pour off any remaining water, and cover with olive oil. Leave to macerate for an additional week.

● **Chef's notes**
Use this spicy mixture for flavoring crostini and pasta, or to accompany meat and fish.
For a quicker result, you can use vegetables preserved in oil (eggplant, artichokes, dried tomatoes, mushrooms, etc.) and mix them with Thai/bird (bird's eye) chili to taste.

Escarole (Endive) Pie ★★

Pitta di scarola

In Calabria, pizza is called *pitta*. In contrast to Neapolitan pizza, the pastry encloses the filling in many recipes, such as this one.

Serves 8
Preparation time: 15 minutes
Cooking time: 30 minutes

Prepare the pizza dough (see p. 31), and let it rise for 4 to 8 hours.
Meanwhile, soak the raisins in water then drain them.
If necessary, rinse the capers to remove excess salt. Peel and crush the garlic. Crush the chili. Grate the provolone.
Clean the escarole (endive), then blanch it for 7 minutes in boiling water. Drain thoroughly and chop coarsely.
Return the escarole to a saucepan and soften with 1 tablespoon of the olive oil, the garlic, and the chili. Season with salt. Add the anchovies, olives, capers, raisins, oregano, and provolone.
Preheat the oven to 400°F (200°C).
Once the pizza dough has risen, divide it into two. Spread it into two rounds of the same diameter (approximately 16 in./40 cm). Lightly oil a deep tart mold with the remaining olive oil.
Line the bottom and sides with one of the two rounds. Pour the escarole mixture into the tart mold, and cover with the second disc. Trim off the excess pastry then seal the edges by pressing them together with your fingers. Prick the surface of the pie in several places with a fork. Bake the pie for 30 minutes. Let cool a little before serving.

● **Suggested food/wine match**
Librandi, Labella Bianco—Calabria IGT

Ingredients
1 quantity pizza dough (see p. 31)
1 lb. 12 oz. (800 g) escarole (endive)
1 tablespoon raisins
1 tablespoon capers in salt
2 cloves garlic
1 Thai/bird (bird's eye) chili
5 oz. (150 g) provolone cheese
1 ½ tablespoons olive oil
1 oz. (30 g) anchovy fillets in oil
¼ cup (2 oz./50 g) black olives, pits removed
1 tablespoon oregano
Salt

Equipment
1 deep tart mold 11 in. (26 cm) in diameter

Technique
Pizza Dough >> p. 31

Ingredients

Macaroni

4 cups (14 oz./400 g) durum wheat semolina flour
2 eggs
½–⅔ cup (120-150 ml) lukewarm water
Salt

Ragout

1 lb. (500 g) pork (chine)
4 oz. (100 g) sausage meat
1 clove garlic
2 onions
A few sprigs of parsley
A few basil leaves
1 stick celery
Thai/bird (bird's eye) chili (to taste)
2 oz. (60 g) ricotta
14 oz. (400 g) peeled tomatoes or 1 lb. 8oz. (700 g) fresh, ripe tomatoes
1 tablespoon olive oil
3 cloves
1 teaspoon fennel seeds
½ cup (120 ml) red wine
1 tablespoon tomato paste
1 bay leaf
Salt

Equipment

1 knitting needle

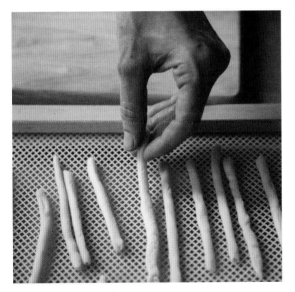

Hand-Cut Macaroni with Pork Ragout ★★★

Maccheroni al ferretto con ragù di maiale

There are several traditional forms of pasta in Calabria. Among the most common is *maccarruni* (macaroni), which can also be called *scialatielli, fusilli lunghi*, or *fileja*, depending on the area (see pp. 162–64).

Serves 4
Preparation time: 1 hour
Resting time: 30 minutes
Cooking time: 1 hour 30 minutes

Prepare the macaroni.
Pour the flour onto the counter or into a bowl; in the center, lightly mix the whole eggs, lukewarm water, and salt. Gradually incorporate the flour, using your fingers or a fork, being careful not to let the mixture overflow.
When all the flour is incorporated, knead the pastry as firmly and thoroughly as possible for 10 to 15 minutes, until it is very smooth. Cover in plastic wrap and let rest for 30 minutes.
Shape the pastry into long sausage shapes of less than ½ in. (1 cm) diameter by rolling them with the palm of your hand. Cut them into pieces 2 to 3 in. (6 to 8 cm) long.
Thread one onto a knitting needle and roll it backward and forward, pressing down with the palms of your hands until it is long and thin. Gently remove the needle. You should now have a hollow tube. Place on a dry cloth, then repeat until you have shaped all the pieces of pasta into macaroni.

Make the ragout.
Peel and chop the garlic. Peel and finely chop the onions.
Wash the parsley, remove the stalks, and chop. Wash the basil leaves, and the celery, and chop them. Chop or crumble the chili. Grate the ricotta.
If necessary, peel the tomatoes (after plunging in boiling water for a few seconds, then in cold water).
Cut the meat into small pieces. Sweat without letting it color in a saucepan with the olive oil, the sausage meat, cloves, and fennel seeds. Add the chopped onions, celery, garlic, and parsley, and continue to cook gently. Deglaze with the wine. Add the peeled tomatoes, the tomato paste, basil, bay leaf, and the chili. Season with salt and let simmer for approximately 1 hour.

Boil a saucepan of salted water and cook the macaroni for 3 to 4 minutes. Combine with the sauce and the grated ricotta.

● **Suggested food/wine match**
Odoardi, Terra Damia—Calabria IGT

Ingredients

1 quantity Bolognese sauce (see p. 52)
1 lb. (500 g) rigatoni
5 oz. (150 g) provolone cheese
2 eggplants
Sufficient quantity of oil for deep frying
½ cup (3 ½ oz./100 g) cooked peas
1 teaspoon olive oil, for oiling mold
½ cup (3 ½ oz./100 g) grated Parmesan
2 tablespoons kosher salt
Salt, pepper

Equipment

1 deep tart mold

Technique
Bolognese Sauce >> p. 52

Baked Rigatoni Gratin ★

Rigatoni al forno

Recipes for baked pasta are very popular in Italy. They make substantial, one-course dishes that can be prepared in advance, and also provide a good way of using up leftover pasta, ragout, etc.

Serves 4
Preparation time: 1 hour
Resting time: 1 hour
Cooking time: 30 minutes

Cut the provolone cheese into small pieces.
Cut the eggplants into slices approximately ¼ in. (5 mm) thick. Place them in a colander, sprinkle with the kosher salt, then leave for approximately 1 hour to allow excess moisture to be drawn out.
Heat the frying oil. Rinse the slices of eggplant, dry them thoroughly with paper towel. Deep-fry (or broil) them and again use paper towel to remove excess grease.
Cook the pasta al dente (according to the packet instructions).
Drain and combine with two thirds of the Bolognese sauce, the peas, half of the eggplant, and the provolone.
Lightly oil the tart mold with the olive oil. Preheat the oven to 340°F (170°C).
Pour the rigatoni mixture into the mold, cover with the remaining eggplant and then the rest of the Bolognese sauce.
Sprinkle with Parmesan and bake for 30 minutes.

● Suggested food/wine match
Cantine Lento, Dragone Rosso—Lamezia DOC

● Chef's notes
You can replace the Bolognese sauce with the ragout of pork from the previous recipe (p. 379), or add béchamel sauce to the Bolognese sauce when mixing it with the pasta.
It is not necessary to first sprinkle the eggplants with kosher salt if they are very fresh.

Lamb *alla Calabrese* ★

Agnello alla calabrese

Calabria is sheep and lamb country, and lamb features heavily in the region's cuisine.

Serves 6
Preparation time: 15 minutes
Cooking time: 10 minutes

Rinse the capers and anchovy fillets under running water if they are very salty.
Roughly chop the capers, anchovies, artichokes, mushrooms, and oregano, then mix everything together to make a chunky paste to serve as a sauce with the lamb.
Cut the meat into medium-sized pieces. Chop or crush the chili.
Season the meat with the chili and salt.
Heat the oil to 320°F/160°C. Sprinkle the counter with the flour.
Roll the pieces of meat in the flour, then deep-fry them for 10 minutes.
Drain and place them on paper towel to remove excess grease.
Serve the lamb immediately, accompanied by the sauce.

● **Suggested food/wine match**
Librandi, Gravello Rosso—Val di Neto IGT

Ingredients
2 lb. (1 kg) lamb (leg or shoulder)
¼ cup (1 ¾ oz./50 g) capers in salt (or vinegar)
1 oz. (30 g) anchovy fillets in salt (or oil)
4 artichokes in oil
2 oz. (60 g) mushrooms in oil
A few oregano leaves
Thai/bird (bird's eye) chili (to taste)
Salt
2 tablespoons flour
Sufficient quantity of oil for deep frying

Techniques
Anchovies in Salt >> p. 26
Artichokes in Oil >> p. 23

Ingredients

4 slices of swordfish (14-16 oz./400-500 g)
A few sprigs of parsley, plus extra to garnish
1 lemon
Scant ½ cup (100 ml) olive oil
1 pinch of oregano
1 tablespoon capers in salt (or vinegar)
1 clove garlic
Salt, pepper

Swordfish in *Salmoriglio* ★

Spada in salmoriglio

Calabrian cuisine gives pride of place to swordfish; it has been harpooned from May to September in the Straits of Messina (between Calabria and Sicily) for centuries.

Serves 4
Preparation time: 20 minutes
Marinating time: 1 hour
Cooking time: 6 minutes

Prepare the *salmoriglio*.
Wash the parsley, remove the stalks, and chop (reserve a little to garnish at the end). Juice the lemon.
Mix the olive oil with the lemon juice, parsley, oregano, salt, and pepper, and marinate the swordfish for 1 hour in the refrigerator.

Prepare a grill pan or a barbecue. Rinse the capers under running water if they are very salty. Peel and crush the garlic.
When the slices of swordfish have marinated, cook them on a ridged grill pan or barbecue (for 3 minutes maximum on each side), basting often with the marinade.
Pour the rest of the marinade into a saucepan, add the capers and crushed garlic, then reduce for a few minutes over the heat.
Serve the swordfish with the reduced sauce and sprinkle with freshly chopped parsley.

● **Suggested food/wine match**
Statti, Mantonico—Calabria IGT

● **Did you know?**
Salmoriglio is a classic Sicilian sauce that is usually served with grilled fish or meats. Its name means salty or brine, although the main ingredient is lemon juice.

Red Onions from Tropea with Eggplants and Potatoes ★

Cipolle di Tropea, melanzane e patate

The onions of Tropea (PGI) have been grown in Calabria since they were introduced by the Phoenicians.

Serves 4
Preparation time: 45 minutes
Resting time: 1 hour
Cooking time: 35 minutes

Peel the onions and chop them. Peel the garlic and crush. Wash the parsley, remove the stalks, and chop.
Chop or crumble the chili. Peel and dice the potatoes.
Peel the tomatoes (after plunging into boiling water for a few seconds, then into cold water) and cut into quarters.
Wash, trim, and cut the peppers into strips. Wash and dice the eggplants.
Place the eggplant and pepper in a colander, sprinkle with the kosher salt, and leave for 1 hour to drain.
Meanwhile, bring a saucepan of water to a boil and cook the potato dice until al dente. Drain and set aside.
Soften the onions in a little olive oil. Add the garlic and the tomatoes. Leave to cook for 5 minutes, then add the other vegetables (except the potatoes) and cook for an additional 20 minutes.
Mix in the potatoes and season with salt, then add the basil, oregano, chopped parsley, and chili. Cook for a further 10 minutes before serving.

● **Suggested food/wine match**
Librandi Cirò Rosato—Calabria DOC

● **Did you know?**
In the past, this was a recipe for the filling of a hollowed-out roll, which peasants ate at midday.

Ingredients
2 mild red onions, preferably from Tropea (PGI)
2 cloves garlic
A few sprigs of parsley
Thai/bird (bird's eye) chili (to taste)
4 potatoes
2 ripe tomatoes
4 bell peppers
3 eggplants
A few basil leaves
1 pinch of oregano
1 tablespoon kosher salt
Olive oil
Salt

Ingredients

Spiced wine reduction
4 cups (1 liter) grape must or 4 cups (1 liter) good red wine
Scant cup (10 ½ oz./300 g) honey
1 orange or 1 lemon
2 cloves
1 cinnamon stick

Pastry
⅔ cup (5 oz./150 g) lard
5 cups (1 lb. 2 oz./500 g) cake flour
¾ cup (5 oz./150 g) sugar
3 eggs
1 sachet (1 tablespoon/11 g) powdered yeast
1 pinch of salt
1 egg white

Filling
¾ cup (4 oz./120 g) raisins
½ cup (120 ml) rum
3 oranges
3 ½ oz. (100 g) dark chocolate
5 oz. (150 g) dried figs
2 cups (10 oz./300 g) almond and walnut kernels
1 pinch of powdered cloves
1 pinch of cinnamon
1 cup (250 ml) spiced wine reduction (see above)

Icing
1 egg white
1 cup (4 oz./125 g) confectioners' sugar
1 lemon
Small candies, to garnish (optional)

● **Suggested food/wine match**
Librandi, Le Passule Bianco Passito—Val di Neto IGT

● **Did you know?**
The name of these turnovers in Italian comes from the Latin nepitedum, *meaning "eyelid."*

Iced Fig and Walnut Turnovers ★★★

Nepitelle con la glassa bianca

These cakes are from an ancient recipe, and are typical of Calabria. They are traditionally prepared at Easter.

Makes 12 turnovers
Preparation time: 1 hour
Maceration time: 15 minutes
Resting time: 30 minutes
Cooking time: 30 minutes

Prepare in advance.
Remove the lard from the refrigerator so that it softens to room temperature.
For the filling, soak the raisins in the rum and zest the oranges. Grate the chocolate. Soak the figs in water (approximately 15 minutes), then drain and pat dry on paper towel. Chop the figs, almonds, and walnuts. For the spiced wine reduction, zest the lemon or orange.
For the icing, juice the lemon and set aside.

Make the spiced wine reduction.
Place the grape must or red wine, honey, zest of the lemon or orange, cloves, and cinnamon stick in a saucepan, and reduce over medium heat. Strain and set aside.

Prepare the pastry.
Pour the flour and sugar onto the counter. Make a well in the center for the lard, eggs, and yeast. Knead everything together quickly and lightly until you have a smooth pastry dough. Place it in a bowl, cover, and let rest in the refrigerator for approximately 30 minutes.

Make the filling.
Mix the chopped figs and nuts with the raisins, powdered spices, spiced wine reduction, orange zest, and grated chocolate to make the filling. Set aside.

Make the turnovers.
Preheat the oven to 350°F (180°C). Roll out the pastry with a rolling pin to a thickness of ¼ in. (5 mm) approximately. Cut out 4 in. (10 cm) rounds with a cookie cutter or a glass and brush the edges with egg white. Place a tablespoon of the filling in the center, then fold over, and press the edges together firmly to seal them.
Line a baking sheet with parchment paper, place the turnovers on the sheet, and bake for 30 minutes. Leave them to cool on a rack.

Make the icing.
Mix the egg white with the confectioners' sugar using a spatula. Thin the mixture down with the lemon juice, until a coating consistency is reached. Brush the top of the turnovers with the icing, decorate with candies if you wish, and let the icing set.

Puglia
Basilicata

Teresa Buongiorno

Through my dishes, I evoke the memories and emotions of childhood. I like to prepare pasta in our traditional way, made simply from durum wheat semolina, water, and salt. Vegetables also play an important part in the cuisine at our restaurant Già Sotto l'Arco. Agriculture is the predominant activity in Puglia, where the production of top-quality olive oil is recognized throughout the world.

My cuisine is fresh, light, and uncomplicated. It is connected with the local *terroir* and respectful of its raw materials, but I keep an eye on my clients' evolving tastes. With the very first glance, a dish is "devoured" with the eyes; that's why I attach a great deal of importance to its presentation, making sure that it is bright and colorful. I also like taste and texture to be distinct from one another, so that the result is an elegant dish with well-defined flavors.

I married into a family of cooks and became a chef that way. I had no formal training whatsoever, but I have risen to the challenge. Step by step, through experimentation and research, I have found my path. It has been a gradual process but full of satisfaction and reward, culminating in a Michelin star.

Mini Tagliatelle and Chickpeas

This is a traditional dish from Salento.

Prepare the chickpeas.
Put the chickpeas in a large container of salted water and leave to soak for at least 8 hours. Drain them and cook in 4 cups (1 liter) of fresh water for 1 hour, then add the finely chopped garlic and onion, the halved cherry tomatoes, and the bay leaves. Leave the soup to simmer for 1 more hour or until the chickpeas are soft.

Make the pasta.
Meanwhile, mix the flour with half a glass of water and a pinch of salt, and knead until you have an elastic dough. Spread or roll it out into a thin sheet and cut it into tagliatelle approximately 2 in. (5 to 6 cm) long (*tria*).
Bring a saucepan of salted water to a boil and cook the pasta, then drain and mix with the cooked chickpeas. The result will be quite dense.

Assemble the dish.
With a skimmer, remove a portion of pasta and a portion of chickpeas.
Drain well, then fry them in a skillet in 2 tablespoons of the olive oil. Once they are crispy, add them back to the pan of chickpeas and pasta.
Season with salt and pepper and serve with the remaining olive oil.

Serves 4

Preparation time: 40 minutes
Soaking time: 8 hours minimum
Cooking time: 2 hours 20 minutes

Ingredients
1 ½ cups (10 oz./300 g) dried chickpeas
1 clove garlic
1 onion
3 cherry tomatoes
2 bay leaves

Pasta dough
2 ½ cups (9 oz./250 g) durum wheat semolina flour
Salt

3 tablespoons extra virgin olive oil
Freshly ground black pepper

Taralli ★★

Taralli go very well with different antipasti or aperitifs. Originally, they were prepared with the remnants of bread dough. Over time, the recipe has evolved with the addition of olive oil, wine, and flavorings such as fennel seeds, chili, pepper, olives, etc.

Makes 30 *taralli*
Preparation time: 20 minutes
Resting time: 30 minutes
Cooking time: 30 minutes approximately

Knead the flour with the other ingredients. Leave the dough to rest for 30 minutes.
Roll the dough under the palms of your hand to form an elongated "snake," approximately ½ in. (1 cm) in diameter.
Cut into sections of 3 in. (6-7 cm) long. Coil each one round and squeeze the two ends together.
Preheat the oven to 425°F (220°C). Flour a baking sheet.
Bring a saucepan of water to a boil and cook the *taralli* for 1 minute, drain and leave them to dry a little on a dish towel, then arrange them on the baking sheet and bake until golden brown.

● Suggested food/wine match
Rosa del Golfo, Primitivo—Salento IGT

● Chef's note
You can replace the fennel seeds with crushed pepper, with chopped or crumbled Thai/bird (bird's eye) chili, or with pitted, chopped olives, etc.

Ingredients
2 cups (7 oz./200 g) bread flour
Scant ¼ cup (50 ml) water
Scant ¼ cup (50 ml) olive oil
1 tablespoon fennel seeds
Scant ¼ cup (50 ml) white wine
Salt

Ingredients

2 lb. (1 kg) mussels
3-4 oz. (100 g) stale bread (preferably bread
   made from hard wheat)
1 clove garlic
A few sprigs of parsley
1 lb. (500 g) ripe tomatoes
2-3 oz. (70 g) *caciocavallo* or provolone cheese
2 tablespoons olive oil
Salt, pepper

Mussels Stuffed with *Metapontina* Cheese ★

Cozze ripiene alla metapontina

This recipe brings together fish and cheese, which is quite rare in Italian cuisine. It is typical of the cooking of Locana, the old name for the region of Basilicata, which borders Campania, Puglia, and Calabria near the southern "toe" of Italy.

Serves 4
Preparation time: 1 hour
Cooking time: 15 minutes

Soak the stale bread in a little water, squeeze it dry, and break it up. Peel and chop the garlic. Wash the parsley, remove the stalks, and chop. Peel the tomatoes (after immersing for a few seconds in boiling water, then in cold water, or with a serrated vegetable peeler), and dice them finely. Grate the cheese.

Clean the mussels.
Scrape the shells, remove the beard, and rinse. Open them while raw: slide the tip of a knife between the two shells on the straighter side of the mussel and run it all the way round. When the knife arrives at the muscle, bend it slightly to act as a lever and separate the two halves. Preheat the oven to 400°F (200°C) and lightly oil a baking sheet. Place the halves containing the mussel meat on the baking sheet and discard the empty ones.

Soften the tomatoes and garlic in the olive oil in a skillet. Add the crumbled bread. Mix together. Remove the skillet from the heat; add the grated cheese, chopped parsley, salt, and pepper.
Spoon the mixture into each mussel shell and bake for 15 minutes. Serve hot.

● **Suggested food/wine match**
Paternoster, Biancorte—Basilicata IGT

● **Chef's note**
For a simpler and quicker stuffing for mussels, mix bread crumbs, grated Parmesan, chopped parsley, garlic, and chili together in a bowl with olive oil.

● **Did you know?**
Mussels must be eaten within three days of their harvest, eliminating any that are broken or do not close when tapped.
Caciocavallo means "cheese on horseback," and is possibly so called because the cheeses are tied together and matured astride a branch, as if on horseback. The cheese was mentioned by Hippocrates as far back as 500 BCE.

Puglia • Basilicata

Pasta with Meatballs ★

Pasta con le polpettine

This recipe is very common throughout Italy. It originates in Puglia, in the far southeast (the "heel" of Italy's boot), where it is an everyday dish.

Serves 4
Preparation time: 15 minutes
Cooking time: 40 minutes
Pasta cooking time: follow packet instructions

Peel the onion, and then chop. Peel the garlic and chop. Wash the parsley and basil, remove their stalks, and chop. Peel the tomatoes (after immersing for a few seconds in boiling water and then in cold water, or with a serrated vegetable peeler).
Crumble the bread. In a bowl, mix the meat with the bread crumbs, Parmesan, and the egg. Add the parsley, basil, and garlic; season with salt and pepper.
Next shape the meatballs into the size of a hazelnut, and brown them in the olive oil in a skillet with the onion. Sprinkle with flour, and deglaze with the wine.
Add the peeled tomatoes and cook for 40 minutes, moistening the sauce with a little vegetable stock if it becomes dry, and checking the seasoning.
Cook the pasta in salted boiling water, drain. Gently mix the sauce with the pasta and sprinkle with grated pecorino.

⬤ **Suggested food/wine match**
Rosa del Golfo, Portulano—Salento IGT

⬤ **Chef's notes**
You can replace the ziti with malfade (ribbon pasta with a serrated edge), with shell-shaped orecchiette, or long spiral-shaped fusilli (see pp. 162–64).
You can also use different meats for the meatballs, either singly or mixed: veal, beef, pork, lamb, turkey, chicken, etc.
You can make a gratin with any leftovers of this dish by adding grated cheese: caciocavallo, a stretched curd cow milk cheese; pear-shaped scamorza made from raw cow milk; pecorino from fresh, whole ewe's milk, or Parmesan, etc.

Ingredients
7 oz. (200 g) ground beef
3 ½ oz. (100 g) sausage meat
1 onion
1 clove garlic
A few sprigs of parsley
A few fresh basil leaves
14 oz. (400 g) tomatoes
1 slice of white bread
3 tablespoons (1 oz./30 g) grated Parmesan
1 egg
2 tablespoons olive oil
1 tablespoon flour
1 cup (250 ml) white wine
2 cups (500 ml) vegetable stock (see p. 94)
14-16 oz. (400-500 g) *ziti*
(large macaroni, see p. 164)
2 tablespoons (⅔ oz./20 g) grated pecorino
Salt, pepper

Ingredients

1 clove garlic

1 lb. (500 g) broccoli rabe

4 anchovies in oil

2 tablespoons olive oil

1 Thai/bird (bird's eye) chili (to taste)

14-16 oz. (400-500 g) orecchiette
  pasta (homemade or store-bought)

⅓ cup (2 oz./60 g) grated pecorino

Orecchiette with Broccoli Rabe ★

Orecchiette con cime di rapa

Orecchiette are characteristic of the Puglia region, and are usually served with a sauce made from broccoli rabe (*cime di rapa*).

Serves 4

Preparation time: 30 minutes

Cooking time: 15-20 minutes

Peel and crush the garlic. Wash the broccoli rabe, keeping only the most tender stalks, the leaves, and tips. Chop coarsely.

In a skillet, melt the anchovy fillets and the crushed garlic in the olive oil with the chili. Add the broccoli rabe and leave to cook for approximately 10 minutes.

Meanwhile, cook the pasta in salted boiling water (if bought, follow the packet instructions). Drain, add to the skillet, and heat everything together with the grated pecorino.

● Suggested food/wine match

Red wine: Calatrasi, Allora Primitivo—Puglia IGT

White wine: Rivera, Marese Bombino Bianco—Castel del Monte DOC

● Did you know?

Cime di rapa goes under different names, depending on whereabouts in Italy you are. For example, the leaves are dubbed friariélli in Naples and broccoletti in Rome. In English they are known as broccoli rabe or rapini.

Butterfly Chicken *alla Diavola* ★ ★

Pollo alla diavola

Pollo alla diavola, cooked over embers, is a recipe that is prepared in several Italian regions. However, the strong presence of chili links it more to the cuisine of the south.

Serves 6
Preparation time: 15 minutes
Cooking time: 1 hour

Chop the chili and herbs.
Mix the olive oil with the herbs and the chopped chili, season with salt and pepper.
Cut the chicken along the sternum, open it out, lay it on the counter, and flatten it well with a meat tenderizer.
Liberally baste the chicken with the herb and chili oil.
Cook over embers (on a barbecue), turning regularly and basting with more of the oil to prevent it becoming dry. Alternatively, you can cook the chicken on a baking sheet in the oven at 400°F (200°C).
Cook for approximately 1 hour until the skin is a deep golden brown and the meat is tender when pierced with a toothpick.

● Suggested food/wine match
Rivera, Cappellaccio Aglianico—Castel del Monte DOC

Ingredients
1 chicken, weighing 4 lb. (1.8 kg)
1 Thai/bird (bird's eye) chili (to taste)
A few sprigs of thyme
A few sprigs of oregano
1 sprig of rosemary
2/3 cup (150 ml) olive oil
Salt, pepper

Ingredients

1 lb. 12 oz. (800 g) pork loin (or boned rib)
1 onion
2 tablespoons olive oil
1 tablespoon paprika
1 tablespoon fennel seeds
1 cup (250 ml) white wine
10 oz. (300 g) bell peppers in vinegar (preferably Senise PGI bell peppers, homemade or store-bought in a jar)
Salt

Technique
Bell Peppers in Vinegar >> p. 24

Pork *alla Lucana* ★

Maiale alla lucana

Pork is a staple of the cuisine of Basilicata. This dish is traditionally prepared by the family on the day the pig is slaughtered.

Serves 4
Preparation time: 30 minutes
Cooking time: 30 minutes

Cut the pork into small pieces. Peel the onion and chop.
Brown the pork in the olive oil in a saucepan.
Add the chopped onion, paprika, and fennel seeds. Once the onion is cooked, deglaze with the wine and cook for 10 minutes.
Cut the bell peppers into strips and add them to the mixture and season with salt. Cover and leave to cook for an additional 15 minutes over low heat.

● Suggested food/wine match
Il Basilisco, Il Basilisco—Aglianico del Vulture DOC

● Chef's note
If you do not have bell peppers in vinegar (see recipe p. 24, or buy from a specialty store in jars), use two fresh red bell peppers. Peel and cut them into strips, then soften them in a skillet in olive oil, and deglaze with white wine.

Puglia • Basilicata

Anchovy and Potato Savory Tart ★★

Tortiera di alici e patate

Serves 4
Preparation time: 30 minutes
Cooking time: 40-45 minutes

Wash and chop the basil. Peel and crush the garlic.
Wash the cherry tomatoes and cut them in half. Peel the potatoes and cut into very thin slices.
Clean the anchovies and fillet them. If using canned anchovies, drain them.
Preheat the oven to 350°F (180°C).
Line the tart mold with parchment paper. Season the potato slices with salt, olive oil, the oregano, and the garlic. Arrange the slices on the base of the mold. Fan the anchovy fillets out on top and season with the oregano and a drizzle of oil.
Arrange the cherry tomato halves on the anchovies, season with salt, and sprinkle over the basil.
Cover liberally with the bread crumbs and drizzle with olive oil.
Bake for 40 to 45 minutes.

● Suggested food/wine match

Rivera, Fedora—Castel del Monte DOC

● Chef's notes

If the tart browns too rapidly while cooking, cover it with a sheet of foil until fully cooked.
You can replace the anchovies with small sardines if they are more readily available.

Ingredients
1 lb. (500 g) potatoes
1 lb. 5 oz. (600 g) fresh or canned anchovies
A few basil leaves
2 cloves garlic
1 lb. (500 g) cherry tomatoes
1 tablespoon oregano
⅓ cup (⅔ oz./20 g) fresh bread crumbs
Olive oil
Salt

Equipment
One 10 in. (24 cm) tart mold

Ingredients

2 lb. (1 kg) dandelion greens
   (or wild chicory leaves)
2-3 tablespoons (1 oz./30 g) capers
   (in salt or vinegar)
2 cloves garlic
3-4 oz. (100 g) cherry tomatoes
½ cup (1 oz./30 g) bread crumbs
1 tablespoon olive oil
Salt

Dandelion Gratin ★

Catalogna arrancanata

Serves 4
Preparation time: 30 minutes
Cooking time: 20 minutes

Rinse the capers in salt under running water, or just drain the capers in vinegar.
Peel and slice the garlic. Wash the cherry tomatoes and cut them into quarters.
Bring a saucepan of water to a boil and preheat the oven to 400°F (200°C).
Thoroughly clean the dandelion greens (or wild chicory leaves), then blanch them for 5 minutes in boiling water. Place them in an ovenproof dish and arrange the tomatoes, garlic, and capers on top.
Sprinkle liberally with the bread crumbs and drizzle with the olive oil. Bake for 20 minutes.

● **Suggested food/wine match**
Rosa del Golfo, Rosato—Rosato del Salento IGT

Zucchini with Fresh Mint ★

Zucchine alla menta

Serves 4
Preparation time: 20 minutes
Cooking time: 10 minutes

Peel the garlic and cut into slices.
Heat the frying oil.
Wash the zucchini, cut them into rounds about ¼ in. (5 mm) thick,
and deep-fry them.
Drain and place on paper towel to remove excess oil.
Prepare a marinade by boiling the vinegar for 5 minutes with the garlic
and some of the mint leaves. Season with salt. Once the mint leaves
have cooked, remove them with a slotted spoon and discard.
Layer the zucchini and remaining mint leaves alternately in a shallow
dish. Pour over the marinade and leave to cool.

● Suggested food/wine match

Rivera, Furfante Bianco Vivace—Puglia IGT

Ingredients
2 lb. (1 kg) zucchini
2 cloves garlic
1 cup (250 ml) wine vinegar
1 large bunch mint
Sufficient quantity of oil for deep frying
Salt

Ingredients
Candied cherries or bigarreau cherries in syrup
Confectioners' sugar

Pastry cream
4 egg yolks
2/3 cup (4 ½ oz./130 g) sugar
2/3 cup (2 oz./60 g) all-purpose flour
2 cups (500 ml) milk
1 vanilla bean
Butter

Choux pastry
1 lemon
1 2/3 cups (6 oz./180 g) cake or all-purpose flour
1 stick (3 ½ oz./100 g) butter
2 ½ teaspoons (10 g) sugar
1 pinch of salt
4-5 eggs

Sufficient quantity of oil for deep frying
   (ideally lard)

Equipment
1 pastry bag with a rosette pastry tip

Doughnuts for Father's Day ★★★

Zeppole di San Giuseppe

Makes 12 doughnuts
Preparation time: 1 hour
Cooking time: 10 minutes
Cooling time: 1 hour

Make the pastry cream.
Whisk the egg yolks with the sugar until pale and light. Add the flour in a stream and mix it in thoroughly. Slit the vanilla bean lengthwise and scrape the seeds into the milk. Incorporate the milk into the mixture gradually. Pour the mixture into a saucepan and cook over low heat, stirring continuously. As soon as it begins to simmer (do not let it boil in case it separates), remove from the heat and pour it onto a baking sheet or into a shallow dish.
Melt a little butter and brush the surface of the cream with it so that it does not form a crust. Cover with plastic wrap and cool in the refrigerator.

Prepare the choux pastry.
Zest the lemon. Sift the flour. Bring 1 cup (250 ml) water to a boil in a saucepan with the butter, sugar, and salt. Off the heat, add the sifted flour all at once and stir vigorously. Remove from the heat once the mixture comes away from the sides of the pan.
Let cool, then stir in the lemon zest and add the eggs one at a time (using a whisk or a food processor). You may not need all the eggs: the choux paste is ready when a small peak formed with a spatula still holds its shape. Heat the oil to 350°F/280°C. Cut out twelve 4 in. (10 cm) squares of parchment paper.
Spoon the paste into a pastry bag with a rosette tip and make two circles approximately 2 in. (5 cm) in diameter, one on top of the other, on each square of paper.
Immerse them in the frying oil and cook until golden brown. Remove the doughnuts with a slotted spoon and place on paper towel to eliminate excess oil. Leave to cool, then carefully detach the paper squares.
To serve, decorate the doughnuts with the chilled pastry cream, place a cherry on top of each, and sprinkle with confectioners' sugar.

● Suggested food/wine match
Di Majo Norante, Apianae—Moscato del Molise DOC

● Chef's note
If you plan to prepare the choux pastry and pastry cream in advance, wait until the last minute to decorate your doughnuts to prevent them becoming soft.

● Did you know?
These doughnuts are traditionally baked on the Feast of St. Joseph, on March 19, which is also Father's Day in Italy. Also known as Bignè di San Giuseppe *and* sfinge, *other fillings include ricotta with chocolate, candied fruits, and honey, or savory versions stuffed with anchovy.*

Sicily

Accursio Craparo

My style of cooking? Indefinable, because it is continually evolving. The local *terroir*–complex, rich, and of infinite possibility–is the main factor that influences everything I make, with such products as olive oil, capers, almonds, pistachios, and even its wild plants. From this starting point, I reinvent traditional recipes while selecting the best ingredients. The resulting dish must of course taste good, but also be light, distinctive, and clearly definable. Besides, the way I present a dish in itself conveys a message to the person who will taste it. The elegance of the whole composition must convey our profound respect for the raw materials and for the locality.

My main objective is to improve and perfect the humble dishes of traditional Sicilian cooking. I am not averse to trying out new cooking techniques in order to enhance the potential of each ingredient.

It was a perfectly natural choice for me to become a chef. I have been surrounded by a love and passion for cooking since my childhood. It is a family tradition. I have also been fortunate enough to come into contact with excellent master chefs.

Pasta with Two Sicilian Pestos

Make the wild fennel pesto.
Remove the tender sprigs of the fennel and boil them for 1 minute in salted water. In a separate saucepan, soften the fennel stalks and the finely sliced onion with the olive oil, salt, and sugar. Moisten with a little of the cooking water from the fennel sprigs and cook for 10 minutes over low heat. Add a splash of oil and blend well with a stick blender until a smooth emulsion is obtained.

Make the anchovy pesto.
In a small saucepan, soften the sliced garlic and lemon zest. Add the anchovies, candied orange zest, candied tomato, chili, and the anchovy extract. Process everything together in a blender.

Assemble the dish.
Cook the pasta according to the packet instructions and drain.
Heat the cooked pasta with the anchovy and wild fennel pestos.
Decorate with the bread crumbs and serve.

Serves 4
Preparation time: 15 minutes
Cooking time: 15 minutes

Ingredients
Fennel pesto
1 small bunch wild fennel
1 small onion
Scant ½ cup (100 ml) extra virgin olive oil
1 pinch each of salt and sugar

Anchovy pesto
1 clove garlic
1 lemon
1 ⅓ oz. (40 g) anchovies
Candied orange zest (from 1 orange)
1 candied tomato
1 pinch of chili
2 teaspoons (10 g) anchovy extract

11 oz. (320 g) artisanal spaghetti
Toasted bread crumbs

Deep-Fried Rice Balls ★ ★ ★

Arancini

Arancini is Italian for "small oranges," which is what these rice balls resemble when cooked.

Makes 10 *arancini*
Preparation time: 1 hour
Cooking time: 7-10 minutes

Cut the *caciocavallo* cheese into small cubes. Wash the parsley, remove the stalks, and chop. Wash and peel the celery and carrot, then chop. Peel and chop the onion.

Dilute the tomato paste with ¾ cup (200 ml) water. Infuse the saffron in a small quantity of water. Beat two of the eggs in a bowl and season lightly with salt. Prepare two more bowls: one containing the flour, the second containing the bread crumbs.

Brown the ground veal in a skillet with the olive oil and butter. Add the chopped vegetables and cook until they become translucent. Deglaze with the wine. Add the peas, mix together, and then add the tomato paste and half of the chopped parsley; season with salt and pepper. Let cook, stirring from time to time.

Cook the rice al dente (see the packet instructions: in general 14 to 16 minutes in boiling salted water), drain thoroughly, then place in a large bowl and allow to cool.

Stir in the saffron infusion, the one remaining egg, the Parmesan, and the remaining chopped parsley. Have a bowl of water ready next to you. Wet your hands slightly, take a tablespoon of rice, and put it in the hollow of your palm. Shape it into a neat and compact ball. Create a small indentation to hold a teaspoon of the sauce and a cube of *caciocavallo*. Close up the indentation to re-form the ball, using a little extra rice if necessary. Roll it firmly between your hands to prevent it falling apart during the coating or frying process.

Preheat the frying oil to 340°F/170°C. Roll each rice ball in the flour, then in the egg, and finally in the bread crumbs.

Deep-fry in the oil until they are a deep golden color, like an orange. Place them on paper towel to remove any excess oil before serving.

⬤ **Suggested food/wine match**
Calatrasi, Terre di Ginestra, Nero d'Avola—Sicily IGT

Ingredients

3 ½ oz. (100 g) ground veal
1 ¾ oz. (50 g) *caciocavallo*, or other
quick-melting cheese
A few sprigs of parsley
1 stick celery
½ carrot
1 onion
2 tablespoons tomato paste
1 pinch of saffron
3 eggs
2 cups (7 oz./200 g) flour
2 cups (4 oz./110 g) fresh bread crumbs
2 tablespoons olive oil
1 ½ tablespoons (20 g) butter
Scant ½ cup (100 ml) white wine
⅓ cup (1 ¾ oz./50 g) peas
1 cup (7 oz./200 g) risotto rice (e.g. *arborio*)
2 ½ tablespoons (1 oz./25g) grated Parmesan
Salt, pepper
Sufficient quantity of oil for deep frying

Ingredients

1 lb. 5 oz. (600 g) small sardines
2 cloves garlic
A few sprigs of parsley
1 lemon
Scant ½ cup (100 ml) olive oil
2 cups (4 oz./120 g) fresh bread crumbs
1 tablespoon (10 g) grated pecorino
¼ cup (1 oz./30 g) pine nuts
3 tablespoons (1 oz./30 g) raisins
8 anchovies in oil
20 bay leaves
Salt, pepper

Equipment

Wooden skewers

Stuffed Sardines ★★

Sarde a beccafico

Peasants who were unable to afford this dish in its true form (made with the Orphean warbler bird) used sardines instead. The birds are known as fig-peckers (*beccafici*), due to their fondness for the fruits, hence its Italian title.

Serves 4
Preparation time: 30 minutes
Cooking time: 15 minutes

Peel and chop the garlic. Wash the parsley, remove the stalks, and chop. Wash the lemon, then slice it finely.
Clean and gut the sardines, remove their backbones and open out the fillets without separating them, then place on paper towels.
Fry the chopped garlic in a skillet with the olive oil, add the bread crumbs, cook for 1 minute, stirring with a spatula, and then remove from the heat. Add the pecorino, pine nuts, raisins, anchovies, and parsley. Season lightly with salt and pepper and stir everything together until you have an evenly mixed stuffing.
Preheat the oven to 350°F (180°C) and lightly oil a baking sheet.
Sprinkle a little salt on the open sardines. Place a spoonful of stuffing on each one, then roll them lengthwise, beginning at the neck end. Thread them onto wooden skewers, interspersed with the bay leaves and lemon slices.
Place the skewers on the baking sheet, and moisten with a little lemon juice and olive oil.
Bake for 15 minutes and serve immediately.

● Suggested food/wine match
Calatrasi, Terre di Ginestra Catarratto Bianco—Sicily IGT

Pasta with Eggplant and Ricotta ★

Pasta alla Norma

This pasta dish, made with eggplant and ricotta, was named in honor
of Vincenzo Bellini's famous opera *Norma* by the inhabitants of Catania.
Bellini was himself a Catanese.

Serves 4
Resting time: 30 minutes
Preparation time: 20 minutes
Pasta cooking time: follow packet instructions

Wash the eggplant, slice it finely, and place the slices in a colander.
Sprinkle with the kosher salt and let drain for 30 minutes.
Meanwhile, peel and chop the garlic. Wash the basil and remove
the leaves from the stalks. If necessary, peel the tomatoes
(by immersing them for a few seconds in boiling water, then in cold
water), then dice them. Cook them in a skillet with a little olive oil
and the garlic. Add a few basil leaves, season with salt and pepper.
Rinse the slices of eggplant, dry them, then brown in olive oil in another
skillet or on a grill pan (see p. 16).
Grate the ricotta.
Cook the pasta, drain, then mix with the tomato sauce over the heat.
Add the eggplant and remove from the heat.
Sprinkle with the ricotta, decorate with a few fresh basil leaves,
and serve.

● **Suggested food/wine match**
Firriato, Ribeca—Sicily IGT

Ingredients
1 eggplant
1 tablespoon kosher salt
1 clove garlic
20 fresh basil leaves
14 oz. (400 g) peeled tomatoes or 1 lb. 8 oz.
(700 g) fresh ripe tomatoes
Olive oil
3 ½ oz. (100 g) hard, salted ricotta
14-16 oz. (400-500 g) *caserecce* pasta
(see p. 163)
Salt, pepper

Techniques
Grilled Vegetables >> p. 16
Peeled Tomatoes >> p. 42

Ingredients

14-16 oz. (400-500 g) *paccheri* pasta
  (see p. 163)
8 oz. (250 g) swordfish
7 oz. (200 g) cherry tomatoes
A few fresh basil leaves
A few mint leaves
1 chili
1 eggplant
1 tablespoon flaked almonds
1 onion
3 tablespoons olive oil
1 clove garlic
Scant ½ cup (100 ml) white wine
Salt, pepper

Pasta with Swordfish ★

Pasta allo spada

Serves 4
Preparation time: 30 minutes
Cooking time: 20 minutes
Pasta cooking time: follow packet instructions

Clean the swordfish and cut the flesh into cubes.
Wash the tomatoes and cut them in half. Wash the basil, remove
the stalks, and cut up the leaves. Remove some mint leaves from
their stalks. Chop or crumble the chili.
Wash the eggplant and cut into small cubes.
Lightly brown the almonds in a dry skillet over the heat. Peel the onion
and chop it, then soften in a skillet with 1 tablespoon of the olive oil.
Add the tomato halves, the basil, and the chili. Season with salt and
pepper.
Cook the pasta in salted boiling water (see the packet instructions).
Meanwhile, in another skillet, sauté the eggplant in a second tablespoon
of the olive oil.
Remove the eggplant with a slotted spoon, and then sauté the swordfish
and the unpeeled garlic clove in the same pan with the remaining
tablespoon of olive oil. Deglaze with the wine and leave to cook for
an additional 3 minutes.
Mix the swordfish with the eggplant and tomatoes in a bowl with
the pasta.
Decorate with a few mint leaves and almonds.

⬤ Suggested food/wine match
Cusumano, Cubia Insolia—Sicily IGT

Lamb with Mint ★★

Agnello alla menta

Serves 4
Preparation time: 15 minutes
Marinating time: 1-2 hours
Cooking time: 1 hour

Cut the lamb into cubes. Marinate for 1 to 2 hours with the vinegar,
a pinch of salt, and a few peppercorns.
Preheat the oven to 350°F (180°C).
Drain the pieces of lamb, and brown them with the rosemary in the olive
oil in an ovenproof casserole. Moisten with the wine, then cook in the
oven for 1 hour.

Prepare the pesto.
Squeeze the orange to extract 4 tablespoons of juice, stir in the sugar,
and let dissolve. Peel the garlic, then chop it finely with the mint. Mix
with the olive oil and the orange juice, and season with salt and pepper.

Remove the lamb from the oven, mix the pieces with the mint pesto
while still hot, and serve immediately.

● **Suggested food/wine match**
Morgante, Don Antonio Nero d' Avola—Sicily IGT

Ingredients
1 lb. 12 oz. (800 g) lamb leg or shoulder
1 ⅔ cups (400 ml) wine vinegar
Scant ¼ cup (50 ml) olive oil
2 sprigs of rosemary
Scant cup (200 ml) white wine
Salt, peppercorns

Pesto
1 orange
2 tablespoons sugar
1 clove garlic
4 sprigs of fresh mint
Scant ½ cup (100 ml) olive oil
Salt, pepper

Ingredients

1 lb. (500 g) fresh tuna (4 slices, weighing approximately 4 oz./125 g each)
1 clove garlic
A few mint leaves
1 tablespoon fennel seeds
1 tablespoon almonds
2 tablespoons olive oil
1 cup (250 ml) white wine or fresh citrus juice (orange, lemon, or grapefruit)
1 ²/₃ cup (3 oz./100 g) bread crumbs
1 pinch of saffron
1 pinch of oregano
¼ cup (2 oz./50 g) grated pecorino
Salt

Tuna *alla Trapanese* ★

Tonno alla trapanese

In Sicily, tuna are fished for their meat and for their eggs, with which the precious *botargo* is prepared. Since each part of the tuna can be prepared fresh or preserved, it is nicknamed "the pig of the sea."

Serves 4
Preparation time: 30 minutes
Marinating time: 10 minutes
Cooking time: 2 minutes

Peel and crush the garlic. Remove the mint leaves from the stalks and chop. Crush the fennel seeds very finely. Chop the almonds.
Marinate the slices of tuna in 1 tablespoon of the olive oil, the wine (or citrus juice), fennel, and garlic for 10 minutes.
Meanwhile, prepare the coating ingredients: mix the bread crumbs with the saffron, chopped almonds, mint, oregano, and pecorino. Add a pinch of salt.
Thoroughly drain the slices of tuna, then dip them in the bread-crumb mixture, pressing down well to ensure they are evenly coated.
Cook in a skillet over medium heat, in the remaining tablespoon of olive oil, for approximately 1 minute per side until completely golden all over. Serve immediately.

● **Suggested food/wine match**
Miceli, Fiammato—Sicilia Rossa IGT

● **Chef's note**
Serve with orange and fennel salad (see p. 437).

Stuffed Calamari *alla Lipari* ★★

Calamari ripieni alla lipari

Calamari (or squid) are very common in Sicilian cuisine, as are cuttlefish.

Serves 4
Preparation time: 30 minutes
Cooking time: 40 minutes

Peel the 2 cloves of garlic and chop the cloves separately. Wash the
parsley, then chop 2 tablespoonfuls. Chop or crumble the chili.
Drain the capers, then chop them with the olives.
Peel the tomatoes (after immersing them for a few seconds in boiling
water, then in cold water, or with a serrated vegetable peeler) and cut
them into quarters (see p. 42).
Thoroughly clean the calamari (see p. 126). Cut the tentacles into pieces.
Mix with one clove of the chopped garlic, 1 tablespoon of the parsley,
the bread crumbs, pecorino, olives, and capers. Check the seasoning.
Stuff the calamari without completely filling the tubes because they
shrink by almost half during the cooking process. Close them by
inserting a toothpick through the opening of the tube.
Brown the calamari in a casserole with a little olive oil; when the water
that comes out of them has evaporated, deglaze with the wine.
Add the tomatoes, the second clove of garlic, the second tablespoon
of parsley, and the chili.
Cover and let simmer for 30 minutes.

● Suggested food/wine match
Tasca d' Almerita, Regaleali Bianco—Sicily DOC

● Chef's notes
*Squid, like cuttlefish, freezes very well—in fact, freezing makes the flesh even
more tender and easier to cook.*
*You can judge the freshness of calamari in the market by the quantity of their
ink. The more there is, the fresher they are.*

Ingredients
1 lb. 12 oz. (800 g) medium calamari
(4-8 calamari)
2 cloves garlic
A few parsley leaves
1 Thai/bird (bird's eye) chili
2 ½ tablespoons (1 oz./30 g) capers
(in salt or vinegar)
¼ cup (2 oz./50 g) pitted green olives
14 oz. (400 g) fresh ripe tomatoes
4 cups (8 oz./250 g) bread crumbs
¼ cup (2 oz./50 g) grated pecorino
Olive oil
½ cup (120 ml) white wine
Salt

Equipment
Wooden toothpicks

Techniques
Peeled Tomatoes >> p. 42
Cleaning calamari >> p. 126

Ingredients

2 eggplants
1 tablespoon kosher salt
¼ cup (1 ½ oz./40 g) capers in salt
1 onion
2 sticks celery
A few fresh basil leaves
⅓ cup (1 ½ oz./40 g) pine nuts
¾ cup (5 oz./150 g) pitted green olives
7 oz. (200 g) tomato sauce (see p. 50)
4 tablespoons wine vinegar
1 ⅔ tablespoons (⅔ oz./20 g) sugar
3 tablespoons olive oil
Salt, pepper

Technique
Tomato Sauce >> p. 50

Caponata ★

Dating back to the sixteenth century, there are now more than thirty versions of this dish.

Serves 4
Resting time: 1 hour
Preparation time: 30 minutes
Cooking time: 20 minutes

Wash the eggplants, and cut into small cubes. Sprinkle with the kosher salt and leave to drain for 1 hour in a colander.
Rinse the capers. Peel the onion and chop. Wash and peel the celery, and cut into approximately ½ in. (10 mm) slices. Wash the basil.
Rinse the eggplant cubes, dry thoroughly, then cook them gently in a skillet with 2 tablespoons of the olive oil until they begin to soften.
Cook the chopped onion and the celery in a saucepan with the remaining tablespoon of olive oil. When they become translucent, add the pine nuts, capers, and olives, then, 1 minute later, the tomato sauce (see p. 50). Season with salt and pepper and the basil leaves, then cook for 10 minutes. Mix together the vinegar and sugar and pour into the mixture. Let evaporate.
Finally, add the eggplant, cook for a few more minutes, and then leave to cool.
Serve cold.

 **Suggested food/wine match**
Planeta, Cerasuolo di Vittoria—Sicily DOCG

Ricotta Cakes with Candied Fruits ★★

Cassate

Makes 4 individual cakes (cassatas)
Preparation time: 1 hour
Resting time: 30 minutes
Cooking time: 40 minutes

Prepare the sponge cake.
Butter and flour the tart mold. Preheat the oven to 350°F (180°C).
Separate the eggs and beat the yolks with the sugar until pale and light; pour in the flour and baking powder, add the lemon zest and a pinch of salt, and fold everything together with a spatula. Whip the egg whites until stiff then gently fold them in.
Pour into the mold and bake for 40 minutes. Let cool before unmolding. Cut eight rounds from the sponge cake using a cookie cutter. They should be slightly smaller in diameter than the ramekins and approximately ½ in. (10 mm) thick.

Make the ricotta cream.
Dice the candied pumpkin. Split the vanilla bean in two lengthwise, scraping the inside of one half to extract the seeds.
Sieve the ricotta, stir in the vanilla seeds, sugar, chocolate chips, candied squash, and a small pinch of salt.

Prepare the cassatas.
Line four ramekins with plastic wrap. Dilute the sweet wine with a little water. Roll out the almond paste to ¼ in. (5 mm) thickness and line the sides of the ramekins.
Lay a first round of the sponge cake in the bottom of each ramekin and moisten it with the wine. Fill the ramekins with the ricotta cream and finish with a second round of sponge cake and again moisten with wine. Cover the ramekins with plastic wrap and leave for approximately 30 minutes in the refrigerator.

Make the icing.
Mix the egg white and confectioners' sugar with a spatula. Add the lemon juice to soften it to a consistency that can be spread easily.

Decorate the cassatas.
Unmold the cassatas and remove the plastic wrap. Decorate them with the icing, the bigarreau cherries, and other diced candied fruits.

● Chef's notes
Keep the cassatas in the refrigerator until you wish to serve them.
To save time, you can buy the sponge cake ready-made, as it is becoming more and more widely available.

Ingredients
Genoese sponge cake
2 eggs
⅔ cup (2 ½ oz./75 g) sugar
1 cup (3 ½ oz./100 g) cake flour
3 teaspoons baking powder
Zest of ½ lemon
Salt
Butter and flour for preparing the mold

Ricotta cream
1 oz. (25 g) candied pumpkin
1 vanilla bean
1 cup (9 oz./250 g) ricotta
¾ cup (5 oz./150 g) sugar
2 heaping tablespoons (1 oz./25 g) chocolate chips
Salt

Cassatas
½ cup (120 ml) sweet wine (maraschino, Marsala, muscat, vermouth, etc.)
8 oz. (250 g) green almond paste (marzipan)

Icing
1 egg white
1 ⅓ cups (9 oz./250 g) confectioners' sugar
1 teaspoon lemon juice

Decoration
A few bigarreau cherries
A few candied fruits

Equipment
4 ramekins
1 tart mold

Cannoli ★★

Makes 10 cannoli
Preparation time: 1 hour
Resting time: 1 hour 30 minutes
Cooking time: 10 minutes

Prepare the cannoli shells.
Mix all the dough ingredients together well to obtain a smooth dough.
Cover with plastic wrap and let rest for 1 hour 30 minutes in the
refrigerator.
Separate the dough into ten small balls. Roll out into oval shapes
approximately $1/12$ in. (2 mm) thick.
Heat the lard for frying to 350°F/180°C.
Wrap each oval around a cannoli cylinder, sealing the join with the egg
white. Deep-fry until a deep golden brown. Drain on paper towel and,
once cooled, gently pull out the cylinders from the cannoli shells.

Make the ricotta cream.
Slit the vanilla bean in two lengthwise, scrape one half to extract the
seeds. Sieve the ricotta, stir in the vanilla seeds, sugar, chocolate chips,
and a small pinch of salt.

Assemble the cannoli.
Fill the cannoli shells just before serving to retain their crispness.
Slice the candied orange peel very finely. Using a pastry bag and plain
(smooth) tip, fill the shells with the ricotta cream. Decorate each end with
the candied orange peel and powdered pistachio. Sprinkle the shells
with confectioners' sugar (see photo p. 435).

● **Suggested food/wine match**

Miceli, Moscato di Pantelleria, Tanit—Sicily DOC

● **Chef's notes**

*If you want to fill the cannoli in advance, brush the inside of the shells with
dark melted chocolate once they have cooled down. This will prevent contact
with the ricotta cream and keep them crisp. You can keep the shells (cooked
and unfilled) for a few days in an airtight container or in the freezer.*
*To save time, you can buy the cannoli shells ready-made, as they are becoming
more and more widely available.*

Ingredients

Dough
1 ¼ cups (4 oz./125 g) cake flour
1 teaspoon unsweetened cocoa powder
1 tablespoon granulated sugar
$2/3$ oz. (20 g) lard
1 teaspoon vinegar
1 tablespoon sweet wine (maraschino,
Marsala, muscat, vermouth, etc.)
1 pinch of cinnamon powder
Salt

Sufficient quantity of lard for deep frying
1 egg white

Ricotta cream
1 vanilla bean
1 cup (9 oz./250 g) ricotta
$1/3$ cup (2 ½ oz./75 g) sugar
2 heaping tablespoons (1 oz./25 g)
chocolate chips
Salt

1 tablespoon powdered pistachio
Small piece of candied orange peel
Confectioners' sugar for decoration

Equipment
10 cannoli cylinders
1 pastry bag
1 plain (smooth) pastry tip

Ingredients

2 fennel bulbs
5 oranges
¼ cup (60 ml) olive oil
1 teaspoon sugar
¼ cup (1 ½ oz./40 g) pitted black olives
Salt, pepper

Orange and Fennel Salad ★

Insalata d'arance e finocchi

Serves 4
Preparation time: 30 minutes
Marinating time: 15 minutes

Clean the fennel bulbs and slice them as thinly as possible.
Remove all the peel and pith from the oranges and separate them
into segments.
Prepare an emulsion with the olive oil, sugar, salt, and pepper.
In a bowl, mix the orange segments and fennel slices with the emulsion.
Add the olives.
Marinate for 10 to 15 minutes before serving.

● **Suggested food/wine match**
Cusumano, Insolia—Sicily IGT

Sardinia

Roberto Petza

When I was young, I dreamed of becoming a carpenter. As it happened, I enrolled at catering school, which was a real stroke of luck. It allowed me to go and develop my skills in several different countries. Upon my return, fifteen years later, I rediscovered my region. For me, *terroir* is everything. My cuisine is born from the produce that can be found locally, close to my restaurant. However, drawing on my experiences abroad, I now enjoy combining local traditions with different techniques and gastronomic cultures. But to be able to move beyond tradition, you first have to be familiar with it.

New technologies offer me the possibility not only of departing from tradition–by interpreting it in a new way–but also, paradoxically, of being even more loyal to that tradition. Cooking sous vide (in a vacuum-sealed pouch) at a low temperature, applied to a suckling pig, for example, allows me to obtain a result similar to that of cooking in an earth oven, practiced for centuries in the center of Sardinia. However, I am not an unreserved fan of technology. In my kitchen, I still regularly use a charcoal grill for roasting meat.

Soup of Moray Eel and Cherry Tomatoes, Crispy Spelt, and Small Ravioli with *Cas'axedu* Stuffing

Make the ravioli dough.
Mix and knead the ingredients until you have a ball of dough.
Roll out the dough and cut out ravioli shapes in rounds approximately 1 ½ in. (4 cm) in diameter with a pasta cutter. Chill in the refrigerator.

Make the ravioli filling.
Mix all the ingredients for the filling in a food processor until thoroughly combined.
Check that the filling is sufficiently seasoned with salt.
Assemble the ravioli as shown on p. 70.

Prepare the spelt.
In a small saucepan, fry the garlic and bay leaf in the olive oil. Add the spelt, season lightly with salt, and leave to brown for approximately 2 minutes. Cover with water and cook until al dente, approximately 25 minutes.

Prepare the soup.
Cut the moray eels into small pieces and set aside.
Chop the onions finely. Soften them in a saucepan with the olive oil, then leave to cook down over low heat. After approximately 10 minutes, add the diced carrot and cook for 5 minutes; then add the diced leek and celery, the bouquet garni, and the chopped garlic and parsley.
Continue to cook for 2 minutes, then add the moray eel pieces, season with salt and pepper and continue to cook, crushing the fish as much as possible to obtain a thick broth.
Remove the pan from the heat and place in a bowl or container filled with ice cubes, to stop the cooking process. Leave the soup to infuse for at least 20 minutes.
Return to the heat and bring to a boil, skim, and cook for approximately 20 minutes, then strain.

Cook the ravioli for 4 to 5 minutes and then drain well. Bring the strained broth back to a boil, check the seasoning, and add the cherry tomatoes and ravioli.

Arrange a few celery leaves, some snippets of chives, the basil cut into ribbons, the wild fennel, and a spoonful of spelt in each of four shallow bowls. Pour over the broth with the tomatoes and ravioli, which should be really hot. Drizzle with olive oil and serve.

Serves 4
Preparation time: 1 hour
Cooking time: 45 minutes

Ingredients
Pasta dough
1 ½ cups (5 oz./150 g) sifted flour
1 heaping teaspoon (5 g) semolina
8 egg yolks

Ravioli filling
3 ½ oz. (100 g) *cas'axedu* (fresh, raw sheep milk cheese, also known as *cagliata acida*)
Zest of ½ orange
1 small mint leaf
1 oz. (30 g) semi-hard pecorino (medium-ripe)
1 tablespoon extra virgin olive oil
Salt, pepper

Spelt
Scant cup (3 ½ oz./100 g) spelt
½ clove garlic
1 bay leaf
3 tablespoons olive oil

Soup
2 Moray eels, gutted, approximately 10 oz. (300 g) each
2 onions
2 tablespoons extra virgin oil
1 carrot, diced
½ leek, diced
1 stick celery, diced
1 bouquet garni (marjoram, wild fennel, thyme, basil, bay leaf)
1 clove garlic, peeled and chopped
1 sprig of parsley, chopped
12 peeled and candied cherry tomatoes

A few celery leaves, basil, and chives
2 sprigs of wild fennel
Olive oil to serve

Sardinian Gnocchi
alla Campidanese ★★★

Gnocchi sardi (malloredus) alla campidanese

This is one of the traditional pasta shapes of the region, called *malloredus*.
They are generally served with a tomato sauce.

Serves 4
Preparation time: 1 hour
Resting time: 30 minutes
Cooking time for the sauce: 40 minutes
Pasta cooking time: 4-5 minutes

Make the gnocchi.
Prepare the farfalle dough as in the basic recipe (see p. 76). Make
a quarter of the dough into a small ball and the remaining three
quarters into a larger ball. Dilute the saffron in a tablespoon of water
and work this into the small dough ball to give it a yellow color.
Wrap both balls in plastic wrap and let rest for 30 minutes.
Once the dough is rested, make the *malloredus*. Shape both doughs
into sausage shapes of less than ¾ in. (1.5 cm) in diameter that you will
then cut into pieces ½ in. (1 cm) long.
Using your thumb, roll these pieces of dough along the tines of a fork or
on a specially designed grooved gnocchi shaper (see p. 168 and right),
to give them the characteristic shape of small gnocchi: hollow on one side
and scored on the other.
Place both the white and yellow gnocchi on a dry dish towel. (There will
therefore be three times as many white as yellow, saffron-colored gnocchi.)

Prepare the sauce.
Peel and chop the onion. Remove the sausage skin, then cut it into small
pieces. Wash and peel the tomatoes (after immersing them for a few
seconds in boiling water, then in cold water, or with a serrated tomato
peeler).
Soften the chopped onion in the olive oil in a saucepan.
Add the small pieces of sausage and brown them well.
Add the peeled tomatoes, basil, and saffron. Season with salt and cover;
simmer for approximately 40 minutes.

Bring a saucepan of salted water to a boil and cook the pasta for 4 to
5 minutes.
Drain, then reheat for a few minutes in the pan with the sauce,
the pecorino, and the freshly ground black pepper.

● **Suggested food/wine match**
Argiolas, Costera—Cannoanau di Sardegna DOC

● **Chef's note**
You can color the entire quantity of dough with the saffron, if you prefer.

Ingredients
1 quantity farfalle dough (see p. 76)
1 pinch of saffron powder

Sauce
1 onion
4 oz. (120 g) fresh sausage
1 lb. 8 oz. (700 g) fresh ripe tomatoes
1 tablespoon olive oil
14 oz. (400 g) peeled tomatoes
10 basil leaves
1 pinch of saffron powder
⅓ cup (2 oz./60 g) grated pecorino
Salt, pepper

Equipment
Gnocchi shaper (see p. 168)

Techniques
Farfalle >> p. 76
Peeled Tomatoes >> p. 42

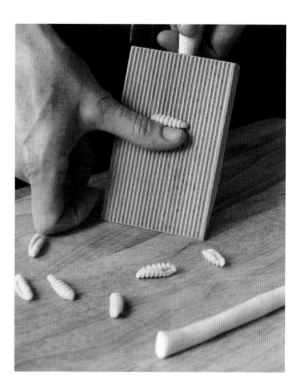

Ingredients
1 quantity farfalle dough (see p. 76)
1 tablespoon olive oil

Stuffing
1 lb. 12 oz. (800 g) floury potatoes
1 clove garlic
1 onion
Either 10 mint leaves
Or 1 pinch of saffron powder
Either 5 oz. (150 g) fresh pecorino, grated
Or scant ½ cup (3 oz./75 g) grated pecorino
   and ⅓ cup (2 ½ oz./75 g) ricotta
Scant ½ cup (100 ml) olive oil
Salt

Sauce
Olive oil
⅓ cup (2 oz./60 g) grated pecorino, or
   tomato and basil sauce (see p. 47), or
   Neapolitan tomato sauce (see p. 51)

Equipment
1 potato ricer
1 cookie cutter (2 ½ in./6 cm diameter)

Techniques
Farfalle >> p. 76
Tomato and Basil Sauce >> p. 47
Neapolitan Tomato Sauce >> p. 51

Sardinian Ravioli
alla Ogliastrina ★ ★ ★

Ravioli sardi all'ogliastrina

These are traditional Sardinian ravioli. They are made with different stuffings, depending on the season or the area. They are always accompanied by grated pecorino.

Serves 4
Preparation time: 1 hour
Resting time: 30 minutes
Cooking time for the sauce: 20 minutes
Pasta cooking time: 4-5 minutes

Make the ravioli dough.
Prepare the farfalle dough as in the basic recipe (see p. 76), with the addition of 1 tablespoon of olive oil. Let rest for 30 minutes.

Prepare the ravioli stuffing.
Boil the potatoes in their skins.
Meanwhile, peel and crush the garlic. Peel and chop the onion, remove the stalks from the mint, if using, and chop ten leaves.
When the potatoes are cooked, peel them, and pass through a potato ricer. Soften the chopped onion in the olive oil in a saucepan.
Add to the mashed potatoes with the mint or saffron, crushed garlic, and pecorino (or pecorino and ricotta); season with salt.

Assemble the ravioli.
Roll out the dough into one thin sheet. Cut out rounds of about 2 ½ in. (6 cm) in diameter using a glass or a cookie cutter. Place small mounds of stuffing in the center of each round. Draw the sides up over the stuffing, to look like an ear of corn. Proceed as follows: first fold the side of the circle nearest to you to the center, then alternately fold over sections of the right and left sides of the circle, sealing them firmly together (see photograph p. 444), making sure that no air bubbles are trapped inside.

Cook the ravioli for 5 to 6 minutes in boiling salted water. Drain, then mix them with olive oil and the pecorino, or with a simple tomato sauce.

● **Suggested food/wine match**
Cantina Santadi, Villa Solais—Vermentino di Sardegna DOC

Linguine with Spiny Lobster ★

Linguine con l'aragosta

Serves 4
Preparation time: 30 minutes
Pasta cooking time: follow packet instructions

Bring a saucepan of water with a bay leaf to a boil and immerse the live spiny lobster; cook for 3 minutes.
Remove and place it on a chopping board with a groove, to collect the juices while it is being cut up.
Peel the tail of the lobster and cut it into pieces, then, using a knife, split the head in two. Keep the juices to add flavor to the sauce.
Peel and chop the onion. Peel the garlic and cut into small pieces. Wash the tomatoes and halve them. Wash the basil leaves. Wash the parsley, remove the stalks, and chop the leaves. Chop or crumble the chili.
Bring a saucepan of salted water to a boil, ready to cook the pasta.
Fry the garlic and onion in the olive oil in a skillet over high heat.
Add the pieces of spiny lobster with their juices and cook for a few minutes.
Deglaze with the brandy and add the tomatoes, basil, and chili; season with salt. Cook for 2 minutes.
Time the cooking of the linguine to coincide with serving the dish.
Drain and mix it with the sauce and the parsley in the skillet.
Serve immediately.

● **Suggested food/wine match**
Cantina Santadi, Villa di Chiesa—Valli di Porto Pino IGT

● **Chef's note**
You can replace the spiny lobster with langoustine/scampi (Nephrops norvegicus).

Ingredients
1 to 2 spiny lobsters, weighing
2-2 ½ lb. (1-1.2 kg) in total
14-16 oz. (400-500 g) linguine
1 bay leaf
1 onion
1 clove garlic
1 lb. (500 g) cherry tomatoes
3 basil leaves
A few sprigs of parsley
1 Thai/bird (bird's eye) chili (to taste)
Scant ½ cup (100 ml) brandy
Olive oil
Salt

Ingredients

2 lb. (1 kg) very fresh sea urchins
14-16 oz. (400-500 g) spaghetti
2 cloves garlic
A few sprigs of parsley
1 Thai/bird (bird's eye) chili (to taste)
2 tablespoons olive oil
Salt, pepper

 Technique
Cleaning sea urchins, extracting the tongues ›› p. 126

Spaghetti with Sea Urchins ★

Spaghetti coi ricci di mare

Serves 4
Preparation time: 30 minutes
Pasta cooking time: follow packet instructions

Peel and chop the garlic. Wash the parsley, remove the stalks, and chop.
Chop or crumble the chili.
Clean and empty the sea urchins, retaining their tongues (see p. 126).
Place the tongues in a large bowl.
Bring a saucepan of salted water to a boil and cook the spaghetti.
Drain, reheat in a skillet for 2 minutes with the garlic and olive oil,
and then quickly mix in the bowl with the sea urchins' tongues.
Add the chopped parsley and the chili. Mix again and serve immediately.

 Suggested food/wine match
Contini, Karmis—Bianco Tharros IGT

● **Chef's note**
If the sauce seems too dry, add a small ladle of the pasta cooking water to dilute it.

Little Sardinian Pies ★ ★

Timballo sardo

This is a recipe of Spanish origin (*panadas*), a survivor from the long Spanish occupation of Sardinia. It is the traditional dish of the towns of Oschiri, Assemini, and Cuglieri.

Serves 4
Preparation time: 45 minutes
Resting time: 30 minutes
Cooking time: 30-40 minutes

Prepare the dough.
Cut the lard (which should be at room temperature) into small pieces. Knead the flour with the pieces of lard, lukewarm water, and salt, until well mixed and smooth.
Cover the dough with plastic wrap and let rest for 30 minutes in the refrigerator.

Make the stuffing (to be adapted depending on the choice of recipe).
For all three recipes, cut the meat into small cubes. Peel and chop the garlic. Remove the stalks from the parsley and chop. Mix the meat with the olive oil, add the garlic, wine, parsley, and any herbs or spices. Depending on which stuffing you have chosen, add the remaining ingredients in the list and season with salt and pepper. Leave for 30 minutes in the refrigerator.

Assemble the pies.
Preheat the oven to 350°F (180°C).
When the dough has rested, shape it into a large "sausage," and cut four slices approximately 1 in. (2 cm) thick and four slices approximately ½ in. (1 cm) thick. Roll out the slices into rounds ¼ in. (5 mm) thick, the four largest to a diameter of 4 in. (8 cm) and the four smallest to a diameter of 2 in. (4 cm).
Place a mound of stuffing in the middle of each of the larger rounds. Moisten the edges of the pastry with a little water. Cover with the smaller rounds and press the edges between your index finger and thumb to create a sealed, fluted border around the pies. You should have 4 small pies.

Bake for 30 to 40 minutes.
Serve the pies hot or cold.

● **Suggested food/wine match**
Agricola Punica Barrua—Isola dei Nuraghi IGT

Ingredients
Dough
2 oz. (50 g) lard, at room temperature
2 ½ cups (9 oz./250 g) durum wheat semolina flour
Scant ½ cup (100 ml) lukewarm water (85°F/30°C)
Salt

Pork stuffing (from Oschiri)
1 lb. 5 oz. (600 g) pork (loin)
2 cloves garlic
A few sprigs of parsley
¼ cup (50 ml) olive oil
¼ cup (50 ml) white wine
Salt, pepper

Lamb stuffing (from Assemini)
1 lb. (500 g) lamb (leg or shoulder)
14 oz. (400 g) potatoes, peeled, diced, and cooked
2 cloves garlic
A few sprigs of parsley
4 dried tomatoes in oil, chopped
¼ cup (50 ml) olive oil
¼ cup (50 ml) white wine
Salt, pepper

Beef and vegetable stuffing (from Cuglieri)
10 oz. (300 g) beef
2 cloves garlic
A few sprigs of parsley
1 ½ oz. (40 g) artichokes, cut into quarters, then finely sliced
¼ cup (50 ml) olive oil
¼ cup (50 ml) white wine
¼ cup (1 ½ oz./40 g) fresh peas, cooked
¼ cup (1 ½ oz./40 g) small, fresh fava beans, cooked
¼ cup (1 ½ oz./40 g) black olives, pitted and chopped
1 pinch of saffron
1 pinch of nutmeg
2 sprigs of rosemary, stalks removed, chopped
Salt, pepper

Technique
Oven-Dried Tomatoes in Olive Oil >> p. 44

Ingredients

1 or 2 sea bass, weighing approximately
  4 lb. (1.8 kg) in total
1 clove garlic
A few sprigs of parsley
2 tablespoons olive oil
A few fronds and seeds of wild fennel
⅓ cup (⅔ oz./20 g) bread crumbs
Scant ¾ cup (150 ml) white wine
Salt, pepper

Baked Sea Bass with Wild Fennel ★

Branzino al forno con finocchietto

Serves 4
Preparation time: 40-50 minutes
Cooking time: 30-40 minutes

Peel the garlic and slice finely. Wash the parsley, remove the stalks,
and chop half of it.
Wash and gut the fish, and then make two diagonal incisions on each
side. Insert some garlic slices and the remaining sprigs of parsley in
the incisions and in the belly cavity.
Mix the olive oil and chopped parsley together and season with salt
and pepper.
Crush the fennel seeds to a powder in a mortar, and mix with
the bread crumbs.
Preheat the oven to 350°F (180°C).
Lay a few large fronds of fennel on a baking sheet.
Brush the fish with the seasoned oil.
Place the fish on the fennel and sprinkle with the bread-crumb mixture.
Bake the fish for 30 to 40 minutes (depending on its size). After
10 minutes, pour the wine around the fish and continue cooking.

● Suggested food/wine match

Argiolas, Is Argiolas—Vermentino di Sardegna DOC

Sospiri Candies from Ozieri ★★

Sospiri di Ozieri

This recipe dates back to 1800 and was traditionally prepared for weddings.

Makes 20 *sospiri* candies
Preparation time: 1 hour
Cooking time: 20 minutes

Prepare the candies.
Preheat the oven to 140°F (60°C). Dry out the blanched almonds in the oven, without coloring them, for 30 minutes, then chop very finely. Place the sugar, honey, and lemon zest in a saucepan over medium heat, add the almonds, and let cook for 10 minutes. Stir in the water and the orange flower water and leave to cool.
Roll out the mixture on a sheet of parchment paper to a thickness of approximately ¾ in. (1.5 cm). Use a small cookie cutter of 1 in. (2 cm) diameter to cut out the candy.
Preheat the oven to 320°F (160°C).
Bake the candies for 10 minutes, until lightly colored on the underside. Turn off the heat and leave to cool in the oven.

Make the icing.
Using a spatula, mix the egg white with the confectioners' sugar to make a firm mixture, then soften it with the lemon juice.
Ice the *sospiri* and let the icing dry completely.
Wrap them individually in colored paper like candy.

⬤ **Suggested food/wine match**
Contini, Vernaccia di Oristano Riserva DOC
Santadi, Latinia—Valli di Porto Pino IGT

⬤ **Did you know?**
In the south of Sardinia, the icing is replaced with superfine (caster) sugar and the candies are known as gueffus.

Ingredients
Candies
9 oz. (250 g) blanched almonds
1 cup (7 oz./200 g) sugar
1 tablespoon honey
Zest of ½ lemon
Scant ¼ cup (50 ml) water
1 tablespoon orange flower water

Icing
2 cups (9 oz./250 g) confectioners' sugar
1 egg white
1 teaspoon lemon juice

Equipment
1 cookie cutter, 1 in. (2 cm) diameter
Colored paper for wrapping the candy

Index

Index

Index

Index

Useful addresses and websites

Australia

Lina's Deli
Bankstown Centro
t224/1A North Terrace
Bankstown NSW 2200
Tel.: + 61 (0) 2 9791 9181

P. R. Raineri Continental
Delicatessen
97 Great North Road
Five Dock NSW 2046
Tel.: + 61 (0) 2 9713 6886

Paesanella
88 Ramsay Street
Haberfield NSW 2045
Tel.: + 61 (0) 2 9799 8483

Pasticceria Papa
145 Ramsay Street
Haberfield NSW 2045
Tel.: + 61 (0) 2 9799 9531

Pino's Dolce Vita Fine Foods
45 President Avenue
Kogarah NSW 2217
Tel.: + 61 (0) 2 9587 4818

Zanetti 5 Star Delicatessen
108 Ramsay Street
Haberfield NSW 2045
Tel.: + 61 (0) 2 9798 4076

France

Astier de Villatte
173, rue Saint-Honoré
75001 Paris
France
Tel.: + 33 (0) 1 42 60 74 13
www.astierdevillatte.com

Ideavino
88, avenue Parmentier
75011 Paris
Tel.: + 33 (0) 1 43 57 10 34
www.idea-vino.fr

Maison de la Truffe
19, place de la Madeleine
75008 Paris
Tel.: + 33 (0) 1 42 65 53 22
www.maison-de-la-truffe.com

Marion Graux Céramiques
50, rue Condorcet
75009 Paris
Tel.: + 33 (0) 6 62 27 23 44
www.mariongrauxpoterie.tumblr.com

Paisano
159, rue Saint-Maur
75011 Paris
Tel.: + 33 (0) 9 51 56 19 68

Rap
15, rue Rodier
75009 Paris
Tel.: + 33 (0) 1 42 80 09 91
www.epicerie.rapparis.fr

Italy

Ceramiche de Simone
11, Via Vittorio Ducrot
Palermo
Tel.: + 39 091 476189

Cotti Ad Arte
26/a, Via Barbaroux
Turin
Tel.: + 39 011 4546410
www.cottiadarte.it

Covo della Taranta, trattoria
salentina
10bis/a, Via Galliari
Turin
Tel.: + 39 011 4270532

La Fabbrica della Ceramica
38, Via autonomia Siciliana
Palermo
Tel.: + 39 091 6251997
www.lafabbricadellaceramica.com

Pentole Agnelli
Agnelli Baldassare spa,
Via Madonna, s/n
24040 Lallio (BG)
Tel.: + 39 035 204 711
www.agnelli.net

Torretti de Ruta Fabbrica Maioliche
Artistiche
S.S. E, 45 Uscita Deruta Sud
06053 Deruta (PG)

Tel.: + 39 075 9711342
Zabbara eccellenze siciliane
49d, Via Saluzzo
Turin
Tel.: + 39 011 6509240
www.zabbara.it

United States

Buon Italia
75, Ninth Avenue
New York City, NY 10011
Tel.: + 1 212 633 9090
www.buonitalia.com

Di Palo's
200 Grand Street
New York City, NY 10013
Tel.: + 1 212 226 1033
www.dipaloselects.com

Eataly Chicago
43 East Ohio Street
Chicago, IL 60611
Tel: + 1 312 521 8700
www.eataly.com

Eataly NYC
200 Fifth Avenue
New York City, NY 10010
Tel: + 1 212 229 2560
www.eataly.com

Faicco's Pork Store
260 Bleecker Street
New York City, NY
Tel.: + 1 212 243 1974

Porchetta NYC
110 East Seventh Street
New York, NY 10009
Tel.: +1 212 777 2151

United Kingdom

East Dulwich Deli
15 Lordship Lane
London SE22
Tel.: + 44 (0) 20 8693 2525

The Gazzano's
167–169 Farringdon Road
London EC1
Tel.: + 44 (0) 20 7837 1586

Gennaro's
23 Lewis Grove
London SE13 6BG
Tel.: + 44 (0) 20 8852 1370

I Camisa & Sons
61 Old Compton Street
London W1D 6HS
Tel.: + 44 (0) 7437 7610
www.icamisa.co.uk

Italian Farmers
186 Stroud Green Road
London N4 3RN
Tel: + 44 (0) 20 3719 6525

Lina Stores
18 Brewer Street
London W1R 3FS
Tel.: + 44 (0) 20 7437 6482
www.linastores.co.uk

Terroni of Clerkenwell
138-140 Clerkenwell Road
London EC1R 5DL
Tel.: + 44 (0) 20 7837 1712
www.terroni.co.uk

Websites

Associazione Verace Pizza
Napoletana
www.pizzanapoletana.org

Athezza (tableware)
www.athezza.com

Consorzio del Formaggio
Parmigiano Reggiano
www.parmigianoreggiano.com

Consorzio del Prosciutto di Parma
www.prosciuttodiparma.com

Cuisinart
www.cuisinart.com

De Dietrich
www.de-dietrich.com

Deruta
www.derutamegastore.com

Eataly
www.eataly.com

The Italian Chef
italianchef.com

Italian Food
italian.food.com

Italian Food Forever
www.italianfoodforever.com

Video sequences (QR codes)

The video sequences show professionals at work and therefore the quantities, cooking times, and other specifics may vary slightly from the recipes in the book, which have been adapted for use in the home. In addition, the sequences show the key steps but do not necessarily include all the details of the recipes in the book. When putting techniques into practice or making recipes, follow the precise indications given in the book.

Acknowledgments

The author wishes to thank the following:
• My mother Leila, for passing on her know-how with enthusiasm and diligence, and my grandmothers, Bianca and Emilia
• Ryma Bouzid and Clélia Ozier-Lafontaine for their faith in me
• Ève-Marie Zizza-Lalu, without whom this book would not have been possible
• Francesca Mantovani, a sensitive photographer, who I wish to thank for perfectly capturing the spirit of my cuisine
• Gilles Weber for his invaluable help and support, without which editing this work would not have been as exciting and charming
• Rita Pinna from Ideavino in Paris for using her impressive knowledge to find the perfect Italian wines to compliment my dishes
• Alessandra Pierini from the gourmet food store Rap in Paris, for her availability, kindness, and quality produce
• Davide and Federica from Paisano, a gourmet food store in Paris, for their availability and enthusiasm
• Fabrice Gour from the Consorzio del Prosciutto di Parma and the Consorzio del Formaggio Parmigiano Reggiano (associations ensuring the quality of Italian cheeses and hams), and Ooyes for their sound advice
• Mr. Auricchio from the Associazione Verace Pizza Napoletana (an association promoting the finest Italian pizzas) for his aid and for casting a careful eye over the chapter dedicated to pizza
• Anne-Sophie Lhomme, the food stylist, for having immersed herself in the culture of my home country
• Paola Nepote for her resourcefulness in her meticulous search for traditional ceramics from Sardinia, Puglia, Basilicata, and Sicily
• Pentole Agnelli for the superb and renowned cookware they so kindly provided
• Ceramiche Torretti-Deruta for the beautiful, traditional Umbrian ceramics
• Cuisinart for their chic electrical appliances, which helped us in the creation of numerous recipes
• De Dietrich for the high performance hot plate and fryer
• Les Céramiques Astier De Villatte for their sophisticated tableware
• La Maison de la Truffe for the delicious truffles they provided
• The charming family restaurant Covò della Taranta in Turin for their kind loan of traditional ceramics from Puglia
• The boutique Cotti ad Arte for their array of traditional southern Italian ceramics
• The boutique Zabbara for their Sicilian products
• Athezza for their beautiful and classic tableware

The photographer wishes to thank the following:
André Bénamoi from Broncolor Kobold for providing the lighting for the filming of the videos